SpringerWienNewYork

Bob Martens
Herbert Peter

ArchiCAD

Best Practice: The Virtual Building™ Revealed

SpringerWienNewYork

Bob Martens / Herbert Peter
Vienna, Austria

The translation of this publication was supported by Bundesministerium für Bildung, Wissenschaft und Kultur

This work is subject to copyright.
All rights are reserved, whether the whole or part of the material is concerned, specifically those of translation, reprinting, re-use of illustrations, broadcasting, reproduction by photocopying machines or similar means, and storage in data banks.
Product Liability: The publisher can give no guarantee for all the information contained in this book. This does also refer to information about drug dosage and application thereof. In every individual case the respective user must check its accuracy by consulting other pharmaceutical literature. The use of registered names, trademarks, etc. in this publication does not imply, even in the absence of a specific statement, that such names are exempt from the relevant protective laws and regulations and therefore free for general use.

© 2004 Springer-Verlag/Wien
Printed in Austria
Springer Wien New York is a part of
Springer Science + Business Media
springeronline.com

Pictures Front Cover
Left above: Thomas Forsthuber, Salzburg (A)
Center above: A-Konsultit, Helsinki (FIN)
Right above: Woods Bagot, Sydney (AUS)
Left below: Werner Nussmüller, Graz (A)
Center below: Walter Hoffelner, Vienna (A)
Right below: Helin & Co. Architects, Helsinki (FIN)

Pictures Back Cover
Left above: STUDIOS Architecture, San Francisco (USA)
Center above: House+House Architects, San Francisco (USA)
Right above: Scheuring and Partner / Lengyel Toulouse Architects, Cologne (GER)
Left below: STUDIOS Architecture, San Francisco (USA)
Center below: Suben/Dougherty Partnership, New York (USA)
Right below: Christoph Oberhofer, Vienna (A)

Translation from German: Pedro M. Lopez
Proofreading: Roderick O'Donovan
Design, Layout and Cover by Herbert Peter and Bob Martens
Printing and Binding: Druckerei Theiss GmbH, 9431 St. Stefan, Austria

Printed on acid-free and chlorine-free bleached paper
SPIN: 10953754

With numerous (partly coloured) Figures

Library of Congress Control Number: 2004109142

ISBN 3-211-40755-3 Springer Wien NewYork

Contents

Preface 6

1. On the Relation between Architecture and CA(A)D 9

　　　1.1 CAAD = Automatic Architecture? 10
　　　1.2 ArchiCAD: Its Inception and Developmental Context 23

2. ArchiCAD as an Intelligent Work Environment 37

　　　2.1 Modeling with Different Tools 38
　　　2.2 Using GDL Object Technology 43
　　　2.3 Hotlink Modules Referencing 66
　　　2.4 Additional Performance Features 70
　　　2.5 Project-related Data Organization 80
　　　2.6 Using Information from the Internal Database 102
　　　2.7 Project-related Communication and Presentation 108

3. Characteristic Applications from Practice 126

　　　3.1 Case Studies from Architecture Offices and Planning Studios 128
　　　3.2 Visualization Strategies 228
　　　3.3 Examples of Non-commercial ArchiCAD Applications 251

4. Developmental Perspectives: Integrated Building Simulation 274

Training Manuals and Reference Sources 283

Internetlinks 283

Trademarks 283

Photo Credits 284

Index 286

Preface

The selection of available specialized computer application publications has increased enormously over the last years. A broad range of software products is already available that are based on the various different experiences of their potential users and buyers. ArchiCAD has been on the market since 1984 and therefore cannot be considered a new product in any way. Instead, it has become a fixture among CAD software packages. However, when you ask for a book on Archi-CAD the selection is rather limited. Of course the manufacturer offers professional training manuals, but the perspective offered here has been missing thus far, although there are highly specialized publications on the subject of GDL Programming. GDL is the abbreviation for *Geometric Description Language*, which is the computer programming language that ArchiCAD is based on.

Although exact figures are not available, it can be assumed that only a small portion of the current users (maybe 20 to 30 percent) is aware of the full range of possibilities and make comprehensive use of them. Honestly, what about yourself? Ultimately, it comes down to the old demand for software that can be used without a manual or the respective laborious training and that is based mainly on intuition. Version 8.1, the current version of ArchiCAD doesn't develop an (emotional) relationship with the user. There is no direct interaction while using the program. The number of ArchiCAD and other Graphisoft product users is considered to be on the rise worldwide and has already passed the 100,000 mark. Additionally, Archi-CAD is distributed in 80 countries in well over twenty local language versions. Did you know, for example, that a Finnish or

Korean version of ArchiCAD is available? The local versions aren't merely editions with translated work menus; they are tailored to comply with the local building codes and regulations, taking regional construction methods into consideration.

Why is it called ArchiCAD? First it was to be called "RADARCH" since "RADAR", a spatial rendering program, was in development at the time. It soon became clear that the pronunciation was difficult and it was agreed that "CAD" should be part of the title. Hence the decision in favor of "ArchiCAD" was made, since language barriers didn't hamper it. What had to be accepted was a similarity with "AutoCAD" (including the potential confusion). The combined syllable allows for more permutations, which are already evident: ArchiPHYSIK, ArchiGLAZING, ArchiFORMA, ArchiFM, ArchiRULER, ArchiTERRA, ArchiWall, etc. Wags see this as part of the Archi-God-knows-what-else wave, but there is, beyond a doubt, a connection to the designations Apple used for its products in earlier times: MacDraw, MacWrite, MacPaint etc.

ArchiCAD is the undisputed "flagship" of *Graphisoft*, the Hungarian software manufacturer. Although the coordination and development headquarters are still located in Budapest, a number of foreign representations were established as well. *Graphisoft* has been a holding company located in Amsterdam since 1996. A network of (key) national and/or regional distributors are involved in the development process along with the sales department. This handbook wasn't conceived only for professionals in the fields of architecture and construction, it is also intended for university students and/or specialized college graduates. The authors are aware of a book's principal problem when it is based on a specific program – rapid aging. The subjects and problems discussed in this book try to throw light on background aspects as well as connections and links. Even though it is necessary to refer to specific ArchiCAD versions, the central idea is to offer universal explanations from a user's perspective.

The book allows for both a chapter-by-chapter approach and a "non-linear" navigation of the contents. By allowing for these possibilities, ArchiCAD helps position Computer Aided Architectural Design as an everyday design and planning tool. Another focal point in this specialized publication is the background information on the various ArchiCAD tools, functions and processes. The uses of these features are explained in a broad array of practical, research and educational applications. We hope the reader will be tempted to exclaim, "I never would have thought that is possible with ArchiCAD". In closing, the book addresses the future: how will things continue? And: what is yet to come?

Dr. Vera Tihanyi (Graphisoft PR Department) provided valuable information that helps reconstruct the company's history. Dr. Wolf-Michael Tschuppik (Vienna University of Technology) offered invaluable editing support for the individual project descriptions. In closing, we would like to give special thanks to all the ArchiCAD users. It was the contribution of a great variety of projects from the respective architecture offices that made it possible in the first place to convey the broad spectrum of applications.

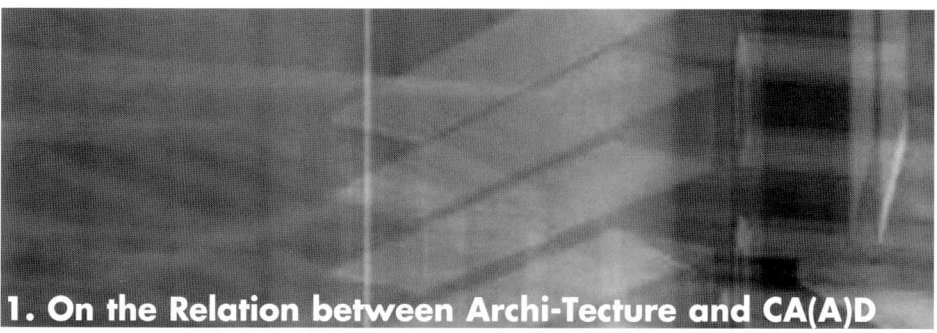

1. On the Relation between Archi-Tecture and CA(A)D

This chapter describes CAAD – Computer Aided Architectural Design – basics. If the "D" in CAAD is interpreted as design as opposed to "drafting", the definition of the concept becomes more far-reaching, since drafting primarily refers to technical drawing and drafting. CAD has long since established itself in many fields aside from the construction sector. The addition of another letter, "A", for "architectural", emphasizes its relationship to architecture, turning CAD into CAAD, however we will not discuss the subject as *Archi*CAAD. This book discusses CAAD in the context of computer aided architectural design, although related fields such as spatial planning and civil engineering are also touched upon. However, this chapter contains more than mere definitions of abbreviations and terms. It describes the developmental history of ArchiCAD, making it possible to explain its significance for architectural production today. The discussion of hopes and ambitions associated with ArchiCAD also helps make a general understanding of the program's development easier. A CAD software product can be developed at a general level and later become specialized for use in specific fields. The reverse sequence is also possible and has been pursued. The software manufacturers' varying approaches define the path taken in development. What is beyond question is that CA(A)D is a small segment of the far greater field of architecture, engineering and construction (AEC). The specialized aspects of architecture were always kept in mind in relation to ArchiCAD, despite the broadening of the horizon of possible applications. User working requirements were integrated in advance.

1.1 CAAD = Automatic Architecture?

After an initial look is taken at the history of the CAAD field, it soon becomes clear that this history covers a maximum period of fifty years. Computer systems are a matter of fact today and life without them can barely be imagined. However, it should be taken into consideration that this wasn't always the case, the *Personal Computer* was introduced only around twenty years ago. This event also marked the birth of (commercial) CAD software packages, some of which are still available today. Although CAD fundamentals had already been developed at a much earlier stage, they remained largely unknown to most CAD users. It took relatively long for it to be even imaginable that professionals in the architectural field would ever start using computers. The process of designing and planning seemed difficult to computerize. After all, pencil-aided design – also called PAD – offers the possibility of "fuzzy" work or creating an unmistakable personal signature.

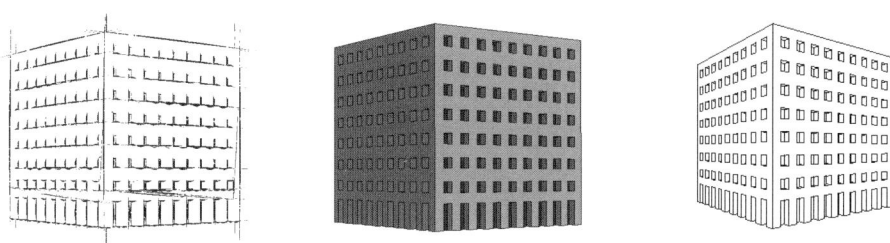

Fig. 1.1a-c Clinical expression vs. drawing by hand? The renderings were created working with computers

A person learns to handle a pencil as a child. "Real" training only comes much later. Drawing has a different status within school education than mathematics or language courses. Drawing is not considered a "killer" subject at a secondary school diploma level by any means. A university-level architecture curriculum generally included classical lectures such as drawing and painting, although computer-aided representation methods were gradually included as the course plans were reformed.

Initially, the attempt was made to imitate traditional work and rendering methods. But there are significant differences in terms of work methods that are registered at a subconscious level. The paper sizes available for analogue drawing are still considerably more comfortable to work with than a 24-inch screen. Zooming in and out is a matter of simple body motions. The hand moves a mouse and the result of the action taken becomes visible in another place – the screen. A personal signature isn't necessarily recognizable, since the sequence of commands creates the same exact result when repeated.

Paper-related media only makes an appearance when the Print or Plot command is executed. Any necessary amount of originals can be generated and kept in a number of places if necessary. But the time factor cannot be fully eliminated, although the evening hours can be used to finish the required plotting (an established invented term, and more will follow). A large format printout conveys a sense of perfection at a superficial level. Tracing paper, on the other hand, shows the manual use of ink and makes corrections visible. Such a drawing can serve as a master draft, but the generations to come would have to accept working with copies of inferior quality. It should be noted that some users let the available paper size dictate the scale they use. Thus a grounds plan will be shown for example in a 1:42 scale so the entire grounds plan is visible on paper.

Who doesn't have a hard time disposing of his own hand-drawn pencil sketches? After all, these are originals that are hard to reconstruct. The cool, clinical character of computer renderings, that can also be multiplied as often as needed, triggers the desire for the inclusion of artistic contents. Image editing software is appropriate for this purpose, the CAD environment is abandoned and mechanisms such as "inverting" and "layering" or special effects filters are used. The goal is to "soup things up", to embellish and enhance.

Fig. 1.2a-b Church project: supplemental editing of photo-realistic renderings (Stefan Klein)

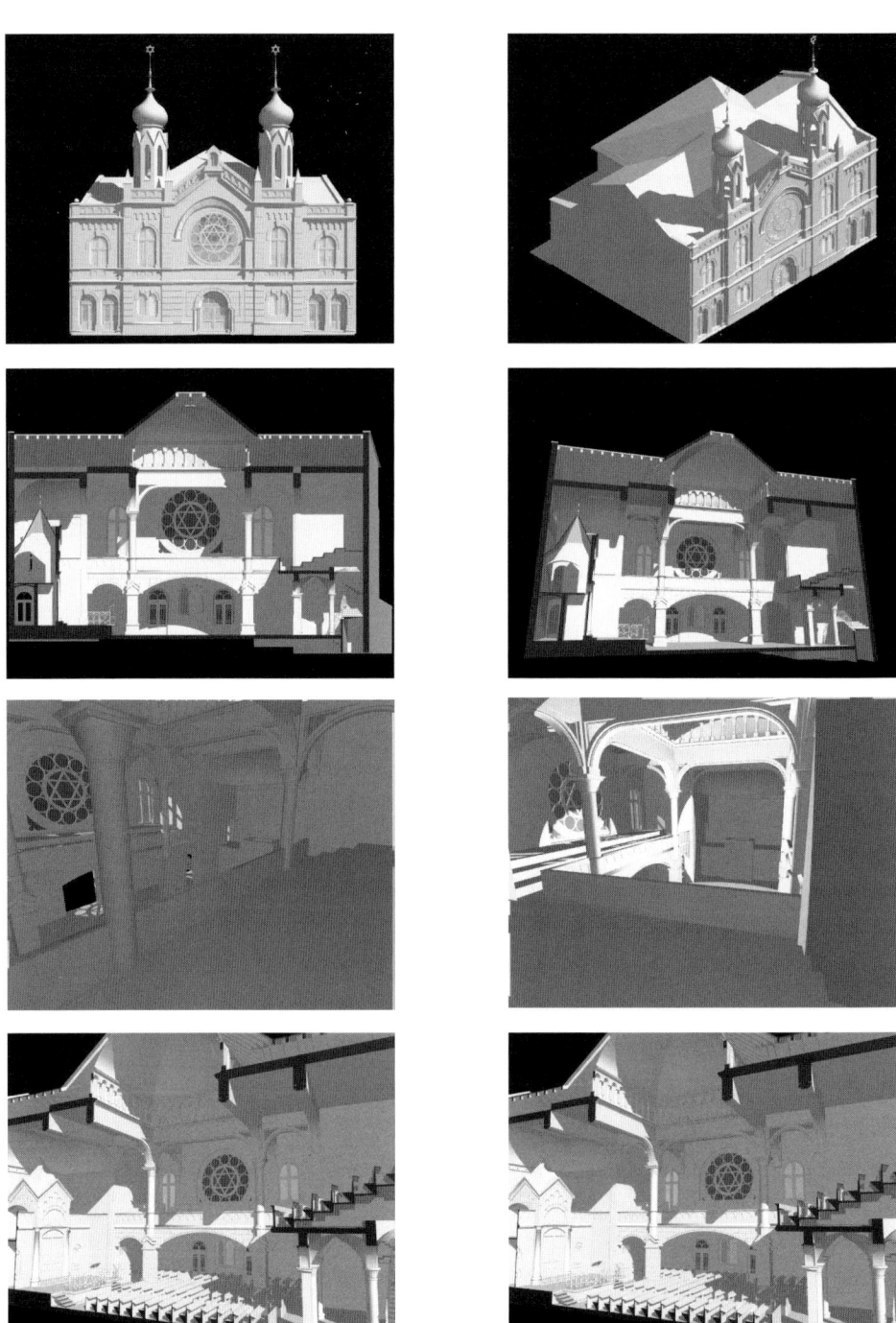

Fig. 1.3a-f A virtual model from various perspectives (Herbert Peter)

A situation in which one and the same digital model is used over the entire course of a project – from the early design phase to its construction – isn't the case most of the time. This consistency is interrupted occasionally, activity shifts from the digital to the analog level and vice versa. Information is lost as a result of these conversions and has to be re-integrated at a later date. The complete model remains in the heads of those creating it when working manually.

Individual drawings are created, which are characteristic parts of the whole. They also try to offer information on the whole effectively. Hence a greater number of drawings has to be prepared as spatial complexity increases. CAD programs that do not offer three-dimensional processing from the very beginning are therefore confronted with the same problems one faces with a conglomerate of unlinked individual drawings that can contain inconsistencies and contradictions. However, it should be kept in mind that three dimensional data inputting requires more time, so it isn't always economical, but it is nonetheless always possible to create images from varying perspectives at any time. The three-dimensional model can also be "picked apart", i.e. it can be taken apart, sliced or opened without destruction. This is possible with the help of the fade-in and fade-out instrument. Hence the model information isn't erased, it is merely filtered. The complete set of data isn't shown for that reason.

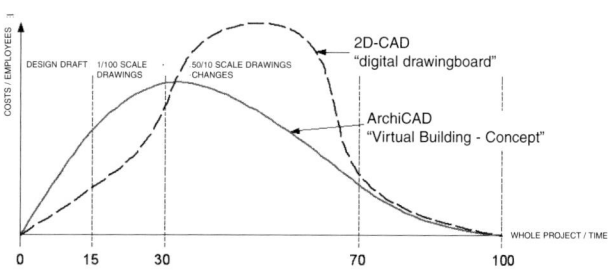

Fig. 1.4 Effort and usefulness: drawing (2D) vs. building model (3D)

A comparison with the automotive sector seems appropriate here, although it may seem a bit worn. The digital model of the vehicle supplies information that determines which computer-aided production line can be used. It would be hopelessly outdated to try to build automobiles on the basis of drawings on paper. CAD is therefore more than just a way of enhancing performance when producing drafts; it has become an indispensable tool for the preparation of the production process. CAD without CAM – computer aided manufacturing – isn't imaginable anymore. It should therefore be noted that the objective is to organize construction processes for different products (many of them "one of a kind"). So the potential of computer aided manufacturing, even if "only" applied in segments, has not been exhausted yet by any means.

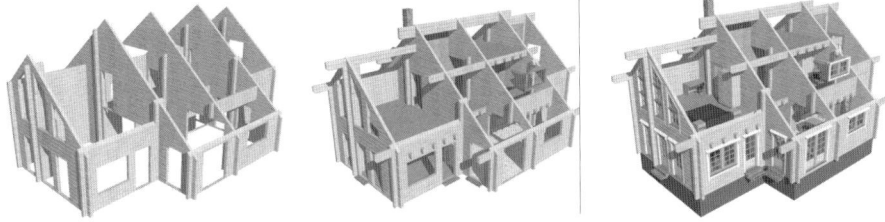

Fig. 1.5 Prefabricated house production with ArchiCAD – building models (LogHome Solution)

Which are the typical "promises" CAAD software distributors make? The following example represents a simplification of a situation in which naiveté or a lack of certain knowledge can be addressed ideally with glib rhetoric. The very first argument mentioned is *increased productivity*. CAD is supposed to facilitate daily office work and foster an effective if not congenial link between man and machine. The assumption that everything can be completed more quickly has not been enough of a sales proposition for some time.

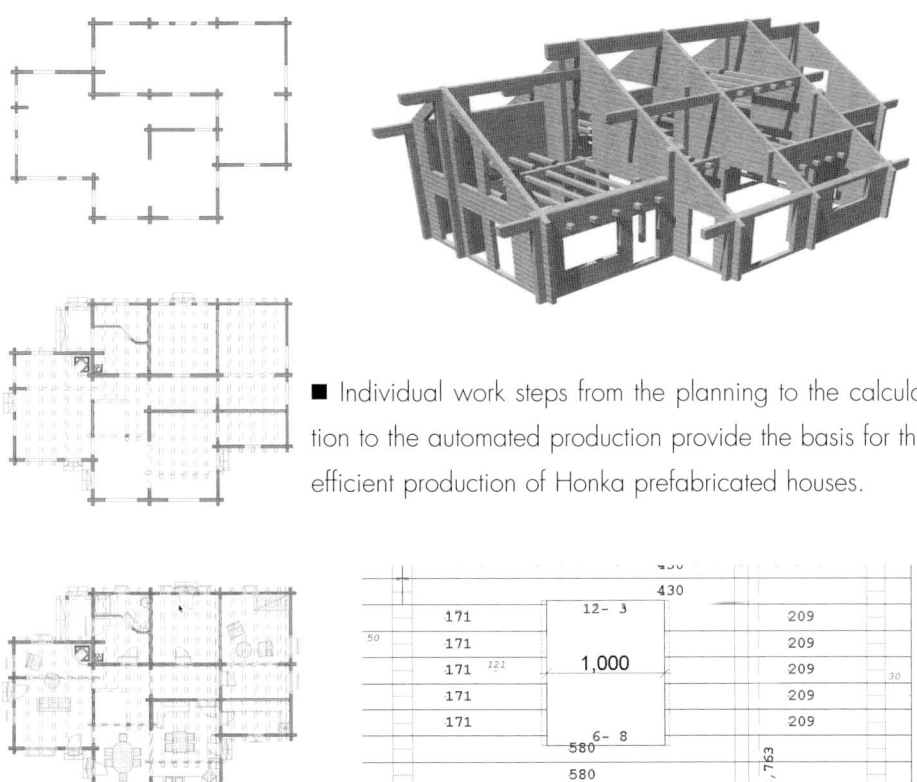

■ Individual work steps from the planning to the calculation to the automated production provide the basis for the efficient production of Honka prefabricated houses.

Fig. 1.6 Elements and planning (Honka, Finland)

Fig. 1.7 Prefabricated house production line (Honka, Finland)

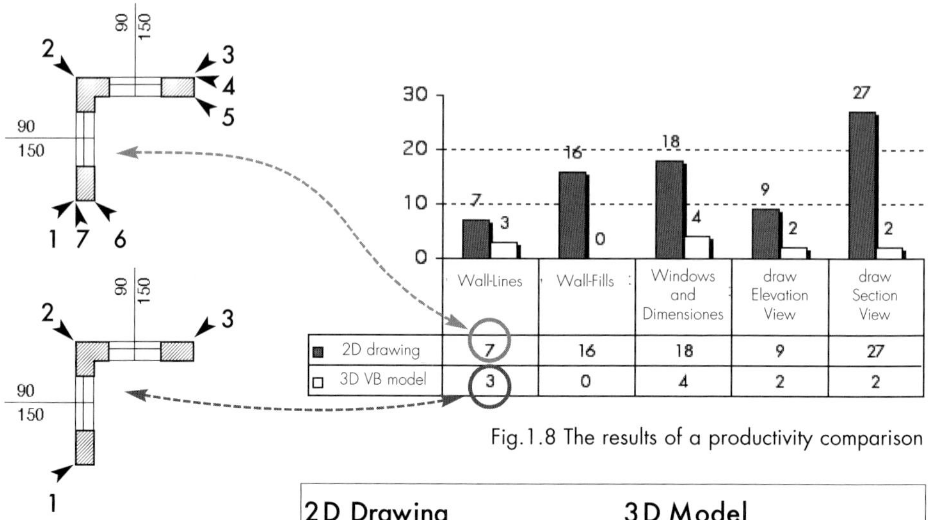

Fig.1.8 The results of a productivity comparison

	Wall-Lines	Wall-Fills	Windows and Dimensiones	draw Elevation View	draw Section View
2D drawing	7	16	18	9	27
3D VB model	3	0	4	2	2

2D Drawing	3D Model
• Wall outlines	• Wall tools
• Hatch filling	
• Window opening	• Window tools
• Draw window symbol	
• Window size calculations	
• Draw view	• Automatic view
• Draw section	• Automatic section
• Draw axonometric	• Automatic axonometric

■ The creation of the above planning segment with a 2D-CAD-Program requires a specific number of mouse clicks. This figure can be significantly reduced using a 3D CAD program. Since this example only discusses a small segment, the time savings during a large project can only be guessed at.

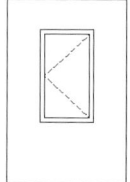
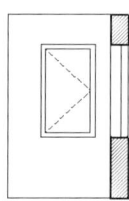
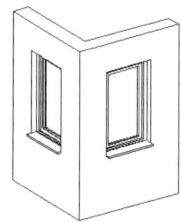

The same development took place with *quality improvements*. Black and white renderings, just as "right" and "wrong", are no longer adequate here. A fundamental question arises here in terms of whether CAD software enhances or limits work possibilities: the only objects that are designed are those the CAD user knows are the simplest to model, without worrying about unpleasant surprises. Hence the software decides on the structural development of the design. The tendency towards the development of "free" building forms, which obviously springs from the desire for "freer" architecture, should be mentioned in this context. The frequent appearance of bubble-like structures – called "blobs", can largely be explained by the existence of the corresponding software options. However, the ease with which such structures are modeled provides a deceptive impression in terms of structural practicability. It is therefore recommendable to approach "new" possibilities with the appropriate caution.

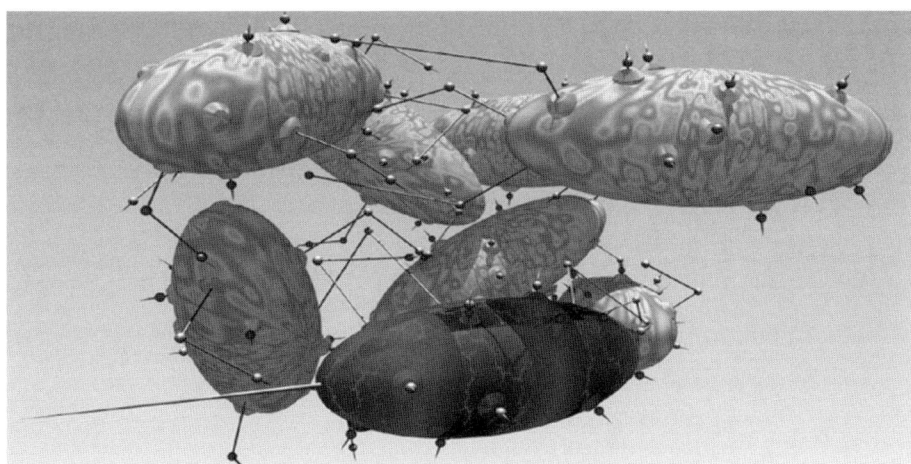

Fig. 1.9 "Free" building forms developed with ArchiCAD (Wilhelm Hochenbichler)

The realization of the (perfect) presentation form is linked to concepts such as status, image and reliability. It should make a professional impression. Even if the larger part of the respective information is produced on a digital basis, sketches are still drawn as work proceeds. However, these are shown to outsiders less frequently since they do not project the perfection of a rendering, i.e., of a photo-realistic depiction.

User friendliness, which used to be the most effective sales point, is almost forgotten in this context. The broad availability of computer systems has led to a decrease in the number of users without any prior (computer) experience. But responsiveness to user behavior or the ability to "learn" or react to the users' idiosyncrasies is destined to remain wishful thinking for a longer period of time still.

What should a CAD-related learning an instruction environment look like? It should be noted in advance that changes are part of the daily routine. This affects the equipment (hard and software) most of all, although the question is also whether training in a pool (classroom) on "unfamiliar" computers represents an ideal learning environment. When the first *Personal Computer* came on the market, their pricing did not encourage purchases at an individual level. Universities invested in the construction of computer pools, which were available to as many users as possible. Today, purchasing hardware at an individual level isn't an insurmountable barrier: more and more users carry their equipment with them in the form of *laptops*.

The course participant's level of previously acquired knowledge has also stopped being an unchanging constant. While some may be bored, others might feel hopelessly overburdened. It shouldn't be forgotten that relevant qualifications can be acquired autodidactially or through independent guided course work. It is also possible to create a responsive Internet environment in which questions can be raised and answered by those who feel able to.

But how can CAAD instruction that takes these factors into consideration be offered? Although it is tempting to just go through a workbook from A to Z, it is impossible to avoid having to discuss fundamental concepts. Practical exercises are indispensable for the coordination of manual and intellectual action. This is thoroughly comparable with driving lessons, and interestingly, a so-called "European Computer Driving License (ECDL)" is offered across Europe now. But a categorization such as those for automobile, truck or bus licenses is missing for computer software. The computer driving license mentioned above only covers basic knowledge (operating system, word processing, table calculations, etc.).

Since almost every secondary school student now has access to computers, changes can undoubtedly be expected. Although some may think computer systems are merely an interactive gaming environment to be used in their spare time, using computers this way also allows for the acquisition of useful experience in terms of practical computer handling. Cramped tension, which befell earlier novices, is barely an issue, and the introduction to computers takes place at an earlier stage. The pace at which this new user community will learn to work with CAAD remains to be seen.

We have strayed from the original subject of CAAD "history" in favor of more general considerations. The massive propagation of CAD took place in the 90's, although the gold rush days in which the number of users doubled every year are long gone. In the meantime, users have decided on one or the other CAD package. It would take "relentless" argumentation to convince them to change products. Which specific performance does the alternative CAD package offer, and how does it compare to my current work possibilities? The so-called "cornucopia" is ultimately a creation of the mind.

The CAAD work environment and the resulting presentation results may not trigger fascination on their own due to the form of rendering. In short: a computer drawing that can be recognized as such isn't going to thrill anyone to bits anymore. Therefore, a shift towards "image creating mechanisms" has taken place. Relevant studies on form generating have been published in great numbers and are available in almost cookbook-like forms. However, the apparent form-content dilemma is becoming harder and harder to cover up. Hopefully, the often-missing critical assessment will be addressed with an ethic for digital renderings. Although some professionals in the field of architecture may still believe in the holy pencil, to put it provocatively, the reciprocal relationship between an architectural design and the use of CAD will become closer and set new standards in the future.

1.2 ArchiCAD: Inception and Developmental Context

The distribution of ArchiCAD began in 1984, Version 1.0 was conceived for the Apple Macintosh Plus, which featured an integrated monochrome screen. The available processor speed was a mere 8 Mhz. Graphisoft had been founded two years earlier in 1982, by Gábor Bojár and István Gábor Tari. These two partners business efforts began with the construction of a pocket calculator, which Bojár describes as the Hungarian tradition of replacing missing computer resources with brains. They developed a special 3D modeling program that used the calculator's full capacity, and thus created the earliest precursor to ArchiCAD-Version 1.0.

Bojár had studied physics at Eotvos Loránd University in Budapest. After graduating in 1973, he became the chief programmer at the university's geophysics institute, where he developed terrain modeling software, among other projects. He was firmly convinced that three-dimensional renderings would improve working conditions for geophysicists considerably. In keeping with this conviction, he used an unorthodox method to convert images into 3D models that had only been rendered in a tabular form until then. The results became an important source of inspiration for both users and program developers. Bojár left the institute in 1981, after the Hungarian economic liberalization began, which triggered his decision. His next project was the three-dimensional modeling of the pipeline system for the nuclear power plant in Paks. After completing that project, he decided it was time to explore and find a market niche for cost-efficient 3D modeling. That was the actual point of departure for the development of the architecture-related software development.

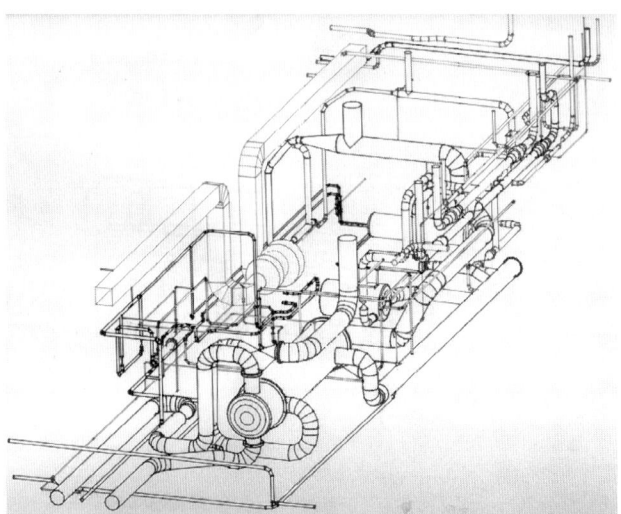

Fig. 1.10 Modeled pipeline system for the Paks Nuclear Power Plant

It wasn't entirely easy to sell the new product. After a number of attempts to woo cooperation partners, *Graphisoft* found one in *Apple*, and thus ArchiCAD was developed for use with *Apple Macintosh* computers. The company then managed to sell ten licenses to an Italian company and four to a German company. By 1988, Graphisoft had become the leading CAD software package for the Apple Macintosh operating system. A far-reaching expansion followed throughout the nineties, which included the establishment of branches outside of Hungary. The release of ArchiCAD for *MS Windows* came in 1993, after years of developing software that ran exclusively with the Apple Macintosh operating system. In the meantime, the number of users was increasing steadily: from 15,000 in 1994, to 25,000 in 1996. Shortly thereafter, ArchiCAD became the first CAD package to offer the possibility of creating QuickTime VR scenes. The introduction of ArchiCAD for TeamWork in 1997 was another milestone. There were 40,000 registered ArchiCAD users worldwide at the time.

Fig. 1.11a-e Graphisoft: "Historical Images"

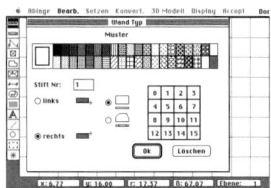

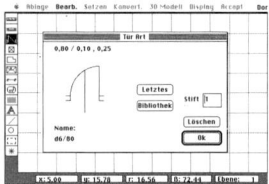

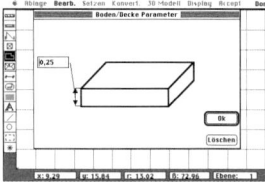

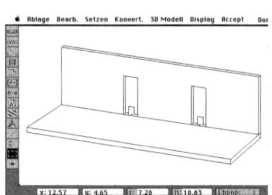

An end to the growth isn't in sight, although the 100,000 mark has already been surpassed, which is a remarkable result for a time period of two decades.

ArchiCAD is distributed as an *education licence*, as well as the *full commercial version*. An inexpensive *student's version* with a few reduced functions (mostly the data exporting features) is also offered. This version is designed to be compatible with the school version. This means that the ArchiCAD documents made with the student's version can be opened with the school version. ArchiCAD has multi-platform capability and the Mac and PC versions are equals. An ArchiCAD Version for *MacOS X* was also released quickly to meet user demands.

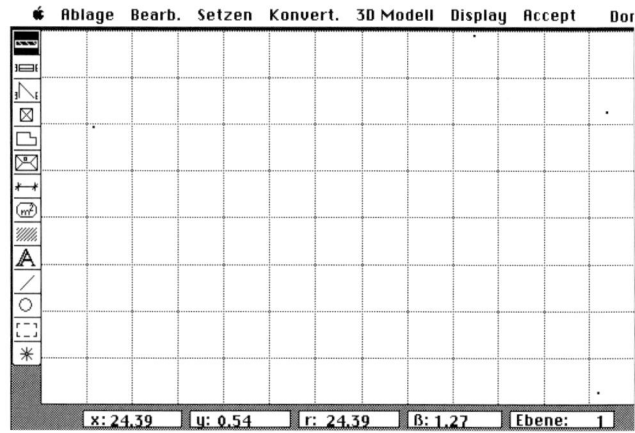

Fig. 1.12 ArchiCAD nostalgia: Version 1.0

- ArchiCAD 1.0: "The revolution on the Macintosh Plus". The first object and element-based CAD program, conceived for architects.
- ArchiCAD 3.0/3.11/3.4/3.43: "The first useable CAD-Program for architects". Also for use in planning large projects.

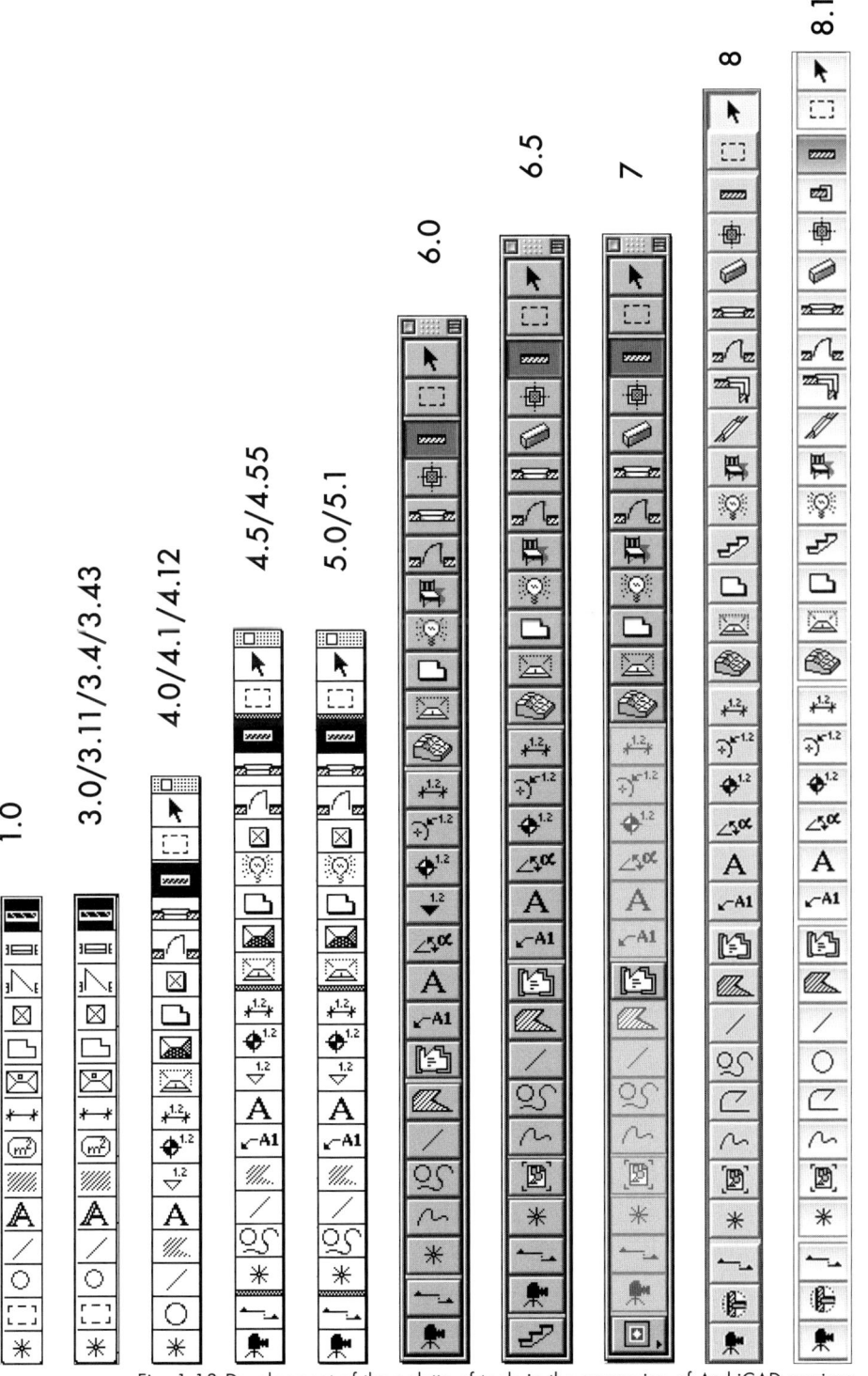

Fig. 1.13 Development of the palette of tools in the succession of ArchiCAD versions

- ArchiCAD 4.0/4.1/4.12: "The Virtual Building Concept develops". New layer handling, height and section calculation tools, new roof construction methods, animation and a refined library concept.
- ArchiCAD 4.5/4.55: "Many new tools". Scrollbars, Separate section/viewing windows, poly curves, light sources, polygons, info box.
- ArchiCAD 5.0/5.1: "Visualization is everything!" QTVR, texture mapping, TeamWork tools.
- ArchiCAD 6.0: "Local program versions, graphical tools" 2D Boolean operations, dynamic sections and views, API, splines, spatial imprint, curved walls, scale-dependent object symbols.
- ArchiCAD 6.5: "Working in three dimensions". Automatic Calculations, Reallife-objects, ellipses, verifiable surface area calculations, beams and imaging tools, 3D room zones, XREFs.
- ArchiCAD 7: "Workflow Management". Project Publisher, stack processing, 3D favorites, half-timbering, automatic 3D grid, interactive mass lists, favorites, Hotlink Modules.
- ArchiCAD 8/8.1: "Speed!" Project Navigator, interactive element lists, solid modeling, 3D Boolean operations, Layout-Book, database-connectivity.

A number of CAD software packages are offered by a variety of manufacturers. The dominant package is Autocad, which was developed by Autodesk, a company that was also founded at the beginning of the eighties. The DXF exchange format that was developed by Autodesk early on almost became the standard. Interestingly, *top*CAD, a 2D software package also developed by Graphisoft, was released too late, since Autocad had become the standard program for 2D drafting work. In view of the tough competition, it is all too understandable that every manufacturer will strive to emphasize the strengths of their CAD software packages and continue developing them. The strength in ArchiCAD's case is the "Virtual Building" concept. Along with the related GDL-Technology, this feature allows for object-oriented work methods. What kinds of objects are being discussed? They are building components (e.g. doors and windows) and furnishings. But this isn't by any means a full examination of the development possibilities. Although the word is not part of the ArchiCAD language, it could be said, "macros" are being discussed here. Make them once and use them time and again is the motto. This process doesn't mean that every succeeding use has to look exactly the same, since parameterization is an important feature. This way, a specific window can have dimensions measuring 100 x 170 cm although the same object can have measurements of 115 x 165 cm in another location. The window object with the newly selected parameters is then cross-referenced in the ArchiCAD document. This keeps the document compact: when used twenty times, for example, the document will only contain 20 cross-references instead of containing the entire pertinent geometry twenty times. Additionally, the GDL format requires around 10 times less memory space than the DXF exchange format despite a much greater information density.

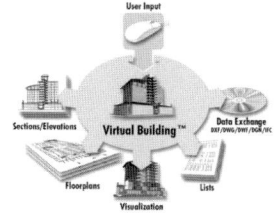

The *Virtual Building* is the central concept of the ArchiCAD product philosophy. The package doesn't solely concentrate on the creation of technical drafts and image renderings. It also focuses on the production of the underlying information, organizing it in a structured project database. In principle, this is meant to cover the entire life cycle of a building – from design planning, to the actual construction of the building and its use, to, as sad as this sounds, its demolition. Hence ArchiCAD offers access to a myriad of information related to the digital building model throughout all its development phases. In the course of the user-specific product development of ArchiCAD it gradually became clear that it is both useful and advantageous to check planning processes against digital line drawings and fine tune planning before construction by comparison with the actual final facility. It wasn't possible to link all the keyed in construction elements in all input windows (section, view and 3D windows) dynamically. The possibility of (automatically) generating or updating views ArchiCAD offers now reduces the amount of work and eliminates a possible source of errors during the correction and redrafting phase. When can CAD be used to its greatest advantage during the design planning phase? An outline of the process can be put together best with an input board. A computer mouse doesn't seem particularly well-suited for such a task. Extensive work on a digital computer model doesn't eliminate the use of analogue drawing implements and paper by any means. On the contrary: the idea of a paperless idea is much closer to being a deceptive fiction.

The Virtual Building Concept was only pursued with determination as of ArchiCAD-Version 4.0. Until then the concentration primarily lay on element-oriented modeling. During this time, for example, it was necessary to save a section outside the actual project document, i.e. in an isolated step. The declared goal now is to administrate all relevant planning and building information in one central project file. As a result, it is possible for excerpts to be generated by the ArchiCAD database with every imaginable form of filter. This comprises both the creation of construction plans and planning documentation, so it includes data that can be used later for building administration purposes. Facility Management (FM) is an up-and-coming field for architecture and planning offices, aside from the classical fields of activity. The spatial data administrated in the Virtual Building Model can be transferred directly to the *ArchiFM* software package and administrated in a SQL database via the "intelligent" ArchiCAD spatial imprint. The linking of graphical and alphanumeric information is guaranteed in this process.

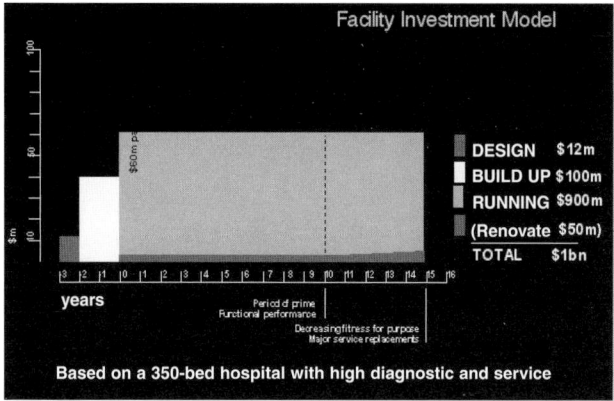

Fig. 1.14 Building life cycle with cost and time axis (John Mitchell, Graphisoft)

Building operators have recognized that the production of data after completing construction is on the one hand expensive and has on the other already been done for large project segments. This explains the increased interest in FM-compatible data structures. It also makes the desire for direct data access and the possibility for the planner include additional information when needed understandable. But it should be kept in mind that every construction plan devised with computer support can basically be exported, but the amount of useful information for the respective FM purposes is markedly lower than the amount ArchiCAD offers. Geometry does not suffice, which makes it necessary to add supplemental information.

Fig. 1.15 Example of a timber block construction that can be dismantled

The possibility of working in three dimensions from the very beginning has already been addressed. It is therefore surprising that a considerable amount of ArchiCAD users are still only using it for two-dimensional drawings. This is probably due to the fact that classical drawing is dominated by orthogonal representation. The third dimension is nonetheless included in ArchiCAD from the very beginning and it can be used in either the 3D or the floor plan window. It also possible to process data that was keyed into the floor plan window in the 3D window.

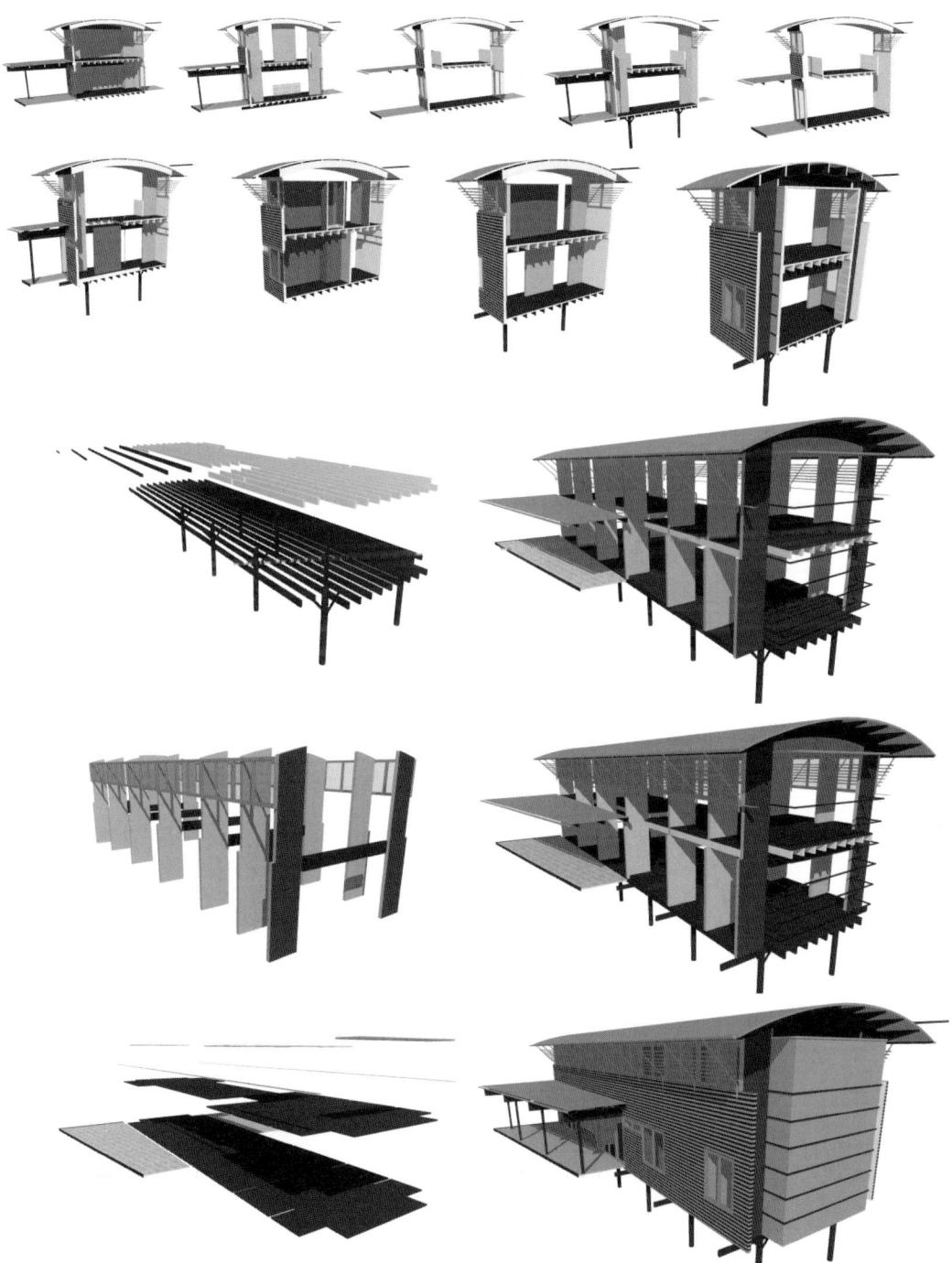

Fig. 1.16 Dismantled components

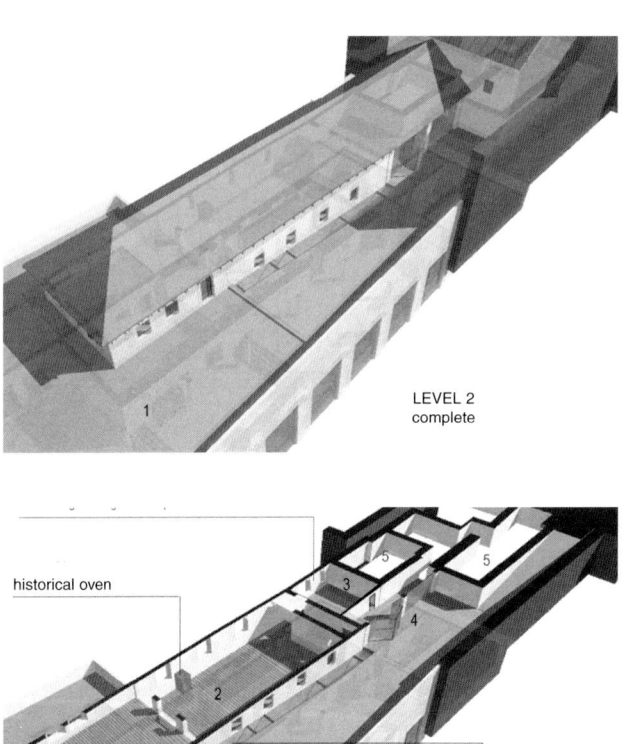

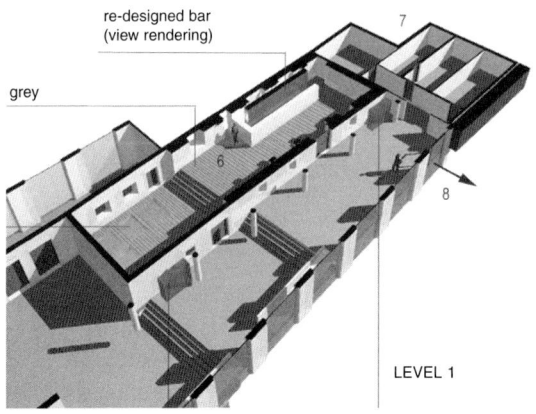

Fig. 1.17a-c Abstract visualization examples

Some may find it disappointing that ArchiCAD doesn't primarily present itself as a pure visualization tool. Although specific products will not be mentioned by name, it is clear that there are competing products that are capable of much greater performance in terms of photo-realism. The question is whether the realism that can be produced is necessary and to the point, whereas an abstract rendering may provide good service as far as conveying information is concerned.

The question, "why even bother with ArchiCAD?" can be considered a provocation: in response, it can be said that the "getting started" phase is convenient, while the program development possibilities are appealing to more advanced users. This represents a balancing act for an all rounder in the service of professionals in the architecture field. The designation "An Architecture Product" shouldn't be seen as a mere advertising slogan. The underlying idea was to create a language of symbols that is related to building construction. This means that tools such as "wall", "slab", und "roof" create a virtual construction site from the very beginning. Once an ArchiCAD novice has started the program, a little house will rise on this construction site. Indeed, it isn't difficult to set up four walls and make the incisions for the placement of windows and doors. The first three-dimensional rendering appears on the screen in no time at all after using the ceiling and roof tools. So initial success can be achieved quickly, although very few users will be tempted to go through life as simple house builders.

The implementation of architecture-specific requirements on the ArchiCAD user interface can therefore be considered a major advantage. These features go hand-in-hand with generally intuitive user orientation and the improved inputting as well partially automatic or semi-automatic measurement calculations and/or wall processing. Work steps are supported in a number of ways, e.g. via an "intelligent" cursor that reacts to the construction components that have already been keyed in and helps the user position components effectively. The multiplication option should also be mentioned in this context. The San Cataldo cemetery in Modena (architect: Aldo Rossi) is a typical example of how this option would have been extraordinarily useful, since it is a façade design that contains a number of repeated incisions within the same axis measurements. A few mouse clicks are enough to achieve this goal.

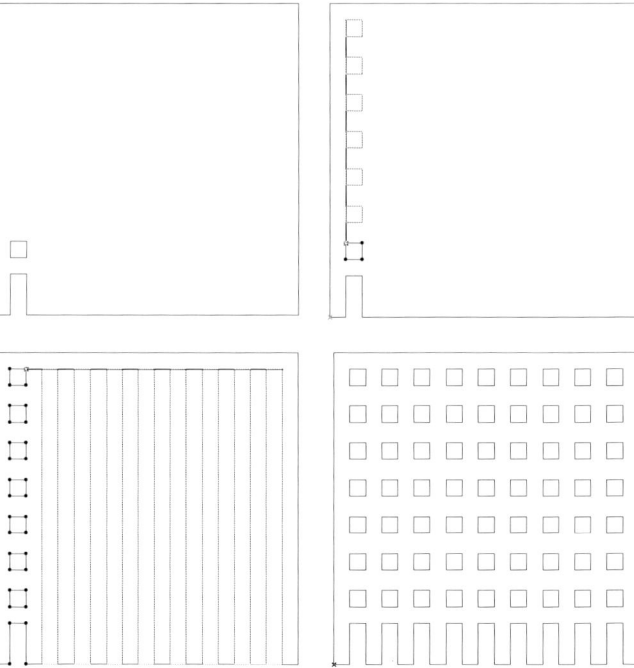

Fig. 1.18a-d "Multiplication" as shown in San Cataldo Cemetery, Modena (Italy)

2. ArchiCAD as an Intelligent Work Environment

After defining the CAAD context in the first chapter and discussing the local development history of ArchiCAD earlier, the focus now lies on ArchiCAD's specific working possibilities. If one looks around in the "CAD kitchens" of the various architecture offices, it becomes clear rather quickly that a significant part of the information produced is still limited to "traditionally" executed two-dimensional (electronic) drawings. But ArchiCAD is capable of much more and these possibilities will be shown in an engaging manner in this chapter. The idea of a thorough, universal data sheet based on a three-dimensional building model is realized with evaluations. The word "intelligent" may seem slightly presumptuous and it is often used as a market barker claim. This may be because of the misinterpreted discussion surrounding "intelligent buildings". However, it should nonetheless be more than just a readily adhering sticker. In this context, "intelligence" is related to the information being transported, e.g., through "automatic updating". This allows for an adjustment to a products changing status. This can be done via GDL technology in a network-supported environment (e.g. the Internet) without any problems. Additional possibilities, such as the creation of GDL objects (library elements) or using the TeamWork option can also be extremely useful. Digital project and document organization have their shortcomings in certain respects. A figure of speech taken from cooking also seems fitting here: too many cooks spoil the broth. Level and floor management will be given close attention for this reason.

2.1 Modeling with Different Tools

The ArchiCAD novice will initially be well-served with the array of standard tools. The rapidly achieved results will motivate him to delve further into the software. These modeling tools are set up in an intuitive manner, but they are at risk of being considered "self-build house construction software". That categorization doesn't do the modeling possibilities justice by any means. Therefore, the following slightly provocative guiding principle should be stated here: "In principle, everything can be modeled with ArchiCAD". However, many users still prefer using an orthogonal language of forms, which relies on flat surfaces. The first thing displayed by ArchiCAD after starting it is a blank drawing document shaped like an empty XYZ space. Every action, which will become visible after being keyed in, appears on the screen from a top view perspective.

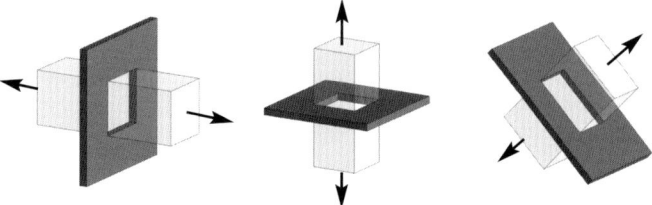

Fig. 2.1 Function scheme wall-ceiling-roof

Slanted surfaces are hard to control in this window (top view), but an additional 2D section window and full access to the element in 3D window offers useful help in such a constellation. As long as there are no double-bended surfaces or similarly complex spatial designs in this representative example, it isn't normally necessary to use the integrated GDL programming technology. "Freaks" have the option of creating their models in GDL, but we will address the respective "how and what" in depth later.

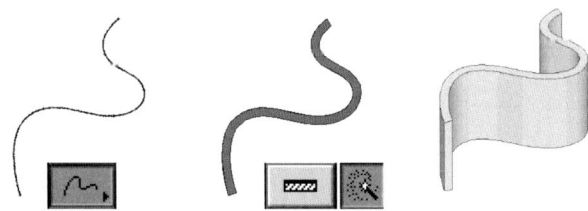

Fig. 2.2 Creating a curved wall

Lines of any form (ellipses, splines, arches, freehand lines etc.) can be converted into partitions and walls and lead to floor plan configurations with a great number of curves. It is also possible to create wall formations with walls of irregular thickness.

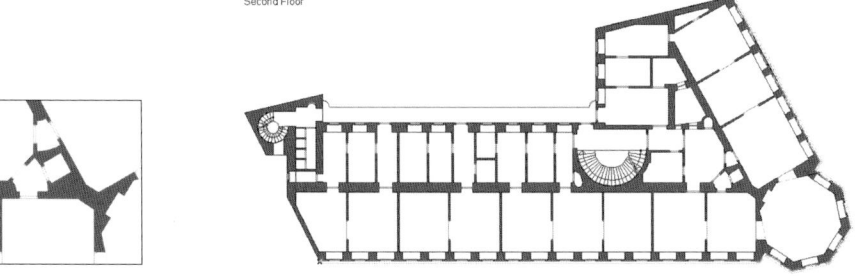

Fig. 2.3 Modeling walls of differing thickness

The desire to be as close to the creative process as possible, in the form of a virtual construction site, led Archi-CAD to favor entering a "wall" via the corresponding wall tool. What makes this tool special are the various predefined wall structuring possibilities. The user can also add user-defined wall structure options to the tool. If the user chooses to set a "slab" instead of using the wall tool (a 250cm thick slab!), the result may look the same, but it is impossible to set windows and doors in this wall-like structure. It would also be possible to use the "wall" tool for the construction of a ceiling, but it would not be possible to make any incisions for openings. Naturally, the experienced user knows a few tricks: he/she would set the wall vertically, as usual, make incisions for windows and then save a horizontal view of the wall and use it in the model. However, this procedure creates a great amount of data to be entered.

Element-type		Story	Layer	User-ID	Librarypart	Width	Height	Surface	Volume
WALL									
		1st. floor	Exterior walls	wall-001		30 cm	300 cm	13.16 m2	3.68 m3
		1st. floor	Exterior walls	wall-002		30 cm	300 cm	20.41 m2	5.85 m3
		1st. floor	Exterior walls	wall-003		30 cm	300 cm	13.16 m2	3.68 m3
		1st. floor	Exterior walls	wall-004		30 cm	300 cm	20.41 m2	5.85 m3
		1st. floor	Beams	wall-005		25 cm	50 cm	1.89 m2	0.47 m3
WALLS		1st. floor total						69.03 m2	19.53 m3
WALLS		all stories total						69.03 m2	19.53 m3
BEAM									
		1st. floor	Beams	Beam-001		25 cm	50 cm	1.89 m2	0.47 m3
BEAMS		1st. floor total						1.89 m2	0.47 m3
BEAMS		all stories total						1.89 m2	0.47 m3

Fig. 2.4 Beam vs. wall tool: apparently visually equal with varying data

Once the user is familiar with the specifics of these tools, he can work without requiring certain characteristic functions, but he is free to experiment. It is also possible and useful to increase the size with the "slab" and "roof" by incremental leaps. This makes it possible to model the construction elements without any problems. A table slab created with the roof tool can then be 14mm thick, for example.

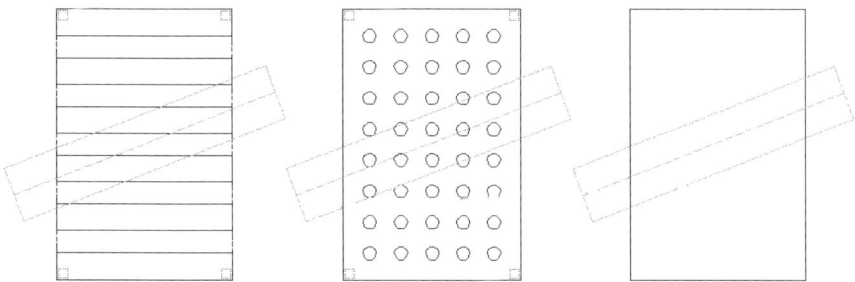

Fig. 2.5a-d Table structure modeling with different tools.

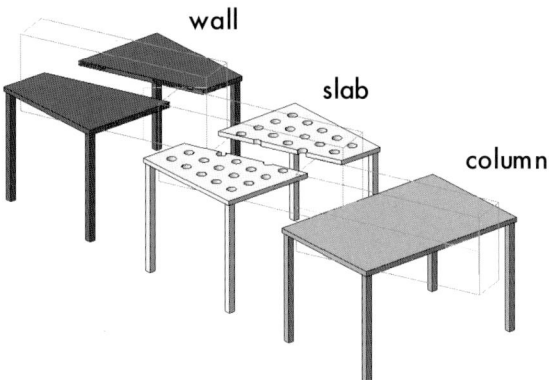

Or the structural volumes required for an urban planning project can be modeled using completely materials with completely different thicknesses. Hence a housing block can be generated with the "wall" tool with a wall thickness of 8m. The question is whether limits actually exist in terms of the project or document size. These are defined by the available hardware, since the calculation of the screen view of particularly comprehensive projects can take longer periods of time.

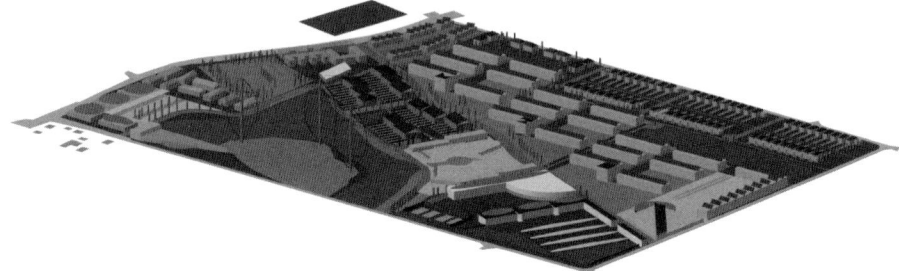

Fig. 2.6 Aspern City Model: standard tool modeling

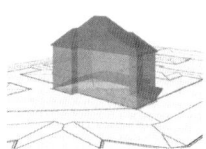

Just as many roads can lead to Rome, it is often the case that there is more than just one single possible way of modeling a specific constellation of forms. But there are also great differences in the amount of work involved in the various approaches.

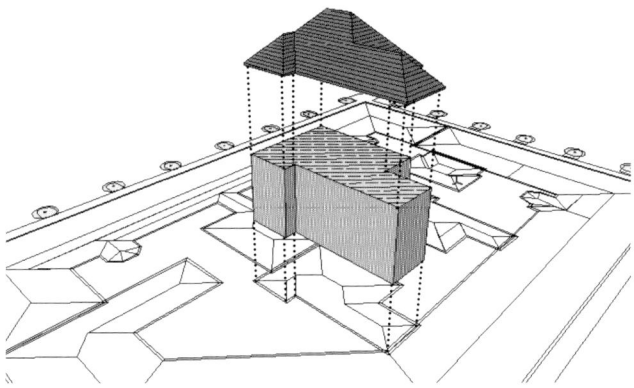

Fig. 2.7 Modeling urban spaces

In concluding, it should be said in this context that the functions included in the standard tools normally satisfy the needs of the average user.

2.2 Working With GDL Object Technology

The basic configuration of the first version of ArchiCAD-Version already contained what was a revolutionary option in 1984: sections of the digital model could be saved as completed segments (called "library elements or "objects") and used in any other place in the same or in different projects. The mere thought that one could create an object once and then use it again and again later caused a stir. The possibility of parameterization that also made it possible to change the object was the real novelty in this context. The workflow up to the parameterization was similar to traditional stenciling work, based on the interior elements and other symbols integrated in the construction plan rendering. In the late eighties and early nineties it was still common practice to use adhesive template foils.

This approach could only be used comfortably with "library elements" that had been predefined or already created, which also helped eliminate the high cost of adhesive foil. The linguistically confusing term (object) library can be explained best from a historical perspective. It doesn't define a collection of books, but of objects. The ArchiCAD-user certainly has no difficulty understanding what is actually meant by "library elements".

The development of an internal ArchiCAD language (GDL – Geometric Description Language) is a story of success. Two of the major advantages of GDL are the open source programming language and the compact file size.

The ability to parameterize objects that were created with GDL is a special feature in comparison to other object formats (ARX, O2C, OFM etc.). This feature also includes the definition of different material and color characteristics and customizable options. Additionally, other, non-geometric information and functional characteristics can be programmed in GDL script language, which is similar to Basic in its fundamentals.

The standard tools actually represent a special form of GDL. The user could create an object and name it a "wall", for example. However, it requires a great amount of GDL scripting to emulate the functionality of the existing wall tool. This is where the idiosyncrasies of architecture come into play. The fact that subjects such as mathematics and geometry have vanished more or less completely from syllabi may explain the lack of programming affinity.

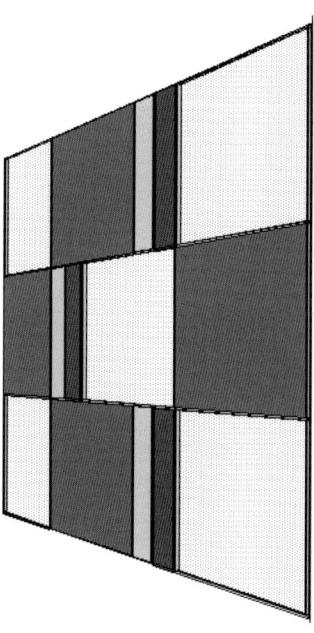

The fear of stunting any (latent) artistic abilities with such activities provides a neat "explanation" for this tendency. The situation delineated here in terms of using a programming language also probably caused the mere discussion of GDL objects to be carefully avoided. GDL scripting has been mythologized unnecessarily, although the current generation of graduates seems to have overcome earlier shyness. "GDL Cookbook 3" by David Nicholson-Cole, which contains skill-building exercises, is an important handbook in this respect.

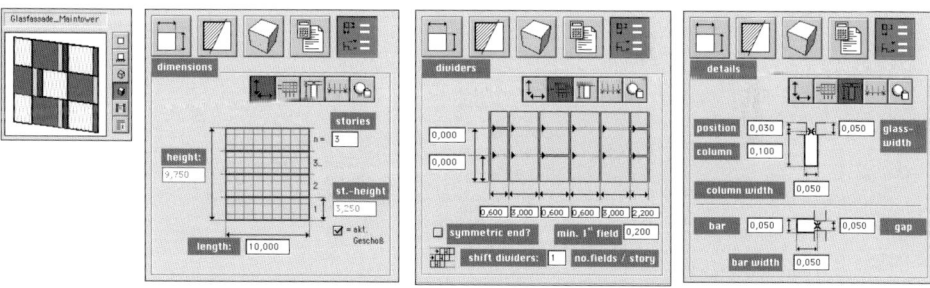

Fig. 2.8 GDL object for a façade system – dialogue window (Result: see page 44)

GDL objects were initially used as planning aids in the form of windows, doors and interior furnishings in early ArchiCAD versions before evolving into central information carriers later. The range is possibilities in growing in this respect. There are "neutral" geometry-oriented objects that can be used as reference for actual construction products, but that do not transport the actual product specifications. A window object contains all the relevant geometric information (sill, frame, sun protection, etc.) along with the scale-based plan symbols and can be created with any set of dimensions. This means that unrealistic values such as 30 x 30 meter large glass surfaces can be entered.

The ArchiCAD-distributor A-Null (Vienna) was the first

company to use the term "real-life object" when referring to GDL objects bearing manufacturer product specifications. The data is minutely adjusted to match the specifications of the respective manufacturer. The only settings saved in the parameter windows are the specifications the manufacturer was able to deliver. This also includes characteristics (colors, materials, etc.) aside from the complete geometric design and non-geometric parameters such as specific performance data (weight, order code, etc.). In this context, the user has the special advantage of being able to link all the individual interdependent parameters, allowing him to proceed with his planning more efficiently.

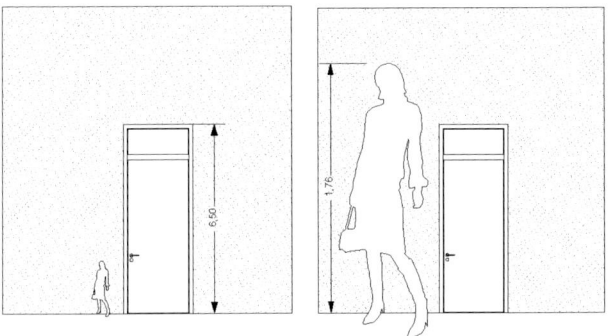

Fig. 2.9 Examples of so-called "unreal objects"

GDL objects can be exchanged without problems between the different ArchiCAD-Version numbers (upwards compatible), as well as between the version editions (full, school and student editions). Additionally, there are peripheral products that support the use of ArchiCAD outside the ArchiCAD program structure. The products are listed on the next pages:

- The *GDL Object Publisher* is a tool used for the publication of comprehensive GDL object libraries by means of HTML pages. These pages can be viewed with a standard Internet browser (Internet Explorer and Netscape Navigator for Mac/PC). A free GDL object web plug-in ("GDL web control") was developed for this purpose. The perspectives points can be chosen at will. The objects aren't simply displayed, they are also parameterized. The GDL object displayed in the open browser window can simply be "dragged and dropped" into the open project document and inserted (as of ArchiCAD Version 7).

- ***GDL Object Explorer*** (only for PC) is a tool used to convert GDL libraries into common (CAD) formats such as IFC 2.0, Art•lantis Render, DXF, DWG, DGN, 3D Studio, Lightscape, VRML, SVF and Wavefront.

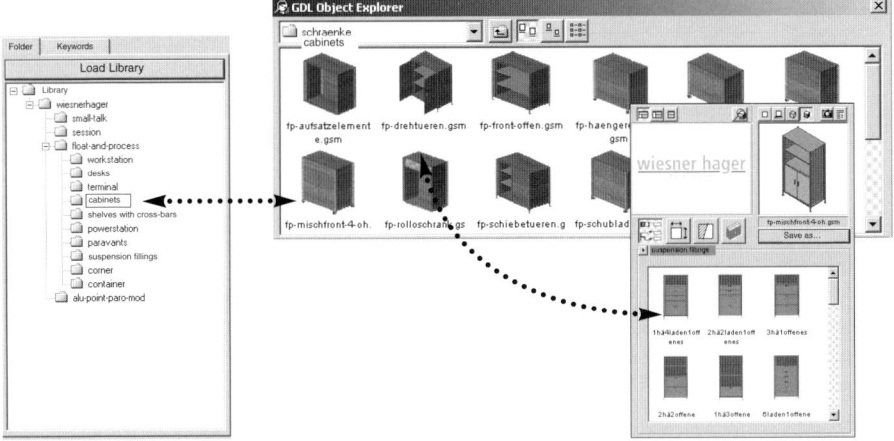

- Autocad users can import GDL objects with the ***GDL Object Adapter*** (only for PC). This ARX application permits the complete integration of the GDL objects, including their parametric characteristics. These can then be used in Autocad 2D or 3D.

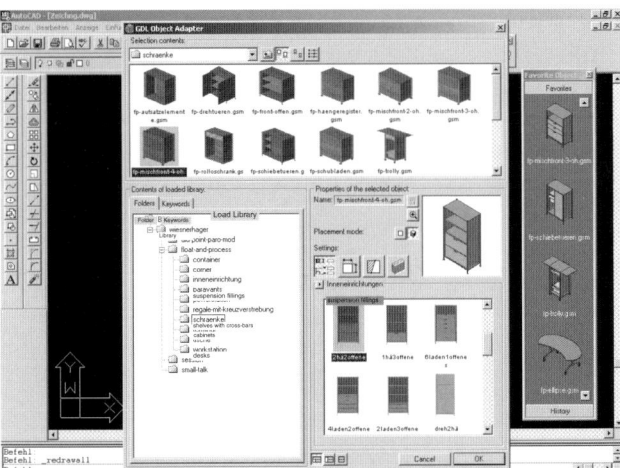

These peripheral products support the spreading of GDL object technology and partly use links to network technology (Internet).

In conclusion, it should be noted that the way the user handles GDL objects is closely related to the user interfaces (so-called "GUI's" or "Graphical User Interfaces"). The potential thereof still seems far from exhausted since the existing data input window isn't optimized for efficient use when displaying complex GDL objects with a great number of parameters.

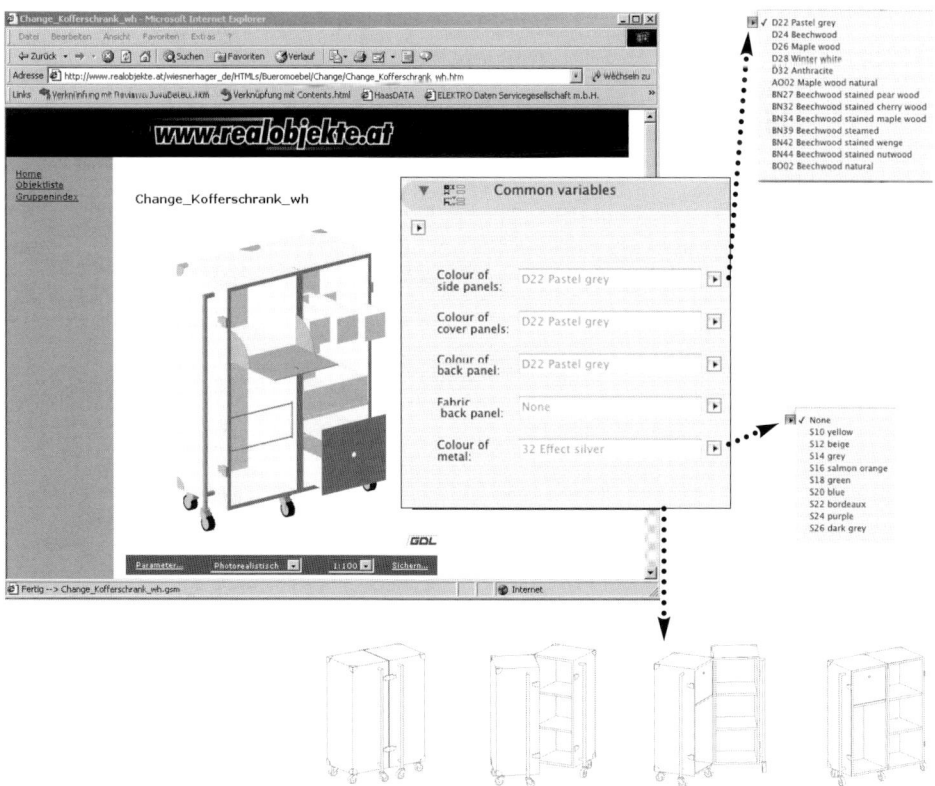

Fig. 2.10 Example: User navigation of a complete GDL object

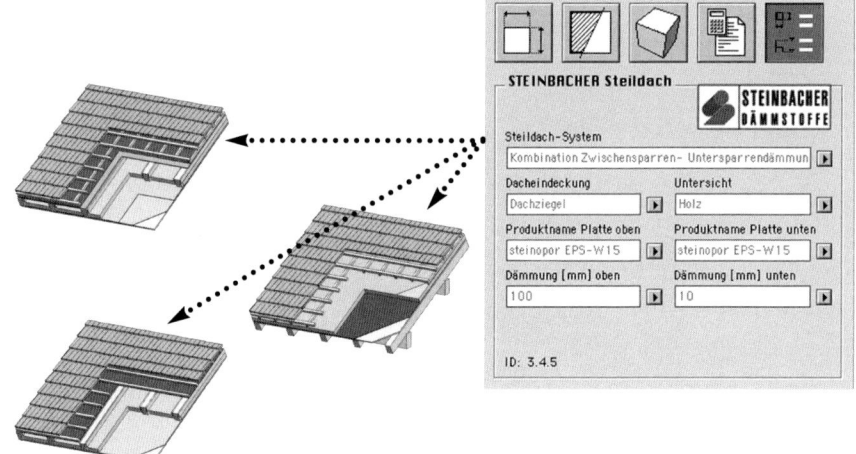

Fig. 2.11 Example: Roof structure object variants

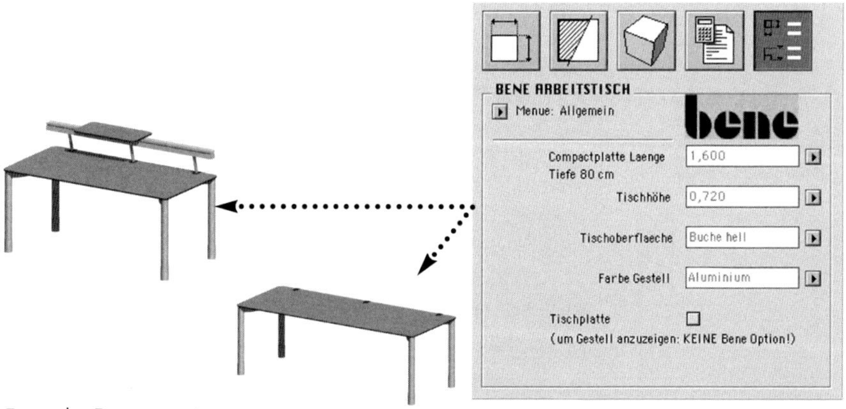

Fig. 2.12 Example: Feature variants

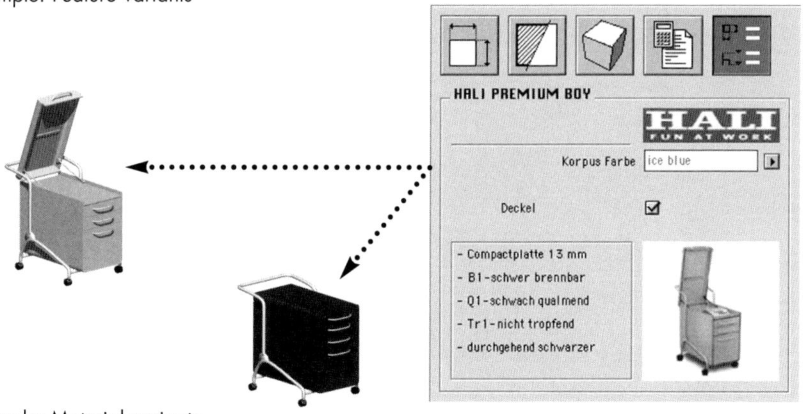

Fig. 2.13 Example: Material variants

2.2.1 Standard Library and Extensions

The ArchiCAD license also includes the so-called "standard library". This is a form of standard feature that is divided into a number of categories (furnishings, doors, windows, construction elements, textures, electric symbols, planning symbols, etc.) and contains a total of around 1.000 GDL objects. Some of the most frequently used standard library objects are bathroom objects, single-leaf windows and single-leaf doors, as well as chairs, tables and chimneys.

■ The young GDL woman in her red GDL dress and the GDL man in GDL jeans (optionally in a GDL wheelchair) have become famous by now.

  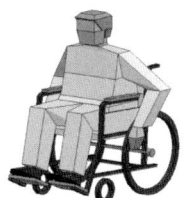

Is it useful to remove superfluous objects, i.e. objects that are never used? Hardly, since the GDL objects are compact and the library, including textures, only takes up 70 MB of memory space. The eleven-part *Graphisoft Collection* is offered as an extension on CD-ROM. Although the composition of the collection may seem a bit haphazard ("The Best of"), it is nonetheless a useful extension to the basic features. There is no obligation to buy the entire selection at once. The most frequently used elements are: *People and More, Architectural Accessories, Texture Library* and the *Office and Business Library*.

The reason for this assortment, which greatly expanded the standard library, was the desire to disseminate the idea of GDL technology:

■ The **Texture Library** consists of over 2,800 surface textures saved as TIFF format files.

 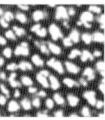   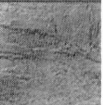

■ **M.A.D. Design** is a collection of 50 GDL objects for European kitchen design, the modern décor range comprises 46 (additional) GDL objects such as lights, crockery, calculators TV sets, etc.

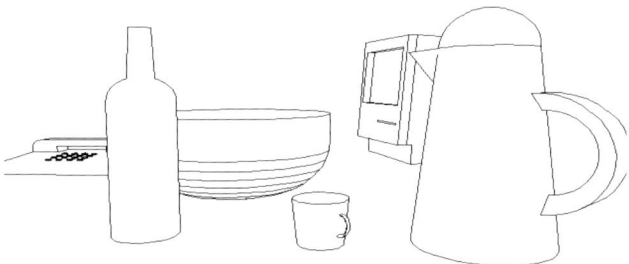

■ **People and More** consists of over 180 GDL objects including human figures, animals, trees, flowers cars, trucks, boats and airplanes.

- *Architectural Accessories* offers around 90 GDL objects that cover elements such as fences, curtains, blinds, roof sills, railing, balustrades, vent covers, flower containers and many other items.

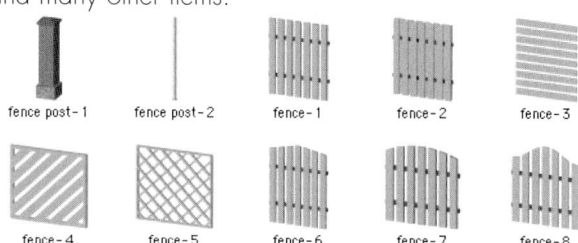

- *Garden Works* provides simplified, realistic modeling of over 40 flower types. The "garden library" contains another 50 GDL objects such as both wooden and metal garden furniture, a range of gardening equipment, playground elements, swimming pools and features.

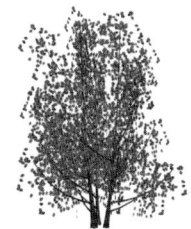

- *Hoshino Residential Library* offers a range of 150 GDL objects such as bathroom furnishings, electric appliances, fences, trees as well as special dining room and kitchen furniture.

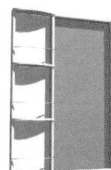
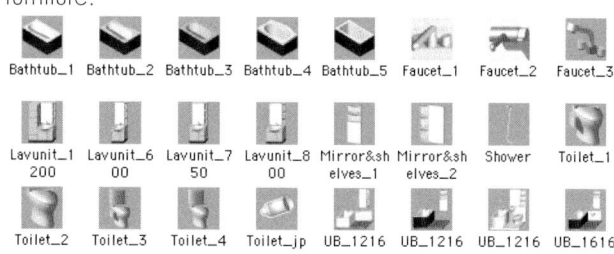

- *Lamp World Library* contains 110 different lamps that can be used in photo-realistic situations.

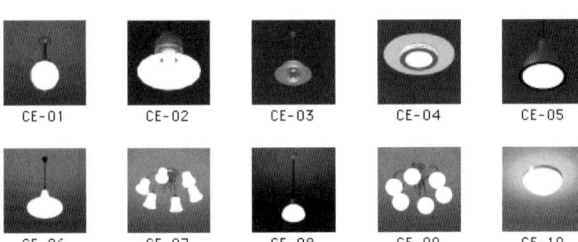

- *Office and Business Library* offers a broad range (300 GDL objects overall) consisting of office furniture and furnishings as well restaurant furnishings and lighting elements, backdrops, etc.

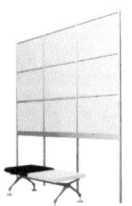
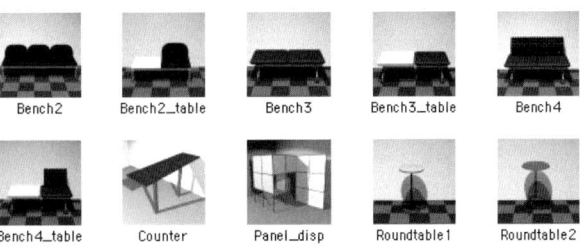

- *Construction Equipment Library* supports the planning of a construction site and includes construction scaffolding, containers, 2D construction site symbols, construction vehicles and many other items (53 GDL objects and 16 textures).

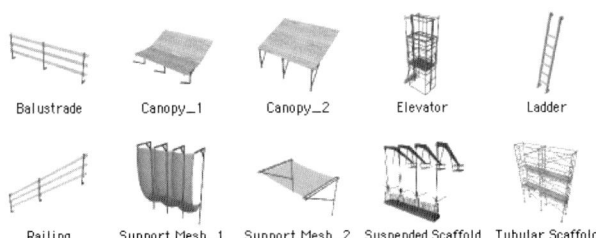

■ *Street and Traffic Library* concentrates on street design and includes cars and other vehicles, street signs as well as public playground facilities.

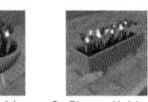

■ *Furniture of Alvar Aalto* offers 99 GDL objects of furniture by this designer.

■ *Furniture of Gerrit Rietveld* offers furniture developed by the designer in the form of 21 GDL objects.

Currently, it doesn't seem likely that any additional software will be created under the aegis of Graphisoft, since third party developers have existed for some time. The Swiss company ArchiMedia released a CD-ROM named "Tree Library" (it includes over 70 trees and bushes in varying degrees of detail).

Fig. 2.14 A selection of the many "objects online" that are available.

If you are looking for a specific GDL objects the http://www.objectsonline.com web portal offers an interesting solution, since it is possible to buy individual objects from their comprehensive range.

2.2.2 Creating your own GDL Objects

Creating your own GDL objects can lead to a potential improvement of workflow steps; the need for the replication of individual draft segments (and/or planning segments) emphatically emphasizes the advantages of CAD-supported planning. It is a major advantage to be able use a GDL object drawn once as a symbol or detail since a GDL object used in multiple situations only has to adjusted once in in the event of a planning change. Every additional use is automatically updated, without any further command by the user. This saves time and also insures no detail is missed during allocation.

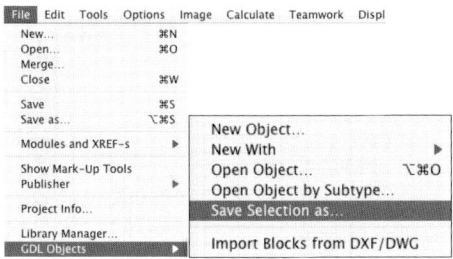

Fig. 2.15 "Save Selection as" as 2D library part directly from the drawing

But it isn't only the completely pre-programmed GDL object that makes everyday work more comfortable. Since the release of ArchiCAD-Version 5.0, it is much easier to create "your own", i.e. user-defined, objects, A specific drawing segment can be marked an ArchiCAD object in the "save as…" menu. The object created in this manner can then be used again in the same document or in any other project document at a later date. The respective position of the elements contained in the file does not change in this process, especially the Z-axis relation.

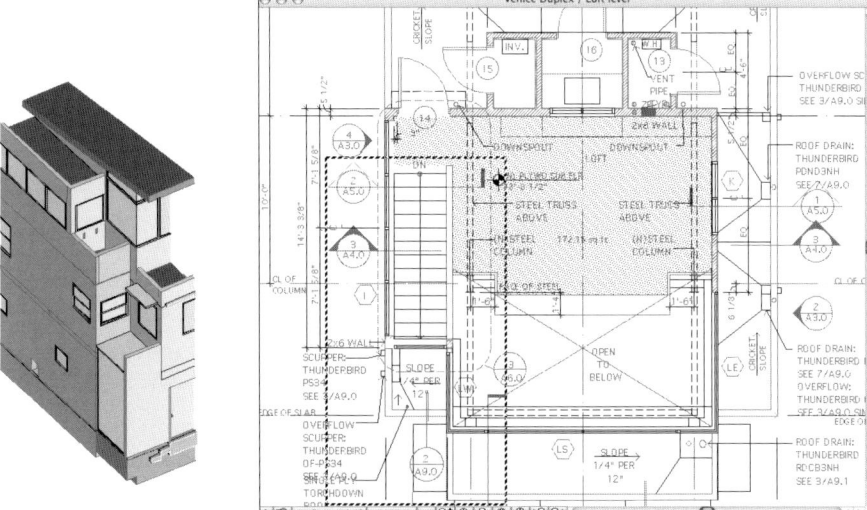

Abb 2.16 Creating an object (3D) used in a project segment

Imagine an undulating wall that should turned through 90 degrees in space and then used as a roof construction, for example. The Z-axis relationship will definitely change. First, the user has to open the 3D window and choose the necessary perspective. The perspective, or more accurately, the sight as it should appear when the created object is inserted. The "save as" menu only offers the *Object/Door/Window* and the *GSM-format* options when the 3D window is in the foreground. It therefore basically possible to create "simple" objects.

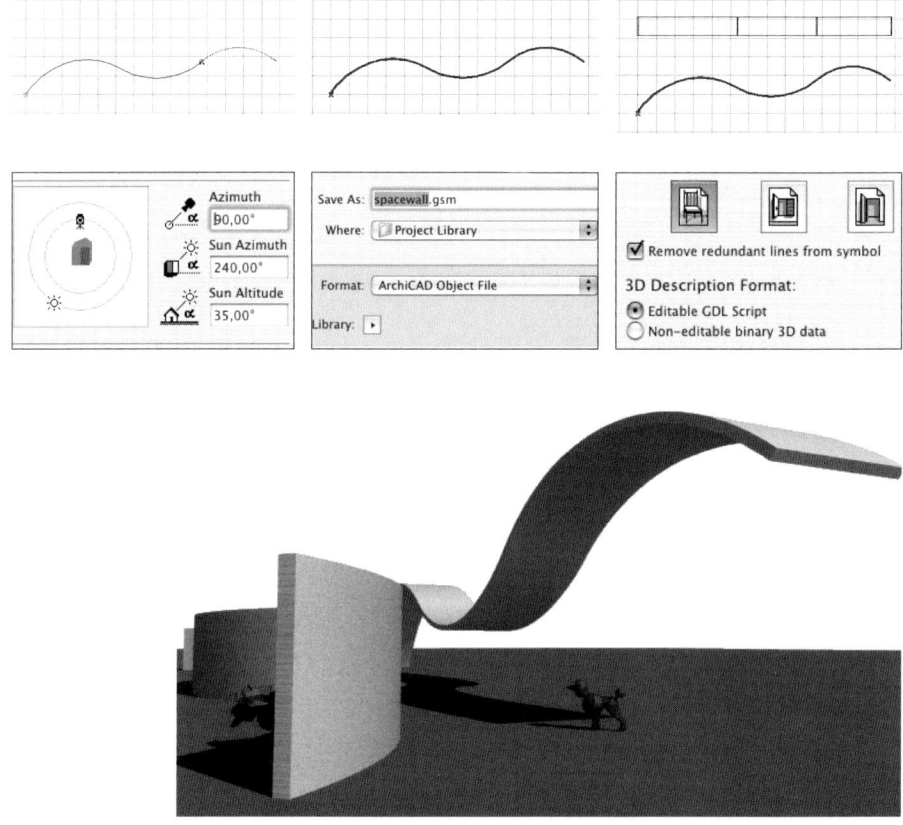

Fig. 2.17a-f The steps required to create an undulating roof

"Simple" objects are those with parameters that allow only a proportional magnification or reduction of the elements contained in the respective object. This means the structural thickness increases proportionally as well if the size of the undulated surface is doubled. The steps described here are based on a graphical construction and would require a re-definition of scope via GDL script changes.

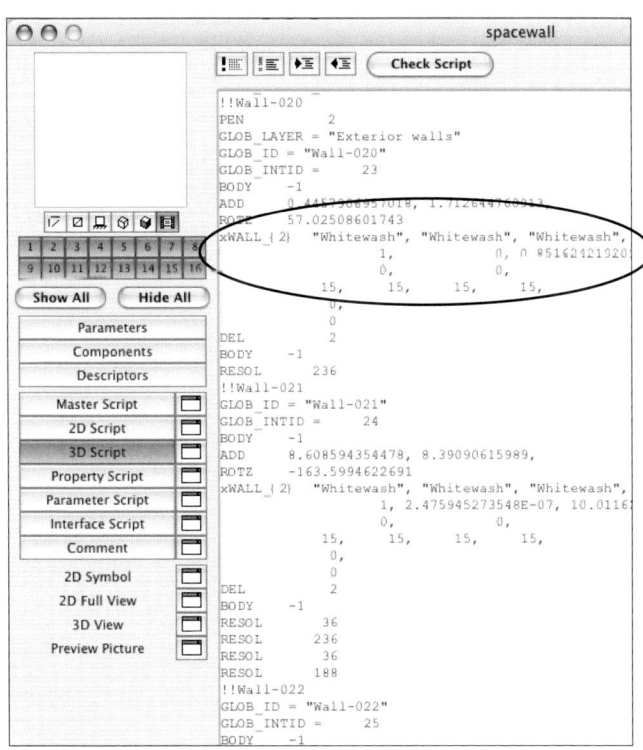

Fig. 2.18 Excerpt from the automatically generated GDL script (see Fig. 2.17)

Until now, it was assumed that only one generation of GDL objects could be created. But it is possible to save a GDL object together with other geometric elements and/or other GDL objects as yet another GDL object.

This mother-daughter situation makes it necessary to create an archive for the mother object. A lack of overview and errant objects can set in if a greater amount of GDL objects is used.

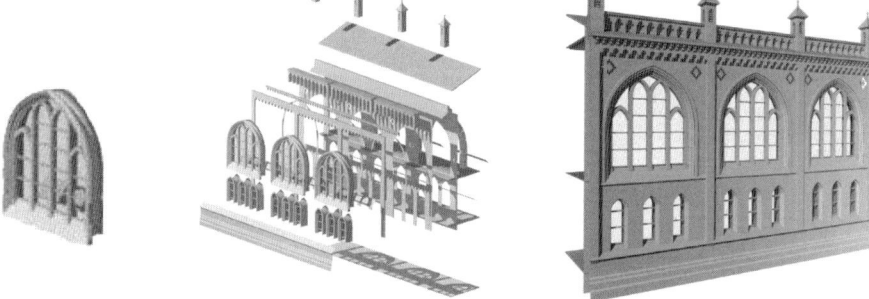

Fig. 2.19 Example of an "object-in-object" situation

In this context, it is important to note that the path to the "origins" is not cut off. The problems involved here also are discussed in the handling of modules in the next chapter.

2.2.3 Planning with GDL Real-life Objects

When you enter an architecture office, you generally walk pass walls of shelving containing large amounts of project documentation. Another problem, aside from the fact that only selected products are collected in these shelves, is creating effective access to the documents. Staff members rely on their own memory or on clues delivered by office colleagues. A much greater problem is the aging of the product collection. Creating catalogs and mail ordering are costly for the producers. A CD-ROM can cut costs significantly, but it should not be forgotten that this medium also has an "expiry date".

It is also important that manufacturers maintain a form of presence of any kind, and there are persuasive arguments for the production of (GDL-based) online construction product catalogs. They can be updated frequently without causing very high costs.

Such catalogs would also offer valuable user habit information. A construction product with X parameters and Y variations describes a number of reallife products. This means that an object used in an ArchiCAD model is a model chosen from the currently actually available selection. The program has the ability to remember as of ArchiCAD Version 7. This makes it possible to trace loaded objects to their origins at a later time.

The so-called "GDL-Alliance" is an independent platform, that is active worldwide with the intention bringing, GDL developers, construction product manufacturers and (CAD) software developers together GDL Technology (Budapest, Hungary) was founded in 2000 to adjust construction products and user support comprehensively and make it more customer-specific. By now, there are branches in Germany, England and the USA. Additionally, Laser-CAD (Sweden) and A-Null (Austria) support manufacurers offering their selection of products via a GDL catalog.

Creating a GDL catalog initially requires the digital modeling of geometric aspects and the options of the physical construction element. It is also necessary to record all possible deliverable variants of real objects and their specific logical links. These are characteristics such as: artcicle number, ordering code, weight, volume, product information, install and use description for administrative and maintenance purposes. The advantage of such an approach is that it allows central updating based on any changes that might be made to the actual products. A change in the script of a programmed object can either widen the selection of product variants or reduce it.

There are no exact figures on the amount of building product manufacturers worldwide. A precise estimate would be risky, but it would seem likely to be a six-digit figure. Which building components are especially predestined for the interactive planning support shown here? More or less everything that is shown in a 1:50 scale plan: the furniture and furnishings, façade systems, wet room equipment, heating and maintenance equipment, etc.

■ Velux, a roof window manufacturer, is one of the pioneers in the field of GDL real-life objects. Although the first generation of real-life objects was immediately related to an ArchiCAD library, a veritable boom has set in over the last two years in terms of parallel availability of such objects (in an Internet-based form).

By now, Velux is using the fourth generation of its building components which includes around one hundred individual windows sorted by size and product name and is based on only eight different GDL objects. Over one hundred different product variants are offered, as well as different material colors in all possible combinations for individual roof windows.

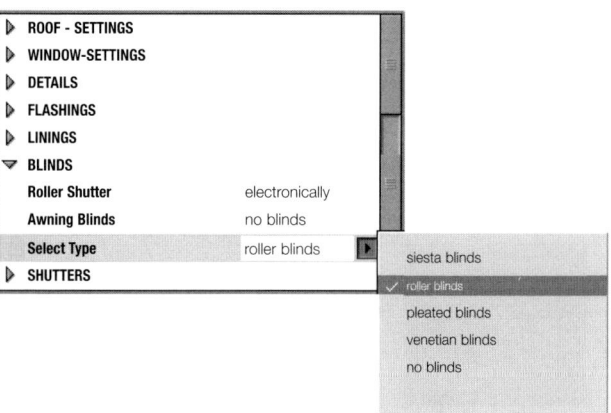

■ Novoferm is another example of a company that offers practical access to the many variants they offer. Novoferm produces metal doors and doorframes as well as metal gates. The range consists of five standard and seven semi-standard products. These products represent 95% of the company's production volume; the other 5% of production are dedicated to special shapes. Over 80,000 different product variants can be generated with the 12 GDL real objects that were created. This insures that the combination variants shown are those available from the (semi-) standard product range.

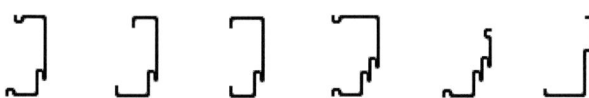

Velux and Novoferm are merely two examples of companies that actually use GDL real objects in the meantime. The amount of building GDL format components continues to increase. Interactive GDL product catalogs are available from both individual manufacturers and in clusters from so-called "object portals". Around 50,000 real-life objects were available by the end of 1999. Five years later, the goal is to have more than 500,000 available.

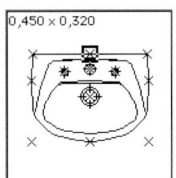
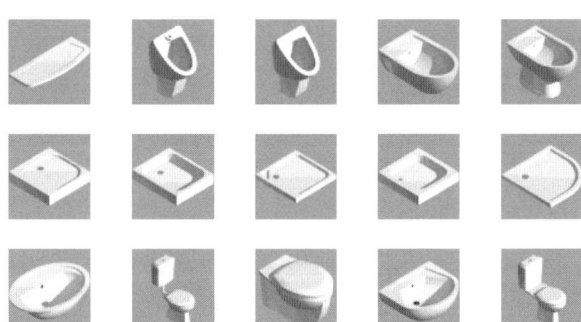

This will undoubtedly lead to the establishment of GDL as an industry standard and insure the independence of operating systems and the software used. Both planners and manufacturers have recognized that it is advantageous to integrate construction elements directly in the CAD software environment. Direct access to real-life objects via an Internet browser was also taken into consideration, outside the CAD environment. It is therefore possible to file a complete construction component order with network support. GDL real-life objects and their variants effectively steer production since the chosen parameters are fed directly into the production line via a database interface. This eliminates laborious steps in between and the related possible errors as well idle or downtimes.

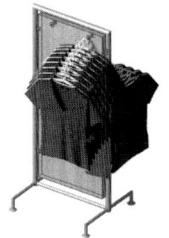

Planning documents printed on glossy paper will disappear from shelves. The CD-ROM merely represents an intermediate stage in the conveyance of information. The search for manufacturer-specific information will increasingly take place on the Internet. Real-life objects found in such searches can be directly integrated in the graphic object. This makes the currently available product information accessible, making outdated product folders and non-existent product types a thing of the past.

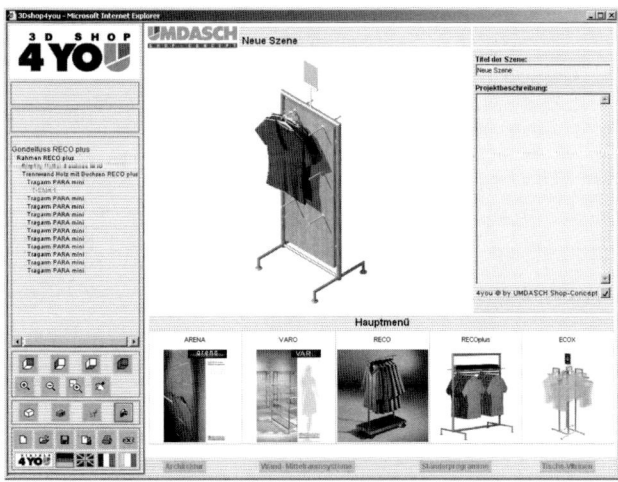

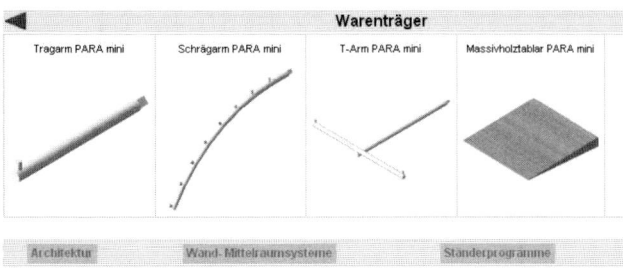

Fig. 2.20 GDL object configuration in a browser ("red square technology")

2.3 Cross-referencing with Hotlink Modules

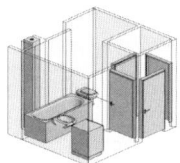

The development of additional, "user friendly" applications for GDL object technology is a high priority for future ArchiCAD versions. This mostly concerns those GDL objects which are built with the standard tools (walls, slabs, roofs etc.). It was noted that the final product has been achieved when an object is generated, any changes in the geometric composition require a change in the GDL script. Any new specifications needed later also require additional programming work.

The solution to this common situation lies in the use of a Hotlink Module that leaves the link to the "ancestors" – the individual geometric solids – intact. If a solid is adjusted within the Hotlink Module, the module information in the specific project document is updated in the corresponding form. This shouldn't be taken to mean that there is no need for object technology when using modules. Module technology is primarily useful as a form of reference for a project document. It should be noted that a Hotlink module can contain different types of elements (including GDL objects). This shouldn't be confused with the creation of so-called modules via the clipboard. This option has been available since the release of ArchiCAD-Version 4.12, dynamic updating is not possible in this mode, but is possible with Hotlink modules. If such a module is adjusted, no change will be reflected in the documents it is used for, since no relevant individual reference exists.

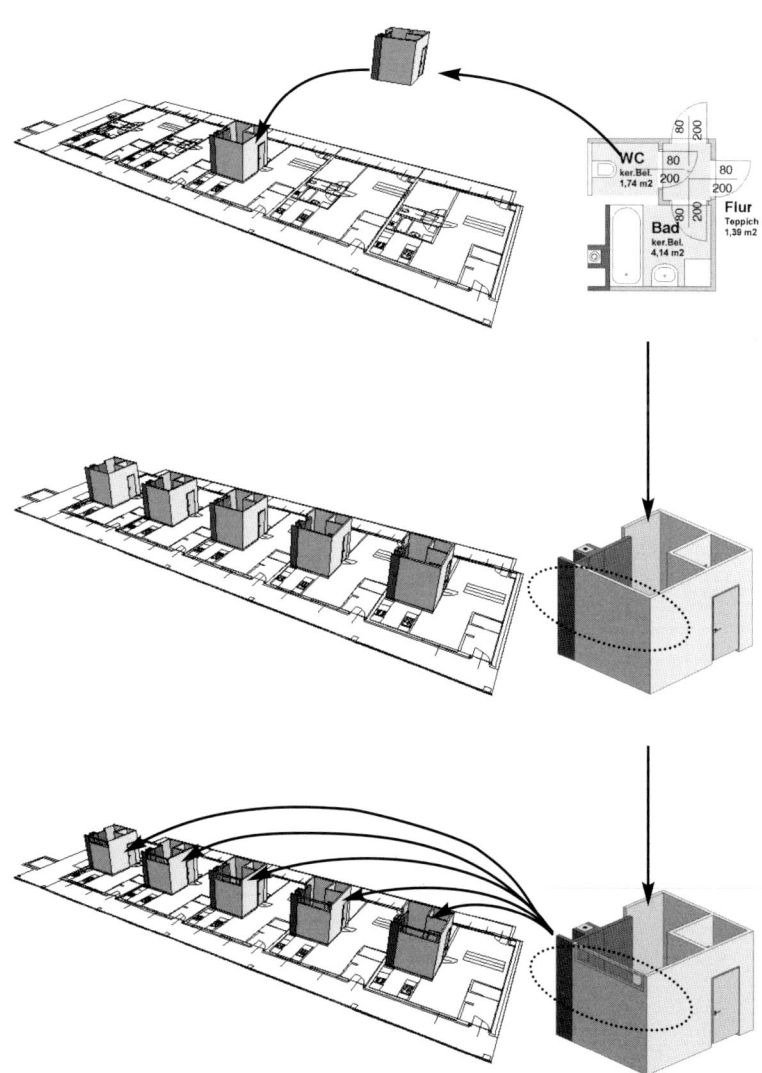

Fig. 2.21 Schematic rendering of Hotlink module use

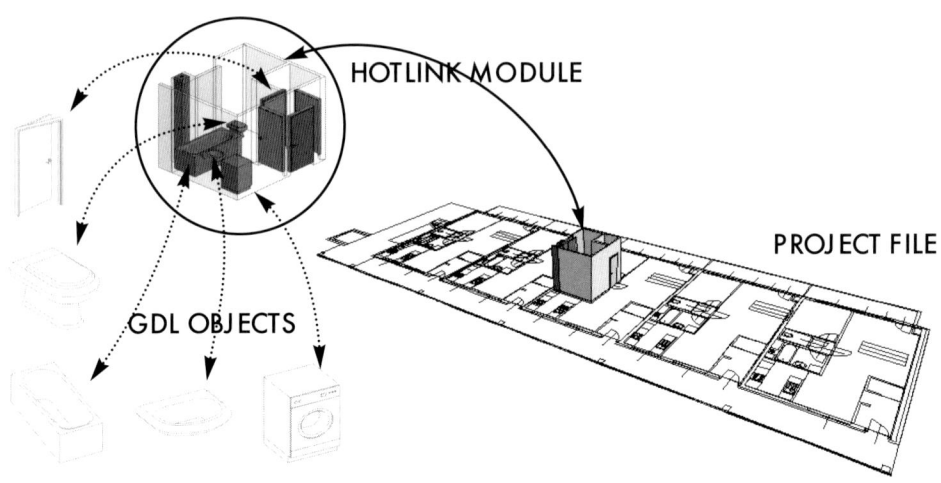

Fig. 2.22 Joint use of a Hotlink Module and GDL object

The repeated use of system components is especially common in housing or hotel project construction, since type variants are generally studied that are not expected to require any changes later. Grids of system components are also used in industrial construction. Although such units could be generated with GDL technology, the changes that could be made later would be limited, i.e. individual components could not be removed without making a manual change to the GDL script.

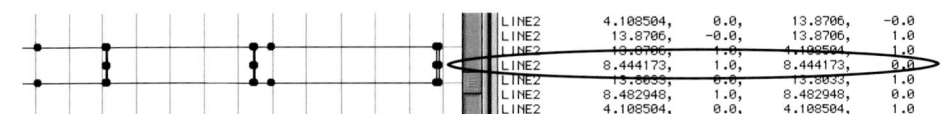

Fig. 2.23 Re-writing of a GDL script at a later time

ArchiCAD Version 6.5 took a decisive step forward in terms of "Hotlink Module" cross-referencing. An easily understandable user interface has been available since that version and also guarantees easy administration of the individual modules within a project document.

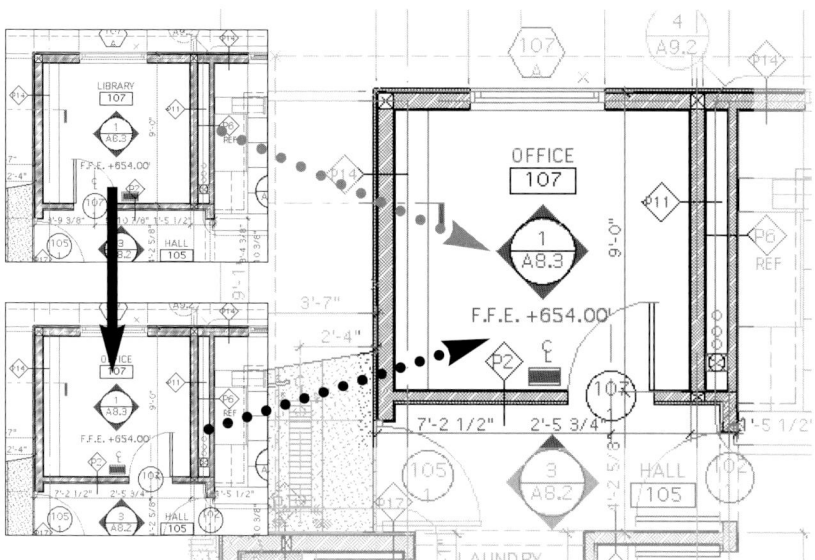

Fig. 2.24 Sequence of updating functions after changing the Hotlink Module

A clear increase in both productivity and quality in comparison to traditional drafting can be achieved using Hotlink Modules. It isn't enough anymore to make a symbolic indication with a quickly drawn line that is then interpreted by a specialist at the realization stage. Every drawn element – especially a Hotlink Module – offers more information than the respective planning segment. All the systems of a virtual building can be structured in advance based on the data that has to be entered. Although it should be added that sketchy structuring can make additional work necessary that is generally complicated. Experience in the field has shown that the potential use lies in a reduction of inputting and documentation work by up to 50 percent.

2.4 Additional Performance Features

The "all-in-policy" seems to be a contradiction at first glance, if you mention modular extension possibilities in terms of "Add-On" in the same breath. Graphisoft and its partners have resolved this contradiction by continuously developing the "Virtual Building" concept and releasing improved versions of ArchiCAD roughly every 18 months. These versions are fully functional architecture tools that do not need any additional software. Parallel to this, since Version 6.0 ArchiCAD contains an external API interface that enables external software developers ("third party developers") to develop specific tools and functions in shorter intervals, which makes it easier for local users to adjust to and maintain. API is the abbreviation for "Application Programming Interface".

The advantage of all these additional features is that they can be completely integrated in the ArchiCAD user interface and can therefore be used like any other standard tool by the user. Without causing confusion, it could actually be said that these are "plug-ins". The additional features that support the creation of the user's own GDL objects will be discussed here first:

- GDL-Toolbox
  (GDL-Modeler) – ArchiData Ltd.

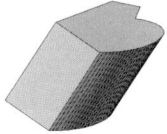 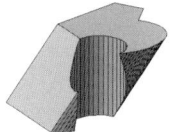 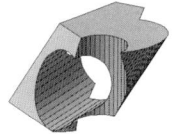

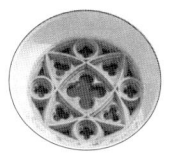
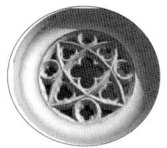

The GDL Toolbox is an API for the creation and handling of complex geometric forms. With the GDL Toolbox, it is possible to create various shapes as both two-dimensional and three-dimensional objects. A parametrical solid created this way can be reduced to its individual parts at any time. Changes made afterwards to individual geometric components at any time can be saved. If objects generated with GDL Toolbox are used on a workstation that does not have this feature installed, the objects still can be used as "standard" GDL objects.

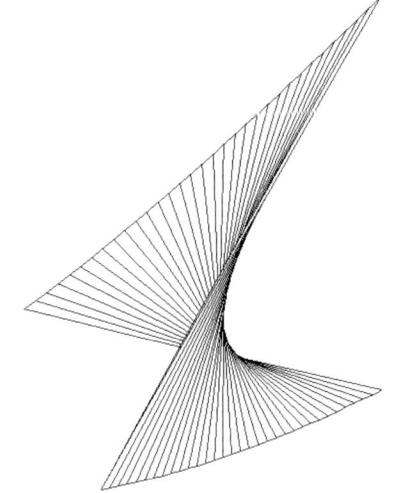

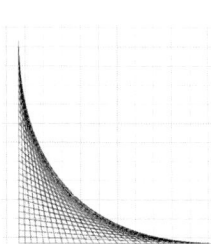

■ ArchiForma
(GDL-Modeler) – Cigraph Tools

One of the special strengths of this Add-On is the intuitive handling of its 3D window. Extruded and rotated shapes aren't the only solids available, the program also enables the user to model prisms, pyramids, cylinders cones, ellipsoids and spheres and the user can also create 3D texts and an additional tool palette can be activated for rotating and extruding. GDL objects processed in this way can be rotated in the 3D window at will and worked on by section level. This feature requires its own library, which has to be constantly available. If this isn't the case, the objects created with ArchiForma will not be displayed.

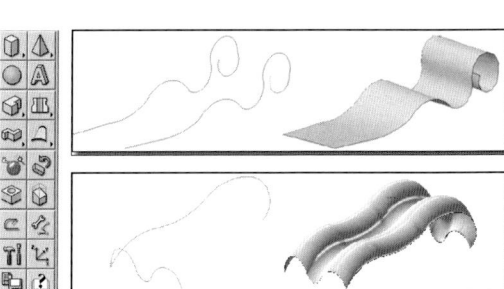

- **Profiler**

(extruded and revolved shapes) – Graphisoft

Here, it is possible to shape extruding solids via a previously drawn profile of a straight or curved route. Rotating solids can also be created in form of GDL shapes. So, if it is necessary to create extruding and rotating shapes, the Profiler (free of charge) represents an easy solution.

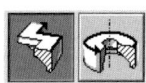

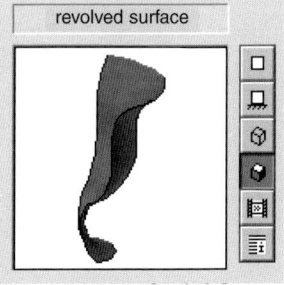

In summary, it should be said that the additional features described here have varying strengths and weaknesses. Normally, it will be the geometrical requirements of the model that are decisive for any potential acquisition. What follows is an overview of other Add-Ons. However, this list is by no means complete, since this is a market segment with many different external suppliers:

- **ArchiFaçade**
(image processing) – Cigraph Tools

Perspectivized images, such as façade images, can be equalized (to scale) with this tool, creating an orthogonal rendering form. The additional tool palette enables the user to crop images digitally.

- **Mesh to Roof**
(creates roofshapes from meshes) – Graphisoft
Elements modeled with the open area tool can be converted into grouped roof surfaces with one set roof thickness. Individual roof surfaces can then be worked on once the group has been broken up (e.g. change of the roof pitch).

- **Reinforcement**

  (drawing and calculation) – Archimage Plusz

  This tool enables users to generate reinforcement planning directly within ArchiCAD in engineering project-documentation. Existing slabs, columns, wall panels and binding beams can be equipped with the calculated reinforcing bars or wire mesh reinforcements.

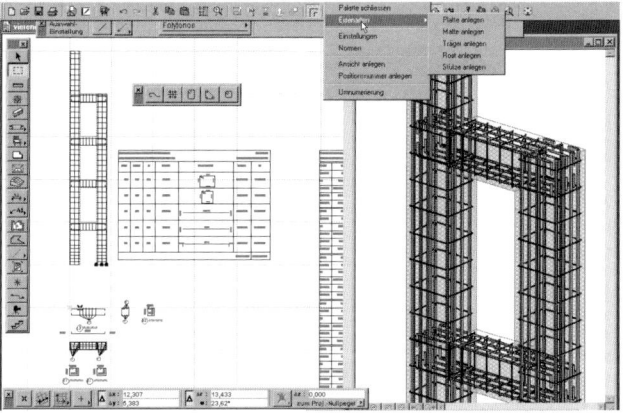

- **HVAC-Tools**

  (Tools for heating and ventilation) – Graphisoft

  Users can create service plans even without detailed knowledge of domestic services. This tool features a comprehensive GDL library for heating and ventilation systems. Information from the 2D drawings of the technical facilities (such as the trajectory of a ventilation duct) including the location of the curves of the respective ventilation duct segment can be visualized in a three-dimensional space. Then comes an automatic adjustment of the T piece size and branches as well as their placement and connections. The tool also offers automatic wall breakthroughs.

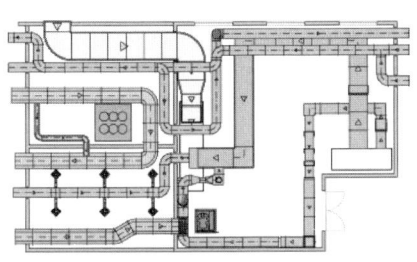
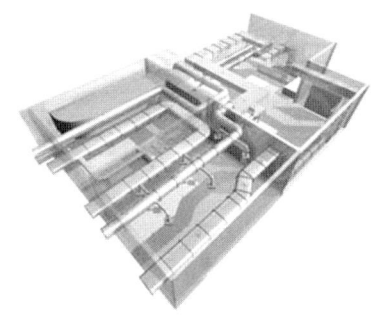

- **ArchiTerra**
(site-modeling) – Cigraph Tools

This tool renders terrain and is applied to imported DXF-data or survey data. A sitemodel can be calculated based on this three-dimensional informations. It is also possible to visualize the contourlines in an equidistance chosen by the user. Guidelines, plateaus, streets, embankments and breakthroughs complete the spectrum of options.

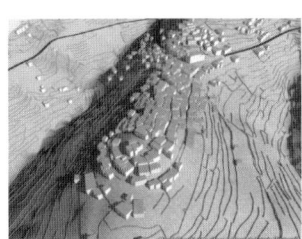

- **ArchiPaint**

    (freehand drawings) – Cigraph

    This connectable tool palette integrates drawing utensils such as a pencil, brush or spray can. Freehand drawings are created in the desired spot via graphical pad.

    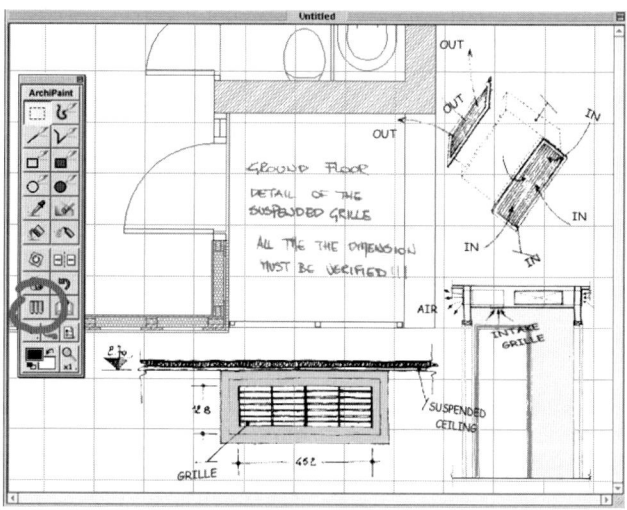

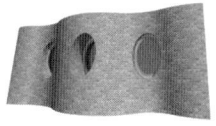

- **ArchiWall**

    (transformation and freeforming of walls) – Cigraph

    This API adds "overlaid structures" to regular ArchiCAD-walls and allows simple prismatic blocks to be transformed into multiform architectural elements. Users can add freeform accessory elements to standard walls in order to create mouldings and other decorations, giving projects a more realistic appearance.

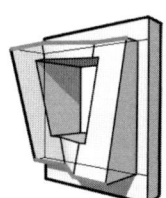 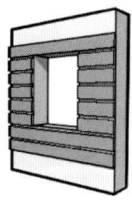 

- **ArchiGlazing**
(modeling of glass structures) – Graphisoft

This plug-in is for upright and slanted façades as well as winter garden glazing and it performs distribution calculations automatically. Tedious measurement work for flat-, shed- and cone-shaped glass paneling is replaced by inputting specific parameter information. Horizontal section heights can be defined in the ground plan rendering and adjacent walls can be fitted to the glass paneling.

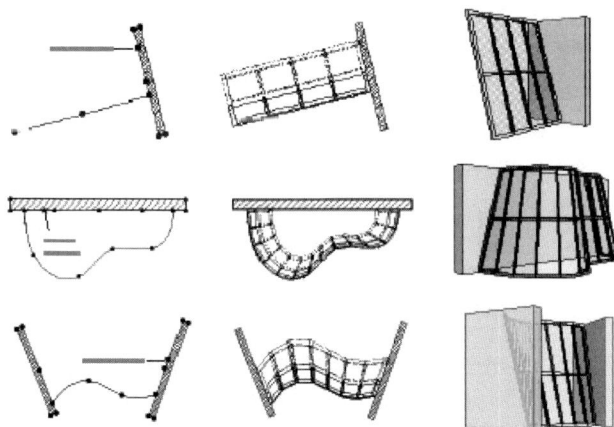

- **ArchiRuler**
(additional 2D tools) – Cigraph Tools
Existing 2D tools can be expanded, which increases their spectrum of applications.

 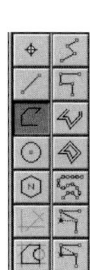 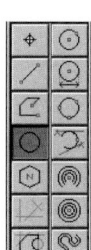

- NCS Colorpalette

    (Color system) – Scandinavian Color Institute AB

    The National Color System gives the user a selection of color hues from the NCS color palette and creates an ArchiCAD material color based on the chosen NCS color. This color system is used all over the world and is considered a standard in many countries.

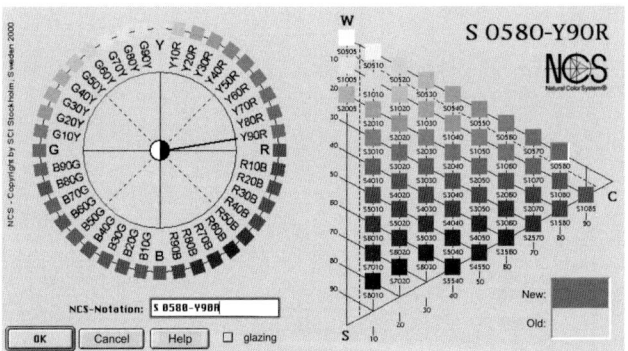

- Check Duplicates

    (deletes double objects in drawings) – Graphisoft

    Double objects are often created due to "coincidental" double clicks on the same mouse position or by copying levels. Objects with the same parameters (type, thickness, height, etc.) that are located in exactly the same place on the grounds plan are activated and deleted where desired.

- Plan2Model

    (create 3D-models from 2D-drawings) - Consistent

    Related geometric shapes are recognized within a two-dimensional grounds plan drawing and automatically or manually modified into the corresponding three-dimensional

ArchiCAD construction components (e.g. walls with window openings, doors and/or GDL objects) via a so-called "conversion library". Once this library has been created, it can be used to process a number of similar planning documents. The conversion is based on a recognition algorithm that generates patterns of structural objects. Two-dimensional drawings based on DXF and DWG files, or data that converts grid points into vectors provide the necessary source material.

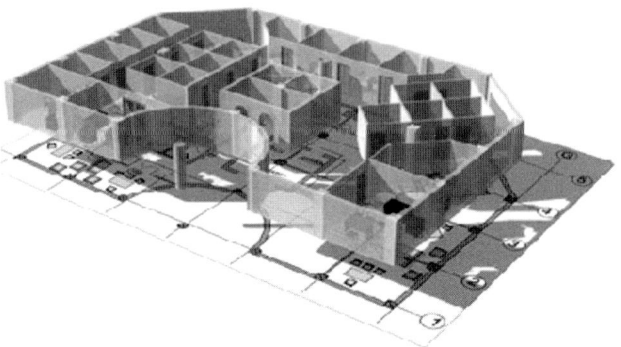

No further explanation of the roof, stair and truss maker (half-timbering modules) are required since they are part of the basic version and are installed as part of the standard installation.

2.5 Project-related Data Organization

The project administration solution applied in practice before computer-aided office work became possible was simple and clear. Neatly drawn plans (on tracing paper) were numbered and stored in a number of drawers after having been recorded in the respective plan book. After CAD equipment became available, this process was copied and replicated 1:1. Hence every (printed) plan draft had a corresponding file that it was based on.

The advantage of such an administration structure primarily lay in the ability to continue using a habitual system. A comparison to cars is appropriate: a car also initially resembled a horse-drawn carriage, although a horse no longer played a role in this motorized transportation form. It took a certain amount of time for another shape to gain acceptance. The development of CAD software packages followed a similar course. When architecture-related software was still in its early stages of development at the beginning of the nineties, nobody had thought of administrating anything other than digital planning documents. The majority of the CAD programs available then ultimately followed a two-dimensional orientation. One (basic) file was duplicated in order to produce various plan printouts and specific planning contents were then added afterwards and all the data that documented the entire document was collected on the hard drive as the project progressed.

The continuing development of the Virtual Building Concept gradually lessened the importance of the administration of individual project files. It became possible to locate all the required planning contents in one project file via a layer group control and relay the result to the plotter. Project administration became perceptibly slimmer and there were no quantitative losses. So much for the theory. In practice, for example, a change of scale from 1:100 to 1:50 caused a disproportional increase in the size of the planning graphics and, most of all, in the font size. So, the work that had been saved on "exterior" administration (the image in the file index) was required for the "interior administration" of the layers. Hence a point was reached where a lack of clarity became evident and users considered the allocation of elements for individual layers more of a chore.

Software manufacturers therefore endeavored to develop a system that makes the administration of project contents verifiable and efficient. One of the first ideas was to introduce so-called "layers" that were analogous to those used in print graphics. Graphical elements such as lines, circles, texts, etc. were set in one layer along with the designated line thickness. The plotting pens used in the beginnings of CAD made it necessary to check how the plotted plan would look on-screen. The line thickness was not included in the layers; instead the pens on the plotter defined it. The system was easy to understand since the pen with the desired line thickness could be plugged into one of the eight available plugs on the plotter carousel. It was also possible to change plan graphics at any time this way. Another advantage was the fact that the carousel offered space for exactly eight pens. Today, it is more or less unimaginable to work with only eight layers, much less structure an entire project document and ultimately print an appealing graphic plan rendering.

Fig. 2.25 Faulty plotting result

The pen plotters described here are no longer in use. But the necessity for layer administration as the key to internal data organization remains current. As far as terminology – with regard to ArchiCAD – is concerned, it is understood that a "layer" refers to a level. There are potential misunderstandings between the terms "layer" and "story". To avoid getting lost in the finer points of language, it is best to use the expression "vertical structuring" for story and "horizontal structuring" for layers.

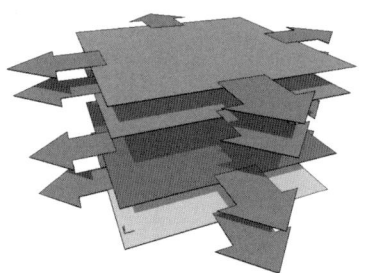 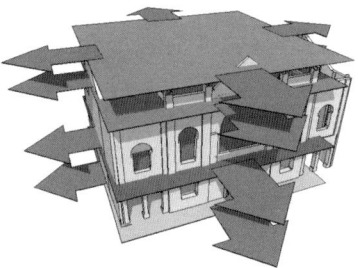

Fig. 2.26 Empty story structure, layer displaying "exterior wall"

Although it sometimes seems that users only communicated with their Personal Computer, the truth is that network-supported work groups are part of everyday life. Conceiving projects to be divided among a number of employees requires coordination between those concerned and a great degree of discipline and internal CAD project planning organization. The spectrum of services a CAD software package should be able to perform should therefore include functions that support team organization. This way, the communication process can be controlled and double execution can be avoided. If what is being produced by the other employees involved can be seen, it is possible reduce the amount of planning errors made. The TeamWork option makes this is possible in the ArchiCAD environment.

2.5.1 Efficient Layer Management

ArchiCAD Version 3.11, which was available in 1989, offered 16 layers, which was twice as much as competing CAD programs offered. However, it still required additional effort to allocate the desired plotter pen numbers to the respective layers. The advantage of 16 layers was nonetheless still greater than the effort involved in assigning the pens, it was still easier to structure planning contents better. It was not necessary to create an adapted file variant of a draft anymore. And this made the actual meaning of the layers clear. The entire project could now be entered and administrated in a single file. So more layers were needed to be able to add more planning contents to a project. The solution to this problem was presented in 1994, with the release of ArchiCAD version 4.55.

This version offered as many freely definable layers as needed. The answer to the question of the maximum amount of layers was of great, if not decisive importance when buying a CAD program at the time. All of ArchiCAD's competitors were compared and tested in terms of their ability to compete. It was trendy at the time to collect so-called "core data" and make simple value comparisons. The decision was often made in favor of the software that had the most top places.

ArchiCAD Version 5.0 was released in 1997, at the same time as this form of "evaluation" of CAD programs (which marked the beginning of ArchiCAD's supremacy) was going on. This version included "layer groups" to simplify layer organization. This control made it clear that it wasn't only necessary to be able to create a comprehensive function, it was also necessary to be able to use it easily.

The simplest form of cataloguing was based on construction criteria, such as exterior walls, interior walls, lightweight wall panels, (sanitary) facilities, furnishings, etc. Since planning graphics (line thickness) is handled independently from the distribution of the drafted elements on the various layers, the user can concentrate on structuring the layers and layer groups. The question of how many layers are useful for a given planning phase cannot be given a general answer. Some CAD guidelines contain a clear indication: the fewer the better. It shouldn't remain unmentioned that every element in a draft has to be allotted to a layer by the user. The respective allocations are ultimately office and user-specific, wrong allocations are sources of errors.

Hence planning work requires control mechanisms that are both time and cost-intensive. The creativity involved in designating layers has an influence on the user's understanding of them; it is an important criterion for verification purposes. The creation of verifiable layer structures has been supported effectively since the introduction of the "favorites palette" in ArchiCAD Version 7. The (automated) allocation of drafting elements to layers is hence easier and more clearly understandable.

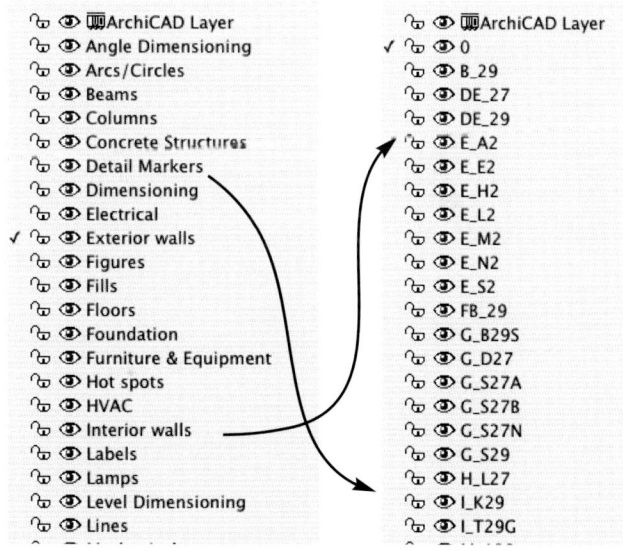

Fig. 2.27 Standard layers vs. layer definition in accordance with CAD structural engineering guidelines

How many layers are required as a minimum? Two layers can be enough, to be precise. One layer could contain the visible drafting elements and the other layer could contain the hidden elements. A third layer could be included in this reduced scenario for cases in which it isn't clear which of the other two layers (visible or hidden) the elements should be located in. Is such a system practicable? Theoretically, the answer is, "yes". The search-and-activate function in ArchiCAD is so comprehensive in the meantime that an item can be found and selected with a few (targeted) search criteria and invisibly inserted in the respective layer.

This idea should now be tried with a design plan, will it work? Is it possible to compile planning documentation without taking a step backwards to the one-plan-is-one-project era? The Virtual Building Concept provides a comprehensive project database as background. The greater the structure of the information in this database, the easier it is to perform a targeted evaluation of the contents of a plan. In the case of our example with only two layers, this means that the database structure offers only limited evaluation possibilities. Thus the possibilities offered by the Virtual Building Concept remain largely unused. If 0.25 mm wide lines are used to symbolize the ceiling breakthrough point and 0.25 mm lines are also used to mark a change in floor surface and both are made visible in the plan and one of lines is to be made invisible, the user will immediately see the limits of the existing structure and be forced to search for the lines line by line. A differentiation via layer allocation is required to sort through sets of identical lines.

Drafting contents with the same meaning (= same planning contents) are therefore logically allocated to the same layer. The ArchiCAD tool used for this is unimportant. The graphic specifications of the drafting elements such as the color and the weight of face are subordinate to the layer structure and can be used independently.

It has already been mentioned that layer designation was rather simple in earlier ArchiCAD versions (numbered from 1 to 16). The possibility of using appealing layer names led users to let their imagination run wild, which resulted in designations that weren't always understandable to their colleagues and caused additional confusion during planning. Although ArchiCAD's competitors also offered alphanumeric layer designations, the number of letters was limited to a maximum of eight. This imitation lead to a "cryptic language" and number combinations that forced users to guess at the contents based on these abbreviations and number combinations. However, this "nomenclature" was difficult to understand for outsiders. The ideal solution came in the form of a useful combination of both approaches: designations such as "structural walls", "non-structural walls", "exterior walls" indicate the allocation clearly and are generally understandable. Things get a bit more difficult when it comes to additional graphic information. The following sample rule for exterior walls can be helpful: "if an element contains graphical contents that compliment an exterior wall consisting of lines or construction component hatchings, it should be on the same layer as the basic information". In this case, they should also be on the exterior wall layer. Thus the allocation refers to both the ArchiCAD tools used and the planning contents.

Why is it useful to use numbering or coding in addition to the layer designations? It functions as an additional classification hierarchy within the layer structure. The code "wall" is used for all layers whose contents have to do with walls, for example. If a user draws elements that cannot be allocated to any existing layer as part of his planning documentation, he merely has to create a new layer and add the groupcode "wall" to it. That makes it clear to others involved that this group of elements are related to the wall layer. This system can also be used for multiple layer allocations when sorting layers automatically by code. The following example shows an especially clever designation. Aa planning progesses additional groups of layers are created and assigned to the individual trades or consultants.

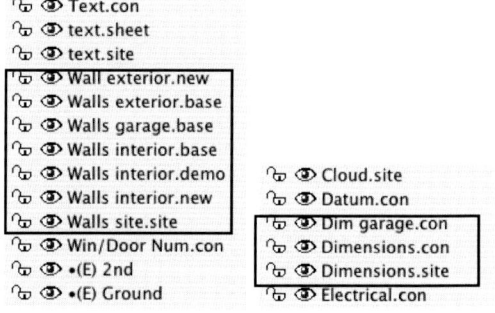

Fig. 2.28 Example of differentiated layer definition

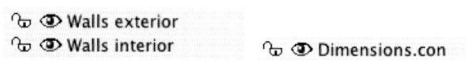

Fig. 2.29 Inadequate differentiation of the layer definition

In closing, it should be stated that the user should develop and use his own office standards based on his immediate work environment. It doesn't seem useful to just adopt structures defined by others, especially in a place where a great number of persons will be working on one project document, a situation in which the logical follow-up of individual inputs, even without consultation, is of great importance. A well-founded layer structure is useful, but it should be considered in advance. After all, it is the Virtual Building Model with the integrated project database structure and not the planning printout that is an important chapter. Adaptations performed afterwards involve additional work.

2.5.2 Practical Story Management

When compared directly with other CAD software products, ArchiCAD features one major difference to the others in form of a floor management function. A useful structure is available for the administration of all vertical elements in a space. The first version of ArchiCAD already displayed floors "on top of one another", later versions of ArchiCAD were able to display elements in various floors, which led to improved performance in terms of organization and graphic project planning renderings.

The simultaneous use of standard, foundation, roof and mezzanine floors allows for a number of plan renderings in combination with the layer administration function. It is not necessary (any longer) to create and external document structure with outsourced project files. Additionally, floor management facilitates the dimensioning of sections and elevations. The user can choose between an absolute and a relative ground floor-based dimensioning system while entering data. Complicated conversion calculations between relative and absolute heights and possible sources of error can thus be avoided. Integrated story management also offers advantages when handling later changes. The elements of the floor above are automatically set on the upper edge chosen by the user of the base of the floor below. The base layer of the floors above is taken into consideration automatically when the floor height is changed.

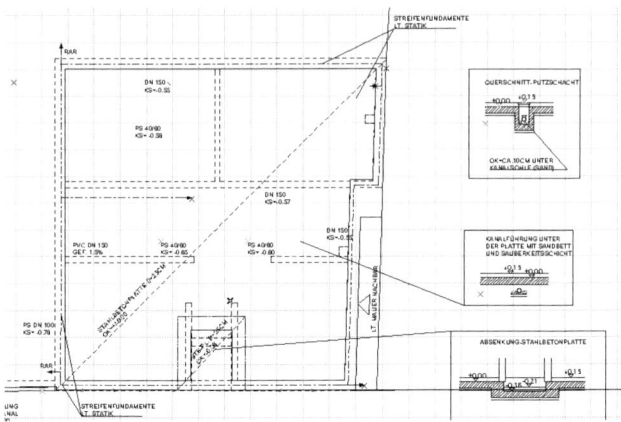

Fig. 2.30 Example: *"foundation story"*

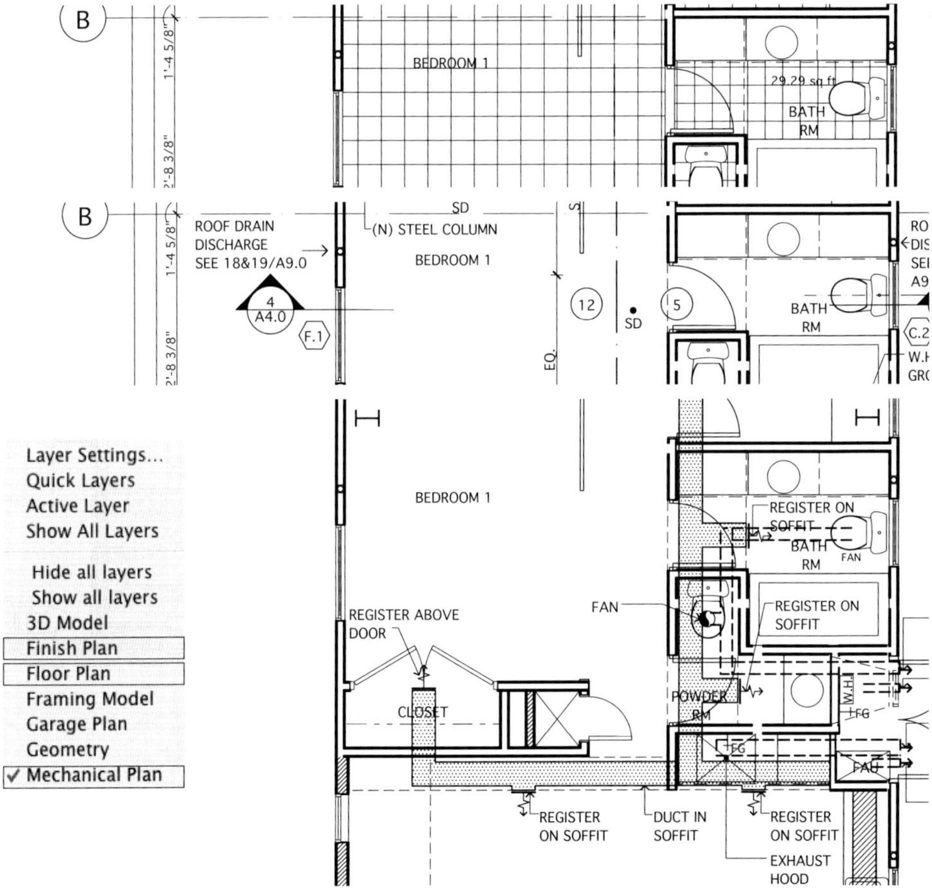

Fig. 2.31 Example: *"regular layer set with an additional story: mechanical plan"*

The sample applications show how the floor structure can be integrated for other uses. Some of the practical solutions shown here seem to contradict the *Virtual Building Concept*, but when looked at closely, they are more of an extension than a reduction of the concept's possibilities. Various building contents can be shown on a number of floors, for example. It is also possible to simplify access to cross-floor planning information in a project. No additional drafting is required if, for example, the garage-based grid on the top floor of a building is supposed to be "translucent".

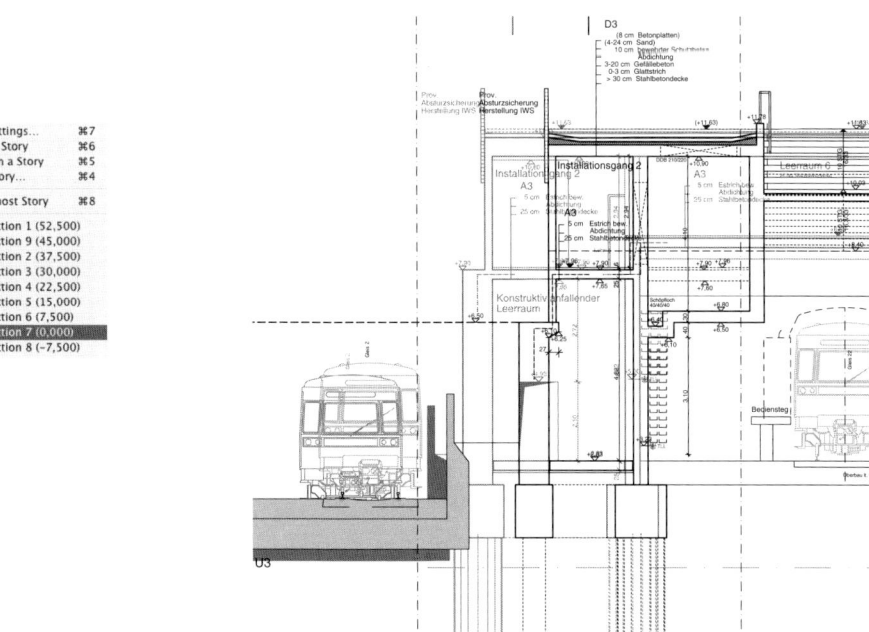

Fig. 2.32 Example: "section/view story" (Architektengruppe U-Bahn)

The vertical structure of the building demands from users that they consider the overlaying of building elements and how they are displayed in the various planning documents. Transparent floor contents help meet this demand, since the user is able to print any ground plan rendering he may require with either complete or segmental information on stories above or below a given location.

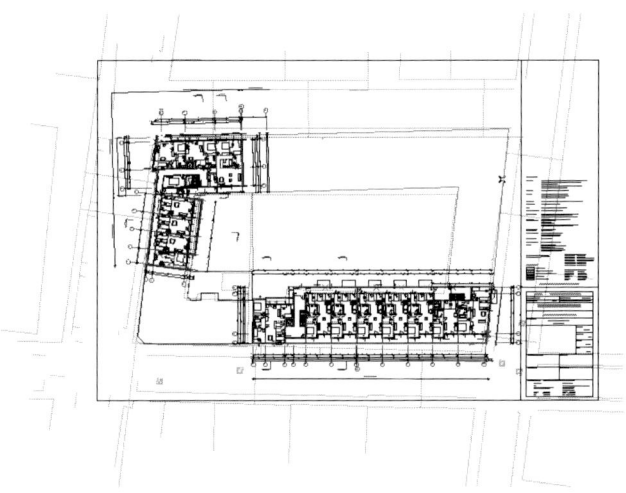

Fig. 2.33 Example: "ghost story" with site plan rendering (Ifsits/Ganahl/Larch)

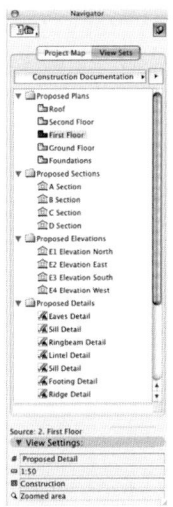

Normally, a site plan including the building outlines is created as a separate planning document. Floor management in ArchiCAD offers the possibility of integrating both such planning and all the loaded relevant surveyor data on the surroundings in a reasonable way. A site plan document can be generated without influencing the grounds plan renderings of the other floors by creating a separate "site plan" floor consisting of data that is not based on imported 2D information, and combining it with the functionality of a transparent floor. The scale contents and the reduced graphical contents of a site plan can be easily stored via navigator settings.

2.5.3 TeamWork Features for Work Distribution

Two separate, basic approaches should be defined in terms of multiple employee access to the same project data. A project can initially be saved as individual drafts (e.g. one file per layer). Complementary drafting segments that may be required can be loaded locally for reference purposes. However, that kind of approach requires additional management software to keep an overview over the entire project. On the other hand, it is also possible to organize data access via a central project file. ArchiCAD chose this path, which is closely related to the Virtual Building Concept. With the TeamWork option, ArchiCAD supports processing and administration structures for projects requiring cross-workstation access. One of the important features is the possibility of creating charts of existing work structures.

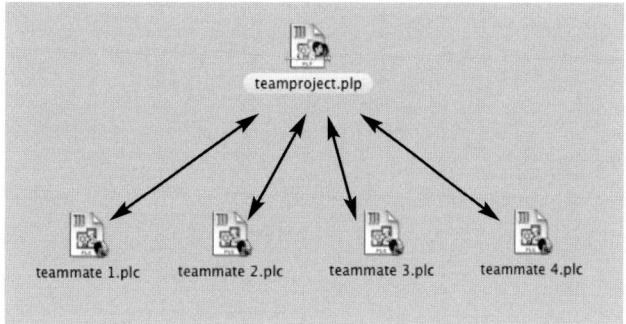

Fig. 2.34 Schematic rendering of a TeamWork file organization

The internal management of relevant project specifications such as building component hatchings, layer designations, the number and height of floors can only be created and/or changed by the so-called "team leader". Team members, can, for example, "reserve" floors or layers for processing in the central TeamWork document.

It is thus possible for all the users concerned to "tug on the same rope", even on a cross-platform basis and over large distances and they all have access to the same project status information. Constant networking is not necessary, but should take place at regular intervals. This means that data that has been entered should be sent to the computer (server) that contains the team project document. This computer can then calculate additions or changes after receiving the data. Drafting is completed in the sketch mode. In principle, as many users as desired can work on a project, but there are mechanisms that regulate specific access and change authorizations. Hence specific project segments can be locked and a conflict recognition mode is available for the floors and layers.

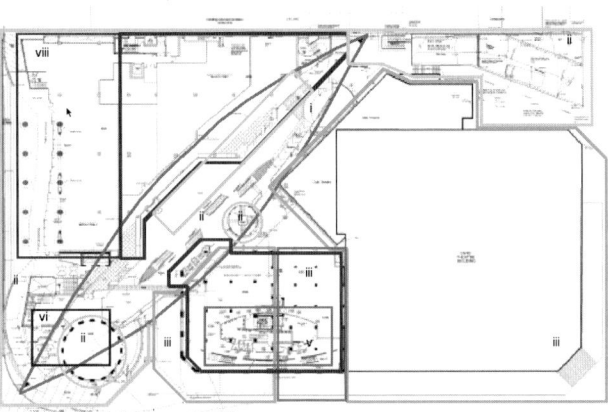

Fig. 2.35 Example: possible reservation of work segments

It is even possible for one user to assume a number of roles (for example: team leader and member) when required. It should also be noted that a number of users can use the same user name, although not at the same time. It is even possible to simulate a team on one single computer, without a network.

If it should become necessary – for whatever reason – it is also possible to switch from a TeamWork constellation to the single document mode.

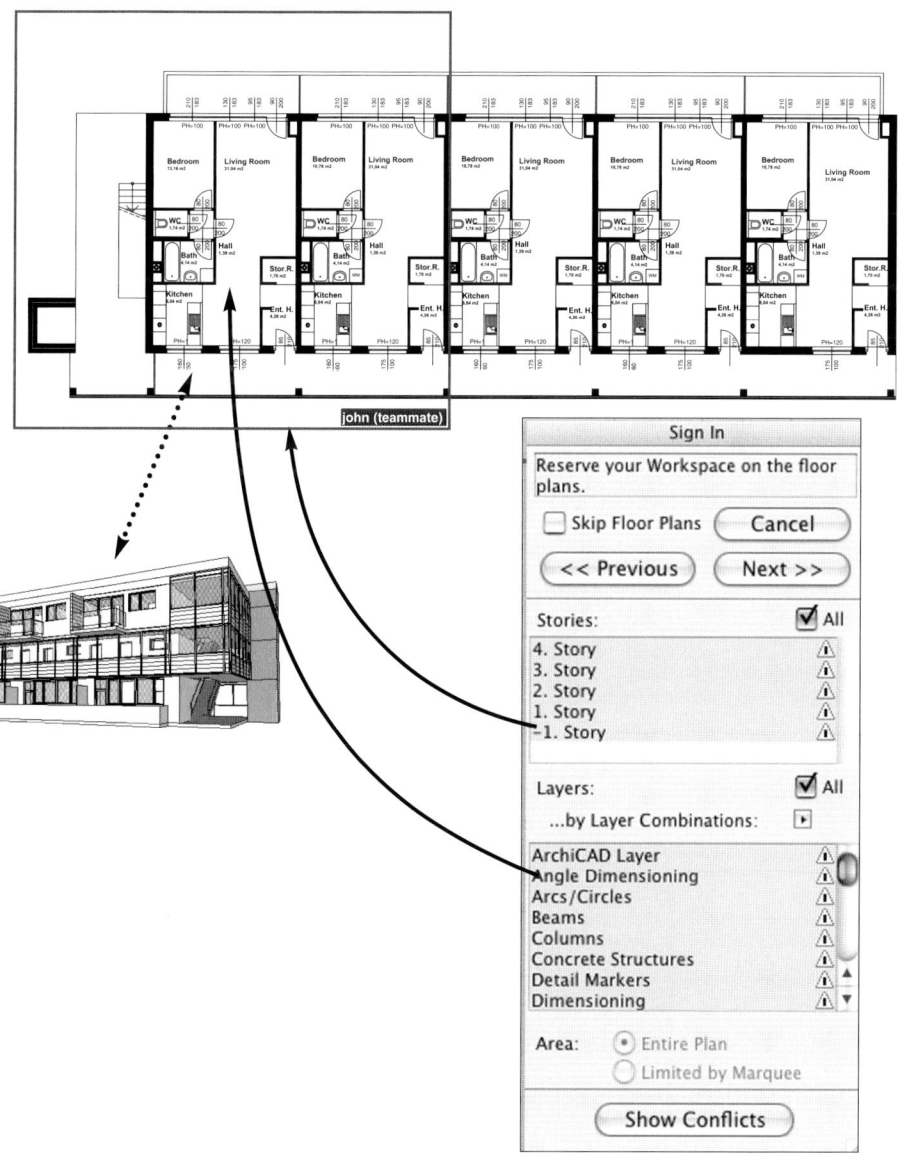

Fig. 2.36 Reserving a work segment

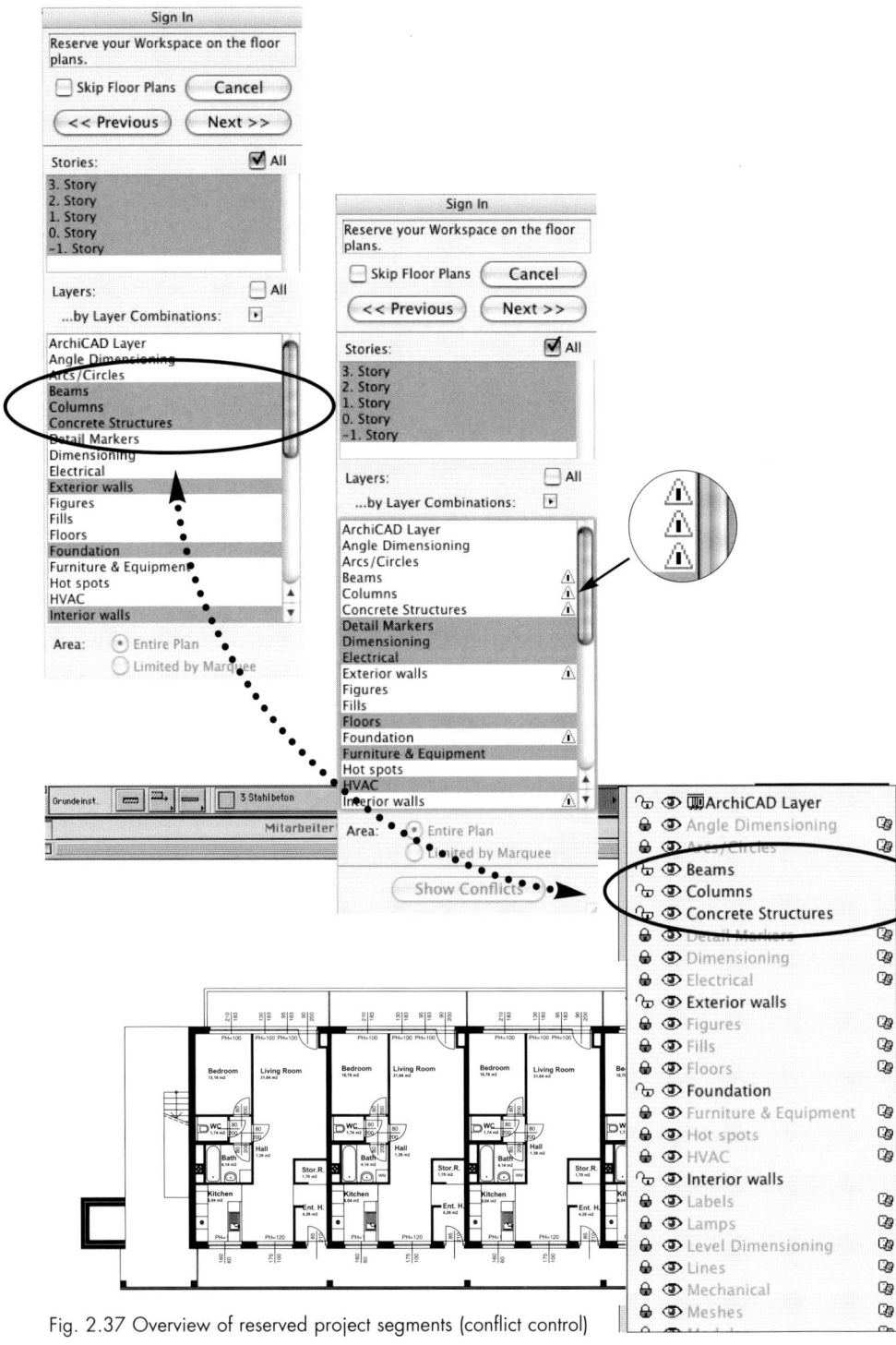

Fig. 2.37 Overview of reserved project segments (conflict control)

What would an alternative approach without the TeamWork features look like? ArchiCAD project documents have to pieced together in this case. Although this is possible, it also requires a certain amount of additional time. A disadvantage is the fact that project segments have to be repeatedly sent back and forth while inputting data, to be able to verify and read data (measurements, parameters, etc.).

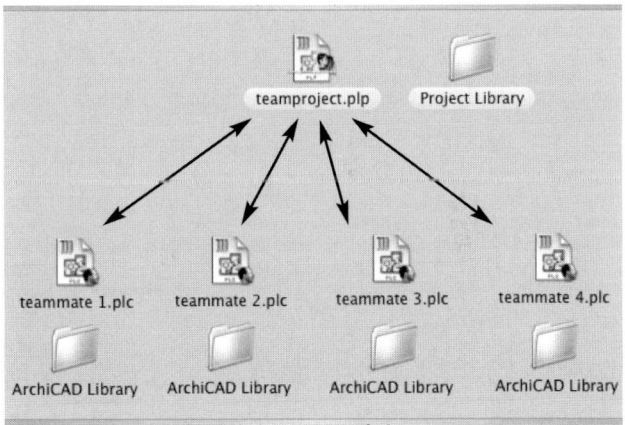

Fig. 2.38 Organization example: Central library

The use of so-called "satellite libraries" means simplified GDL object management in TeamWork project use for the user. The satellite library is no more than an identical (indexed) copy of the object library linked to the original team project. The indexing makes local changes to a standard library GDL object recognizable during the next TeamWork project comparison. The user can choose between the changed and the original GDL object for future reference.

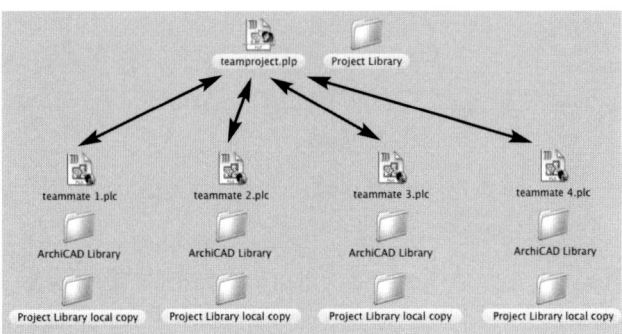

Fig. 2.39 Organization example: Satellite Library

Over the course of the last years, varying application TeamWork functionality forms have crystallized at many different architecture offices. The fundamental question that arises is, when is most helpful to use the TeamWork mode and under which conditions might it be best to choose Hotlink Module features instead?

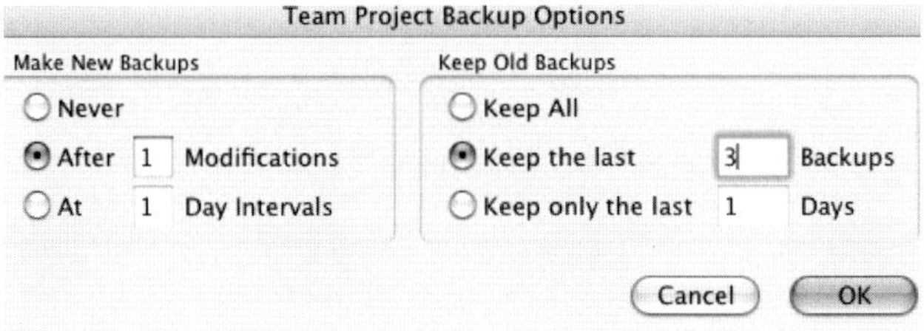

Fig. 2.40 Data saving options

A conclusive answer is not possible, since Hotlink Modules can also be used within the TeamWork mode as an additional project organization method. Practical experience shows that project processing in the TeamWork mode is useful whenever more than three employees are supposed to work together on one project, since the integrated and automatic backup functions in the TeamWork mode are an advantage when compared to the local, manual saving of individual files.

2.5.4 Changing Plans and Document Designation

It is advisable to create a structural segment completion file whenever a change of plans becomes necessary (change of plans due to additional information received). The project file is archived as a verifiable planning status file. As of this moment, the planning change is then completed on a (digital!) copy of this project file. All the planning contents that are no longer required for the new status can then be deleted, since the new planning may use far more detailed structures.

A classical example are is the the deletion of lettering and dimensioning for the planning submission stage (S=1:100). The required new lettering and dimensioning in the execution planning (S=1:50) or in the detailed planning (S=1:1, S=1:2, S=1:5, S=1:10, S=1:20) can be newly made. Parallel to this duplication of the project file, the user should store all the files pertaining to this planning status into a separate directory. A combination of the project name and the corresponding date is the best designation for such a directory, for example "S_Broadway_20041201.PLN". In the case of project variants with the same date, the project name, the variant designation and the current date should be used: "S_BroadwayR1_20041201.PLN", or "S_Broadway R2_20041201.PLN". The "S" stands for submission plan and defines the planning contents. A detail plan for the same project could be named, "D_Broadway_20041201.PLN".

A name should be used that all project staff members can recognize and designations such as: "Today01.PLN", "Today01_NEW.PLN" should be avoided at all costs. Ultimately, such designations are only understandable for a short period of time at best and they are hardly practicable for other employees. It would also be hard for the user himself to reconstruct exactly which planning status a document refers to after a few weeks or even months. Other search criteria such as the date and time of the last change are already integrated in the designation key. It should be noted that a general designation for project documents cannot be prescribed since this would ultimately massively curtail an architecture office's individual freedom. An office specific standard should be instituted that covers the respective requirements and is generally understandable. A designation key should then be handed to each employee.

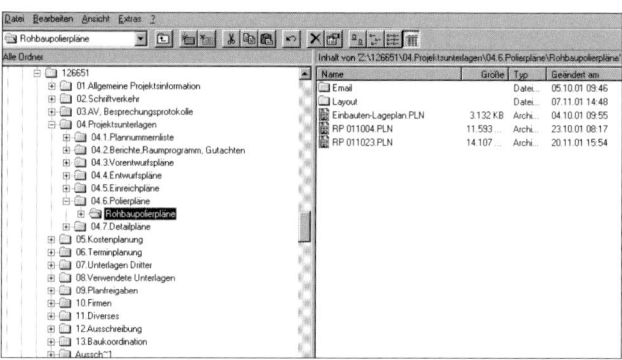

Fig. 2.41 Example: Data management (AXIS engineering services)

The Virtual Building Concept makes it possible to manage the sections and perspectives of a project as well as the floors within a project file. This ArchiCAD functionality allows for quicker updating of all the planning documents affected by any changes. Ultimately, the user can choose between automated updating or an update "at the press of a button". However, the latter system means that the work process, although it will not be stopped, may now have a source of error, if changes have been made to the 3D model without performing the necessary manual update.

2.6 Using Information from the Internal Database

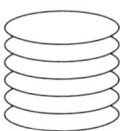

The Virtual Building Concept is based on an integrated project database. So, if a large amount of information exists, the question arises as to which evaluation types can be performed with the given information. The space labeling possibilities, the automatic surface area calculation options and the dynamic linking of the spatial zone with its surrounding (space-creating) elements have been standard for a couple of ArchicAD versions. The space stamp functions are convenient in everyday work processes. Space stamps show the basic information in the grounds plan and are a central part of database evaluation. If a teammate is required to list all floor area categories within the project while completing a competition proposal, he can either perform long, wearisome calculations or simply press, the "calculate" button within the ArchiCAD environment. Gross volume and total floor area calculations in a building are another example of a case in which database access gives the user an overview of expenses immediately, if needed.

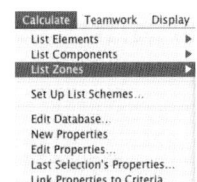

Within the project completion process, the creation of architectural space reference book, containing the spatial program and the functional program of the building should be seen as a central task. Sometimes manual aids such as table calculation programs are also employed, which require additional work time. Thorough use of the integrated software functions leads to cost savings and therefore a long-term reduction of planning-related work (elimination of errors, unnecessary inputting work, etc.). Sample space reference books for standardized room types meeting the structural engineering requirements can be used in these cases. These include the areas of preliminary structural work and completion as well as hygienic, electric and heating, ventilation equipment. Specialized planners can be integrated in the process at an early stage for these purposes.

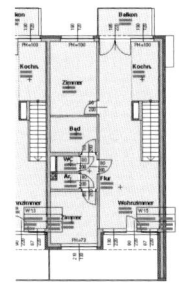

A "room reference book" should be structured in a way that puts the project at the top layer of the hierarchy and that breaks buildings according to stories, room categories, areas and functions. Bordering elements that create further spaces are given a clear room coding ("room ID"). The allocation of a room to a user category, or to a story or area (eventually a department) defines the exact room position in the building. The respective roomname (bedroom, office, hall, etc.) can be defined in the next hierarchy layer with a number of room categories and used on many stories.

Rooms listed by flats								
Flat	RoomNo.	Roomname	Story	Floor finish	Room height	Perimeter	Wall surfaces	Room m2
04	05	Hall	Groundfloor	Carpet	2,50 m	4,72 m	5,49 m2	1,39 m2
	06	Bathroom	Groundfloor	Tiles	2,50 m	8,20 m	23,11 m2	4,14 m2
	07	WC	Groundfloor	Tiles	2,50 m	5,32 m	14,33 m2	1,74 m2
Flat 04	total					84,80 m	210,84 m2	61,09 m2
F05								
	01	Living Room	Groundfloor	Carpet	2,50 m	28,34 m	70,59 m2	31,04 m2
	02	Bedroom	Groundfloor	Carpet	2,50 m	13,30 m	35,44 m2	10,78 m2
	03	Kitchen	Groundfloor	Tiles	2,50 m	10,02 m	28,82 m2	6,04 m2
	04	Hall	Groundfloor	Tiles	2,50 m	9,52 m	20,47 m2	4,26 m2
	05	Storage	Groundfloor	Tiles	2,50 m	5,38 m	13,36 m2	1,7 m2
	06	Hall	Groundfloor	Carpet	2,50 m	4,72 m	5,49 m2	1,39 m2
	07	Bathroom	Groundfloor	Tiles	2,50 m	8,20 m	23,11 m2	4,14 m2
	08	WC	Groundfloor	Tiles	2,50 m	5,32 m	14,33 m2	1,74 m2
Flat 05	total					84,80 m	210,84 m2	61,09 m2
F06								
	01	Living Room	Groundfloor	Carpet	2,50 m	28,34 m	70,59 m2	31,04 m2
	02	Bedroom	Groundfloor	Carpet	2,50 m	13,30 m	35,44 m2	10,78 m2
	03	Kitchen	Groundfloor	Tiles	2,50 m	10,02 m	28,82 m2	6,04 m2
	04	Hall	Groundfloor	Tiles	2,50 m	9,52 m	20,47 m2	4,26 m2
	05	Storage	Groundfloor	Tiles	2,50 m	5,38 m	13,36 m2	1,7 m2

Fig. 2.42 Example of a "space reference book"

An area is understood as a summary of the individual rooms in either the same zone and/or use category on one or more floors. An additional summary of areas between different buildings is also possible. A room reference book manages both graphic and alphanumeric data that can be clearly matched with a room coding system. This collection of data can then be handed over to the operator or the building user once the project is completed:

- The *building technology collection* manages all preliminary structural work and completion data. It is comprises the wall, floor, ceiling surfaces and the substructure. Additional information such as net and gross room volume, the number of room corners and room contours can also be recorded here.

- All *space creating elements* including their surfaces are specified in the furnishings collection, such as the tiles on a wall and possible dust guards.

- All the *windows* and *doors* allocated to a room, including their surface areas and jamb depth can be documented in a corresponding collection. Product and finish-specific attributes can be included. The type of finish or the type of metal fittings etc., used can also be defined here.

Necessary basic data that is required for the creation of complex evaluations in ArchiCAD are already included in the active library data sets, but it is also possible to create user-specific extensions and perform changes and updates.

The user can also create a number of task-specific data sets that contain components, descriptions and units (quantities, mass, weight etc.). It is also possible to group them under data keys based on user-specific logic. Characteristics can be organized according to construction elements such as walls, supports, roofs or materials such as concrete, wood/timber, and steel or by work steps such as foundation, electrical wiring and furniture.

Every data key contains an alphanumeric key name and key code. The data keys are sorted alphabetically according to the corresponding codes and it is also possible to create key hierarchies. This is possible with the numbering, which serves identification and description purposes. Personally generated data sets have to be loaded on the active library to be available in the ArchiCAD environment. Data sets and construction elements always have to be linked with the "component-objects" function and the objects have to be created and available in the object library.

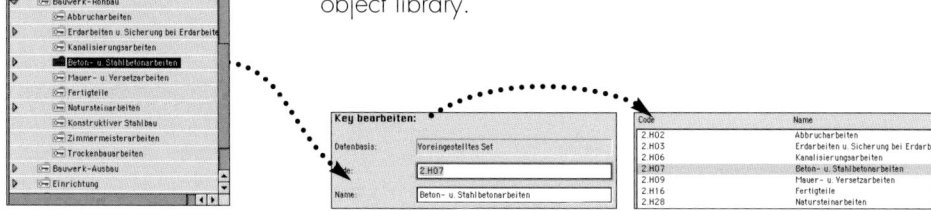

Fig. 2.43 Database settings and the corresponding "keys"

ArchiCAD differentiates between the linking of data sets with drafting elements (e.g. walls, windows, etc.) The element (e.g. a light-weight concrete wall) has to be selected individually and linked with the "individual link" function, with the "component-objects" function.

The feature "Linked Property Objects" can be used should it be necessary to create a general allocation of element hatching or material types. This way, every time a characteristic matches the criteria, the amount is updated on the amounts calculation list.

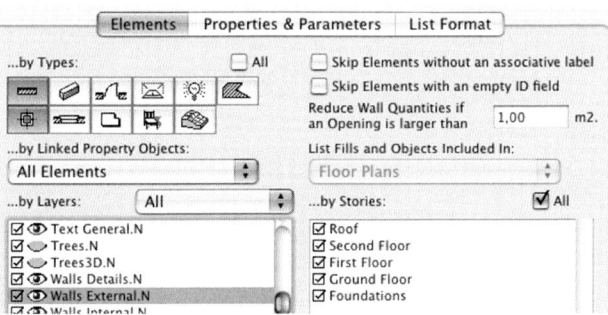

Fig. 2.44 Database: Quantity selection

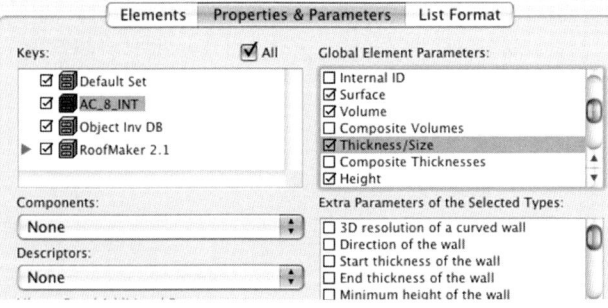

Fig. 2.45 Database: Attribute selection

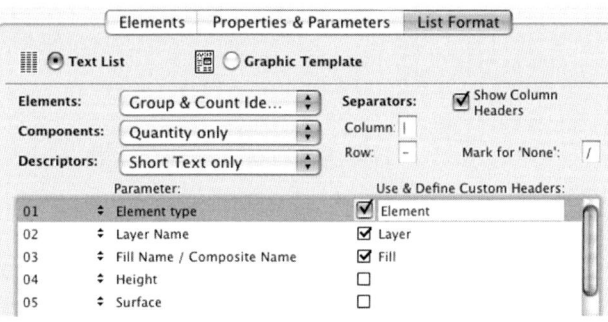

Fig. 2.46 Database: List sequence

Schemes with element lists should primarily be used to sort, count and record construction elements in ArchiCAD projects. The information in the element lists can be related to element parameters, components and descriptions and should be used when it is necessary to sort and count components or to calculate amounts and quantities, as well as to generate price lists or other similar data. The criteria in the stock lists can also be based on element parameters.

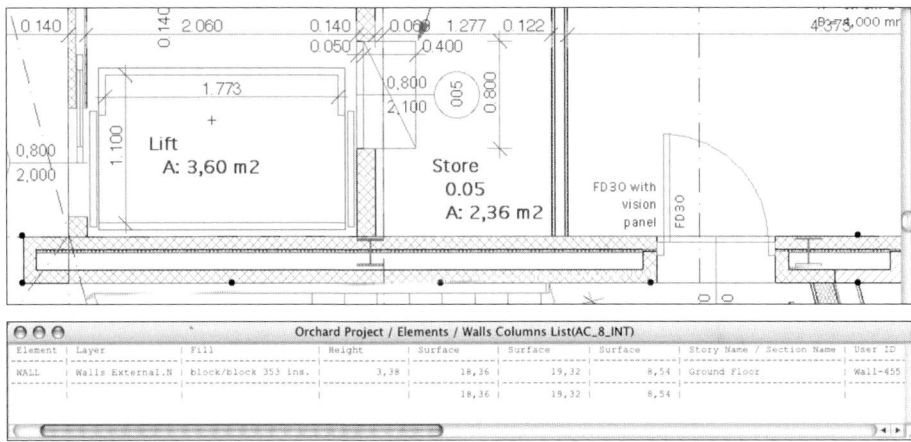

Fig. 2.47 Database: Example of a bill of quantities

2.7 Project-related Communication and Presentation

When looked at closely the means of communication used in traditional design and planning presentations are not significantly different to paper-based media. The information carrier that is used on-site provides the basis for interpretation and the planning symbols which make it possible to build the real building. The analogous physical scale model should also be mentioned here, since detailed models can make a great impression on the observer. A lay person's lack of ability to understand technical construction plans can be responsible for a potential communication problem. Such a person could be compared to an illiterate person who has to accept what is written as the true rendition of what is said. Someone who can read will hardly doubt what is written since he does not know the underlying communication. Visualizations such as perspective-view renderings are useful instruments for conveying information in such constellations. This "insight" isn't anything new, but which points of view are shown? Are they positions people can assume? A bag full of tricks filled to the brim is available for these cases.

In architecture, graphical renderings are usually complemented by a verbal declaration of intent of another form of communication. Internal communication – between the various project staff members concerned – should also be taken into consideration aside from external communication with various parties. After all, it is the staff that is able to interpret the technical symbols on a planning draft.

The roles of "architect" and "structural engineer" themselves are defined by varying perspectives that are reflected in the planning of one and the same building section.

A new generation of tools was introduced in ArchiCAD Version 6.5 that supports, for example, communication between the protagonists in the building process. This simplifies everyday work steps during a project. The ProjectXchange features, which consist of the project publisher reviewer and marker, are useful (Internet-based) tools in this respect. Those concerned can add comments after preparing the required plan renderings with publisher. This can also be done without using ArchiCAD since the plan renderings prepared for this purpose can be viewed in an Internet browser. It is also possible to add comments with the "redlining features". One-click batch processing of the required grounds plans, sections, perspectives or visualizations is also possible with the help of the publisher. Mass lists of the virtual building can also be generated and exported into a selected data format and made available to the specialized planner via the "ftp upload" function. The reviewer includes the redlining function as well as direct Internet browser information access. This makes it possible to import comments added to the published draft back into the original project file. The project marker used for this purpose simultaneously provides information on the current changes as well as all other changes and comments made earlier by the external user. Changes can thus be verified and easily documented. ProjectXchange therefore gives the user and effective information flow control and organization tool.

2.7.1 Visualization Strategies

A large array of visualization instruments is available to every user, in accordance with the (tired) statement, "an image says more than a thousand words". For a time, it looked like photo-realistic computer renderings were going to become an Olympic discipline. Indeed, it became increasingly difficult to establish whether and to which degree a presented rendering (either partial or complete) was "artificial" or "natural". The eye recognizes differentiating elements quickly. The rendering of traces of use and a wealth of detail, just think of vegetation structures, would definitely overburden a computer (or even an entire computer network). But is it all really necessary? The ArchiCAD (photo-realistic) visualization palette shows a certain restraint in this context. It offers a comfortable range of standard functions that makes use of abstraction. Additional features, such as image editing techniques are available if needed. This means that retouching and supplementary imaging can be used as a means of manipulation. An additional rendering level can be employed if the intention is to offer "more" photo-realistic quality. Graphisoft favors an ArchiCAD-Art•lantis link in this context, which makes "ray tracing" (= the rendering of mirrored images, reflections etc.) possible. Comprehensive modeling work makes it necessary to enter the required information layer-by-layer. It is also necessary to consider in advance the materials to be used for model organization purposes. Other software products pursue similar objectives. A number of providers have been established in the field of professional visualization that specifically process such assignments. A comparison with translation seems useful here.

Fig. 2.48 Visualization: German Pavilion, Biennale / Venice (Project: LengyelToulouse Architekten)

Fig. 2.49 Visualization: Former Gymnasium Bitburg (LengyelToulouse Architekten / Project: J. Götz)

Fig. 2.50 Visualization: Adaptation of a movie theater (Project: LengyelToulouse Architekten)

Fig. 2.51 Visualization: Detail of glass façade (LengyelToulouse Architekten / Project: Klaus Müller)

Texts are defined by varying degrees of difficulty and therefore require a degree of familiarization. This is especially the case when the author has turned on his "twaddle maker" and his remarks are given clarity and precision only "in translation". Machine-made translations allow only a global understanding, while more complicated text passages suffer in this process.

Contract visualization takes an extreme position in these considerations. The objective is to create an ideal situation that will set the tone for the decision makers. Computer-supported visualization acts as a ticket to the next round of negotiations. However, it can also act as the opposite, in case a project should be hindered, by creating a photo-realistic rendering to act as a deterrent. Visual angles, the point of view and lighting effects contain important elements. Human figures, vegetation elements and objects for everyday use are also important supplementary visualizations elements.

In closing, it should be noted that ArchiCAD users have been able to produce so-called "Quicktime VR scenarios" (QTVR) directly from a project file since ArchiCAD Version 5.0. Therefore, it isn't necessary to buy additional software for this purpose. Free playback programs for all operating systems and/or plug-ins for Internet browsers are available free of charge. The results are hard to show in a book such as this since the interactivity is lost in this medium. The guiding principle behind the use of QTVR is to offer access to panoramic renderings with software extensions using widely available PC technology.

Viewing Quicktime VR sceneries makes a controllable experience of spatial situations possible based on the user's own preferences.

Fig. 2.52 QTVR scenery from the "FAUSTs Laboratory" (H. Peter / K. Wilhelm)

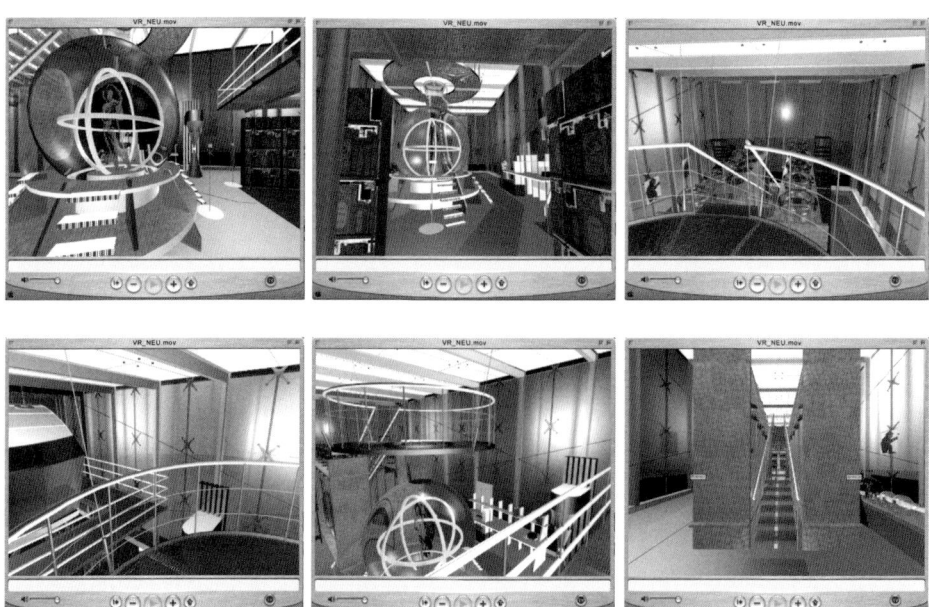

Fig. 2.53 QTVR scenes from the "FAUSTs Laboratory" (Herbert Peter / Kurt Wilhelm)

2.7.2 Printing and Plotting

The screen environment is sufficient for an ArchiCAD user over a certain period of time, but paper-based printouts become necessary at some point. Small format results up to an A3 size can be handed out as prints, while larger formats have to be generated by the plotter. Using the print command isn't a very great problem with certain applications. But the results can be surprising sometimes when handling print-outs from a CAD software product, especially in terms of the colors and line thickness. Printing and plotting problems have become less significant due to the continuing technical developments of recent years, but is still necessary to install the right drivers. It can happen that a fully functional driver is not immediately available for a new printing device when it is introduced. This leads to (minor) problems in terms of printed project renderings. Another potential source of error can emerge if a plotter isn't assigned enough main memory space. This is often the case when a file contains high-resolution images, since the plotter lacks the memory to depict the screening settings on a paper printout. The plot result will then feature missing draft segments, which may not be noticed during a cursory inspection (e.g. certain labels will be missing). Normally, these problems aren't dramatic, if it weren't for the fact that they tend to surface miraculously when there are time constraints or when a reliable result is urgently needed. One disadvantage compared with (paper-based) rendering methods can be identified here: a complete electronic planning draft is hardly useful at the construction site as long as it is only available "on computer" and cannot be delivered in printed form.

It is therefore advisable not to try any new constellations when working against a deadline.

The computer used to generate computer-supported plan renderings should have the right drivers installed (for both the printer and the plotter) and it should be kept in mind that ArchiCAD also offers extended print commands, e.g. it possible to create a scale print-out of a selected plan segment or even of the entire project. It is especially important to check the paper format settings of the connected printer in these cases. However, the scale selected for a plan adjusts the size of the font proportionally as well as enlarging or reducing the drawing elements contained. Unfortunately, the often desired reduction of the size of a plan rendering, while keeping the font size selected (to ensure legibility) earlier is not possible. This is generally desirable when creating a print-out with a 1: 50 rendering scale – a rendering with a great degree of detail – based on an enlarged 1:100 rendering without changing the rendering scale in the planning documentation. The reverse can happen if construction plans (S=1:50) are used to create plans of existing buildings or to be exchanged, which should include renderings in a scale of 1:100.

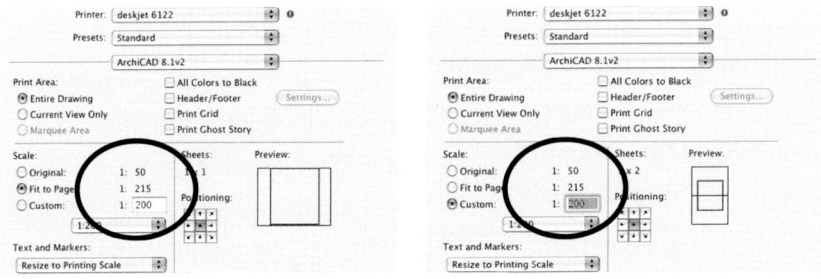

Fig. 2.54a-b Printing dialog: relationship between printing scale and paper format (A4 format)

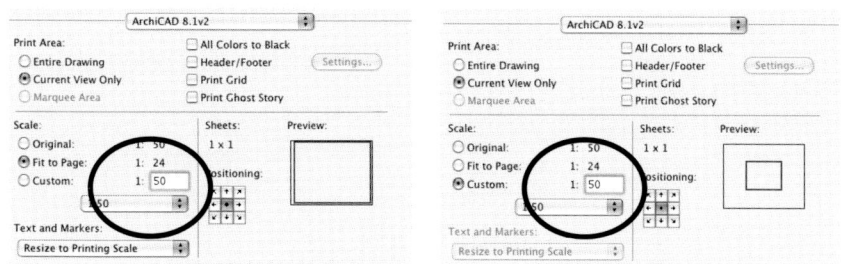

Fig. 2.55a-b Printing dialog: relation of planning segment to normal scale

If a digital planning draft was issued from a printer or plotter, this draft is considered a document since it will ultimately be used at the construction site. Hence document status also contains an element of liability for the planner. It is therefore advisable to send important planning status reports directly to the plotter including the respective date to be archived as a "plot file" in the project structure. Such files should be suffixed with "*.plt". This makes it possible to clarify planning errors or faulty construction segments at any time in the event of contractor questions or legal disputes using dated files. It is also useful to re-plot archived plotting data with the information bearing the relevant date. The printed version of the planning contents should correspond with the contents saved at that time. Any manipulation of the plot file at a later date would be clear based on the file's creation time and date stamp. It is therefore important to record important planning phases in a parallel planning book that can be compiled manually or electronically within the framework provided by office administration software.

The PlotMaker software is included in ArchiCAD as a basic feature. This is a tool used to lay out planning documentation. Aside from offering the possibility of sending planning documentation directly to the plotter (and printer!), PlotMaker also enables the user to manage planning documents. Dynamic updating is possible to direct ArchiCAD data access. The intermediate step requiring PMK format use in earlier versions is no longer necessary.

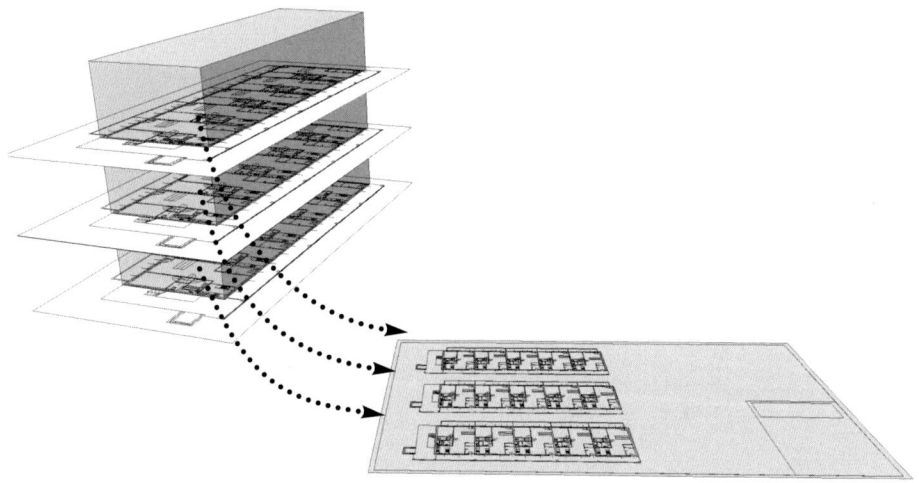

Fig. 2.56 Schematic rendering of the connection between ArchiCAD and PlotMaker

Although PlotMaker can hardly be characterized as outdated and still works as the ArchiCAD document manager par excellence, it can nonetheless be assumed that full integration within the ArchiCAD environment is likely in the future. Basic user requirements haven't changed significantly in the last years since paper-based planning documentation in varying scales and greatly differing graphical contents are still needed. Therefore the motto is: "the faster desired planning contents can be put in the right rendering scale and in a layout, the greater the comfort for the user".

- Is it possible to save a floor plan with a resolution greater than 72 dpi (= screen resolution)? First, it is necessary to "zoom in" around five times, if a resolution of 300 dpi is desired, for example. The entire floor plan will be saved in the selected format (*.tif, *.pict, *.bmp, ...) even if only a segment is visible. Then the file should be opened in an image editing program, before it can be reduced to the "right" size. This pushes the pixels closer together, creating the desired resolution.

2.7.3 Interfaces and Data Exchanges

The exchange of data between users – especially between different CAD software products – can paradoxically be seen as both an aid and an obstacle in project processing. It as improvement since a specialized planner or consultant can receive the respective data directly on his CAD system instead of waiting for printed planning copies. This eliminates the need for repeated data inputting before adding the supplementary information to the existing data. But additional work does become necessary if the coordination required for the exchange of data hasn't been prepared adequately. The amount of work can even increase if the supplementary consultant and specialized planner information has to be imported back, which jeopardizes control over the Virtual Building Model (including the integrated database). This doesn't sound very encouraging and awareness when working with CAD software product-related structures (layer designations and the allocation of planning contents, etc.) is only developing slowly. When two users are using varying internal cross-office standards, they have to institute communication that allows them to coordinate the selection of the contents to be exchanged and the structure in which this should occur and execute the exchange accordingly. The layer designation structure isn't the only decisive element here. The respective user's has to be thorough in terms of only allocating data to the layer it actually belongs to.

The Autodesk DXF exchange format has effectively become the standard in this field. This format makes it possible to exchange both 2D data and 3D data (although generally not at the same time) between two CAD software products while largely maintaining the existing (layer) structures. However, 2D information is primarily exchanged by this means. But for the user, this data quality means a loss of information due to the reduction of three-dimensional elements to the graphical contents of a two-dimensional line drawing. The DWG internal Autocad format has become more important, but the possibility of changing this format at any time (without stating a reason and without the corresponding documentation on the part of Autodesk, the manufacturer can jeopardize the exchange of data in this manner. ArchiCAD users are given support during data exchanges via the configuration table ("DXF-DWG-Config.txt") in the DXF-/DWG- interface. The various allocations and changes during data exchanges can be defined here. An effective exchange of data between two different office standards is possible once the corresponding agreements have been reached with the respective consultant.

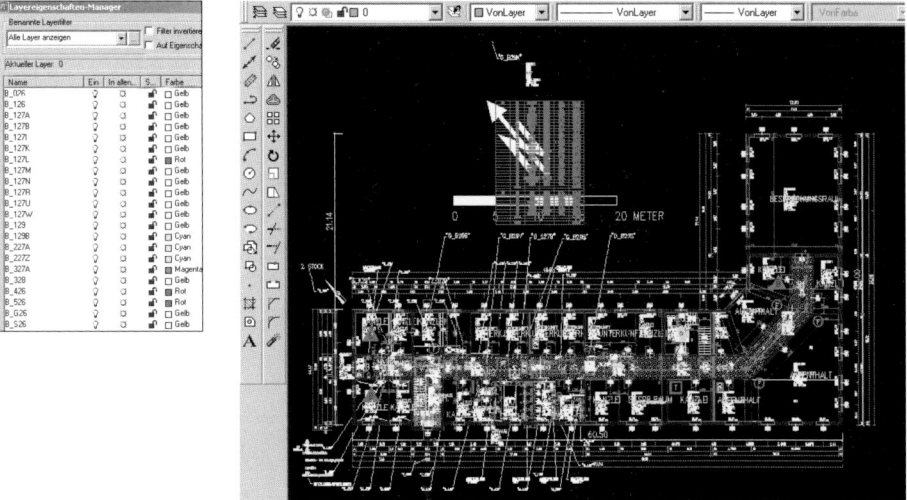

Fig. 2.57 Standardized layer and color samples (source material)

- Sample of a translator table within the framework of an open or save dialog.

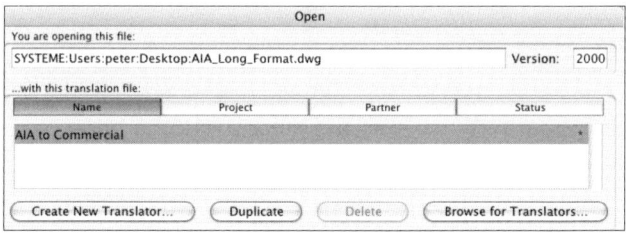

- Allocation of the original layer designations from the source file in the layer structure of the target file.

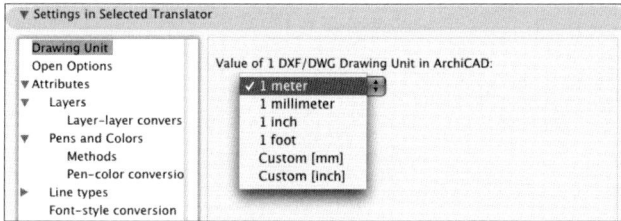

- Result of the layer designations changes after importing them via the selected configuration table.

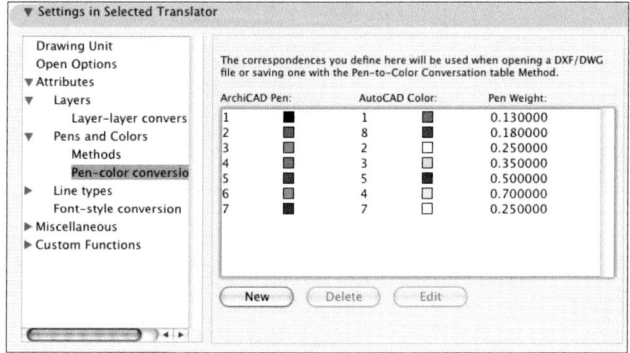

A "merge engine" was already included in ArchiCAD Version 7 for the exchange of data in both directions (i.e. import and export). A selection of data exchange options accompanies the merging of two flows of data without having an immediate effect on existing project data. Options can be bypassed when employing user-specific filters. Ultimately, it is a system of rules based on "if – then ties". It is possible to keep certain elements unchanged, deleted or allocated to a specific layer during a merging process, for example. But changes to data originally stemming from the architect can be added in a way that eliminates any possible discrepancies with the current project status. That type of planning information can be allocated to a desired layer and compared to the planning status depicted on the existing 2D line drawings.

The so-called "XREF technique" is not an individual format type in the Autocad environment. It is an abbreviation for eXternal REFerence and can be understood as an element converter. It is a form of config-file. The referencing process makes project data in other planning documents visible in the representational project file via DXF or DWG formatting without having to import the entire file. This function merely creates a reference linking the user's own project file and the contents of the referenced file. If a change is made to the original, the referenced drawing contents are also updated. The main disadvantage of using external references is the fact that the referenced file influences layer management. The layers in the references are added to the existing layers. This lack of clarity can then prove to be disadvantageous.

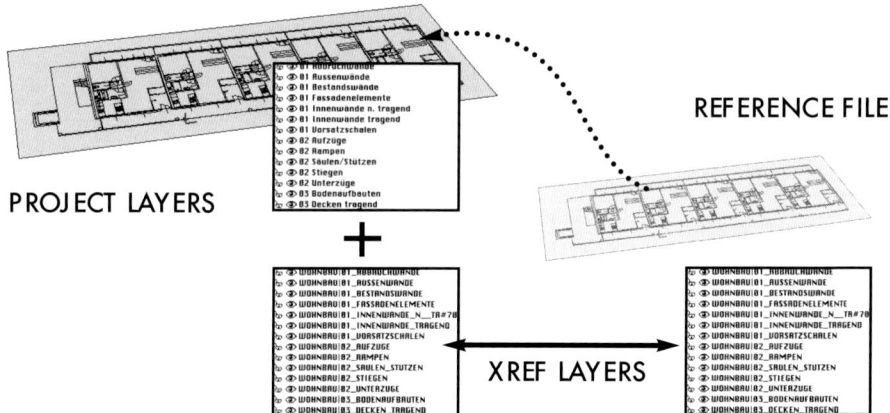

Fig. 2.58 XREF reference file level structure

The Hotlink Module technique can be used to avoid this type of problem. The complete layer structure remains intact within the Hotlink Module, but that module is only allocated to a single layer in the project file.

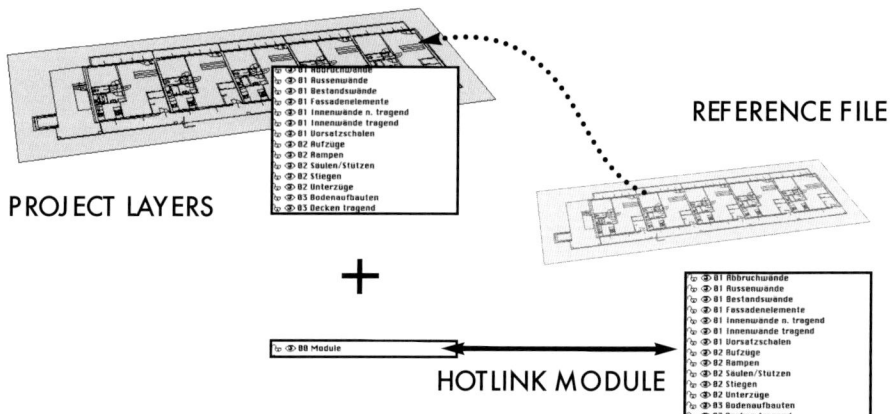

Fig. 2.59 Layer structure and reference file in a Hotlink Module

A remarkable revolution in the development of interfaces for CAD software products began with the introduction of IFC (Industry Foundation Classes) as an independent industry standard. The advantage of IFC over DXF lies in in the fact that the non-software-dependent description of construction elements was an objective from the very beginning. This could then be interpreted according to specific rules by the respective software manufacturers within their applications. This view makes it possible to look at building from other perspectives apart from the architect's, giving the specialized planners and consultants, while minimizing the room for interpretation in terms of the construction element for specialized planners and consultants. The corresponding plan rendering can then be generated with the respective CAD tool and then be integrated in the individual work environment of the respective consultant or specialized planner

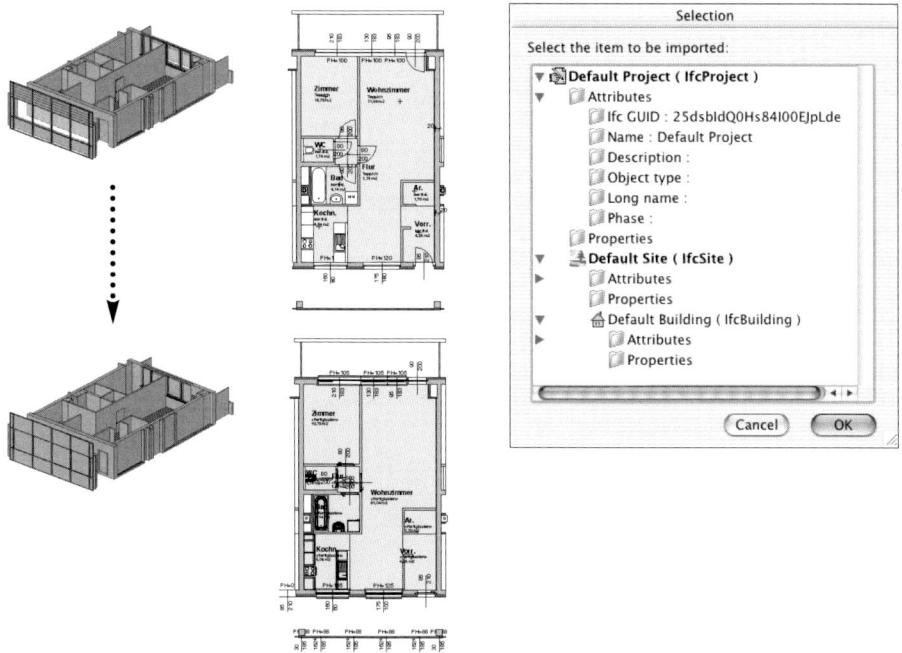

Fig. 2.60 IFC - function sample: results of a comparative data transfer (ArchiCAD, IFC)

3. Characteristic Applications from Practice

After discussing the ArchiCAD "intelligent" work environment in detail in the second chapter, we will now explain how it is used in practice. The topics already mentioned were the following:

- Three-dimensional Modeling and Visualization
- GDL Object Technology
- Hotlink Module Technology
- Level and Floor Management
- TeamWork Features
- Project Management /Data Organization/ Interfaces
- Database Usage

It isn't assumed that masterful use of ArchiCAD is only possible if all the available commands are used in some form at the same time. The surrounding conditions in an existing project situation are therefore of major importance and should help ensure proper command selections. For this reason, the observations in this chapter focus on a variety of ArchiCAD applications. It should also be noted that effective explanation methods vary from subject to subject. Therefore, it isn't surprising that visualization isn't all that difficult, while explaining database applications is much more challenging in a book.

Some of the program's functions could definitely be explained much better interactively on a screen. But it should be kept in mind that interest won't last long if such an explanation merely amounts to the presentation of a "beauty contest". It seems enticing to simply present the final results of other users initially, although close examination shows that the underlying "making of" is of much greater significance. The object isn't merely to show results in the form of images, but rather to present the information that led to the respective result. In this respect the motto is: "Please feel free to make use of this and improve it as you wish".

Some of the renderings used in this chapter were specifically generated for explanation and discussion purposes. This was possible thanks to user project data contributions. These examples allowed us to take a look behind the scenes and gather information on individual ArchiCAD user habits. Naturally, this wasn't possible with all the sample projects shown here. An Internet search is a typical way of finding additional examples, since it is easy to "publish" materials of varying provenance online. The Graphisoft Internet portal (http://www.graphisoft.com) and local ArchiCAD distributor Websites are definitely interesting starting points for an Internet search.

3.1 Case Studies from Architecture Offices and Planning Studios

The kaleidoscopic nature of the examples submitted became clear as the projects were compiled. For this reason, it seemed appropriate to create a sequential outline of categories. The first approach to this categorization was based on the size of the computer-aided projects completed in relation to the size of the architecture office using CAAD software. This proved difficult since a smaller office can also work on large-volume projects, while larger offices have also been known to complete compact projects, for whatever reason. The other question is where the border between large and small lies. The underlying motive here is the desire to show as broad a spectrum of applications as possible. To underline this objective, "extreme" positions are described at the end of each case study. These are meant to cover everything, "from a city to a chair," so to speak.

Attempting to categorize projects in relation to the variety of construction tasks is very similar to taking a classical construction course. The goal is to be aware of the danger of a "rigid corset". Keep in mind that the linking of the extensively discussed subjects (such as layer and floor management, Hotlink Module Technology, TeamWork features, etc.) is important in terms of categorization. This makes it possible for a hotel structure to be used as a hotel after revitalization is completed. The fact that it is a revitalization project isn't of primary importance, unless a change of function takes place. Every example within a category is first explained in brief. The specific ArchiCAD uses are discussed next, since it isn't possible to explain everything with images. Information on the rights to the images shown, Website availability and similar information as well as project-related data such as staff member lists and photos are included in the photo credits. The impressive amount of user support for this publication deserves special mention since it allows for the effective conveyance of user experiences with ArchiCAD. After researching office presentations it became clear that, not surprisingly, photographs of the finished products – built reality – are generally shown. Computer-aided visualization products are hardly published on architecture office Websites anymore, because their actual function no longer exists after the completion of construction. Hence we requested submissions of visualization products created during the planning phase (for example: which image renderings were of key importance?). "Before and after" comparisons are also included in certain cases.

 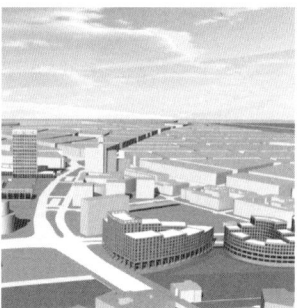 

3.1.1 Large-Scale Applications and und 3D Urban Modeling

The "Archi" prefix in "ArchiCAD" suggests that urban planning applications are not possible. Yet the study of the surrounding context – including the construction of a model – is undoubtedly one of the primary duties of those involved in creating architecture. Even if the name "ArchiCAD" does not allow for special expectations – "UrbanCAD" might be the more appropriate designation in this case – it is possible and useful to work with urban planning models without any hindrances. The modeling of structural bodies with standard tools (wall-ceiling roof) has already been explained earlier. It is more than a mere advantage to be able to create "digital styrofoam" models quickly with a reasonable amount of effort. The results of these efforts can be reproduced as required and made available in various different places when needed. Things become more complex when the intention is to create three-dimensional models of urban hubs and link these models to digital city maps. Updates are the order of the day in terms of the continuous evolution of construction, which makes the sustainability of the model data structures a central issue. However, architects are rarely entrusted with such tasks, although they certainly make use of model segments in their work.

- U3 Subway-Erdberg – Subway train yard roofing project
  AGU-Bahn, Peichl+Partner, COOP Himmerlb(l)au, Vienna (A)

The Vienna Department of Public Works used sites they already own for this project. The plans include the building of a roofing slab for the expansion of the train yard that is scheduled to be built. Later, a new urban district will be constructed on the slab. The proposal made by the "Architektengruppe U-Bahn" was chosen as the lead project in a certification process. This basically consists of a sequence of buildings of varying heights parallel to the Danube Canal and Erdbergstraße. A continuous mall will be built between these two lines of buildings.

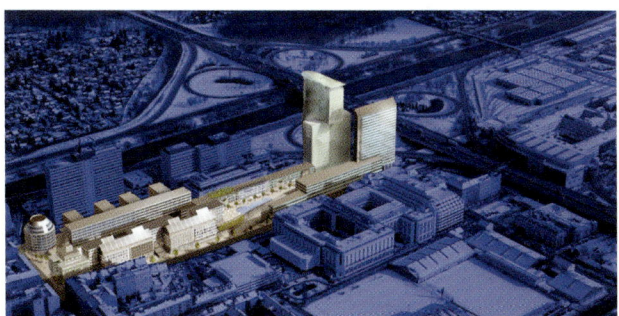

The use of ArchiCAD within a heterogeneous conglomerate of architects and CAD software products is the most striking characteristic of this project. The project is being processed with two-dimensional CAD software products as well as ArchiCAD. For this reason the usability of the virtual three-dimensional building model is limited. The individual specialized planners (structural engineers, building technicians, drainage specialists and electrical planners) deliver their respective planning levels as two-dimensional,

DWG format drawings. The data is then loaded into the ArchiCAD project. Although it would be possible to use Hotlink Module and XREF technology, the decision was made to work without referencing in this case.

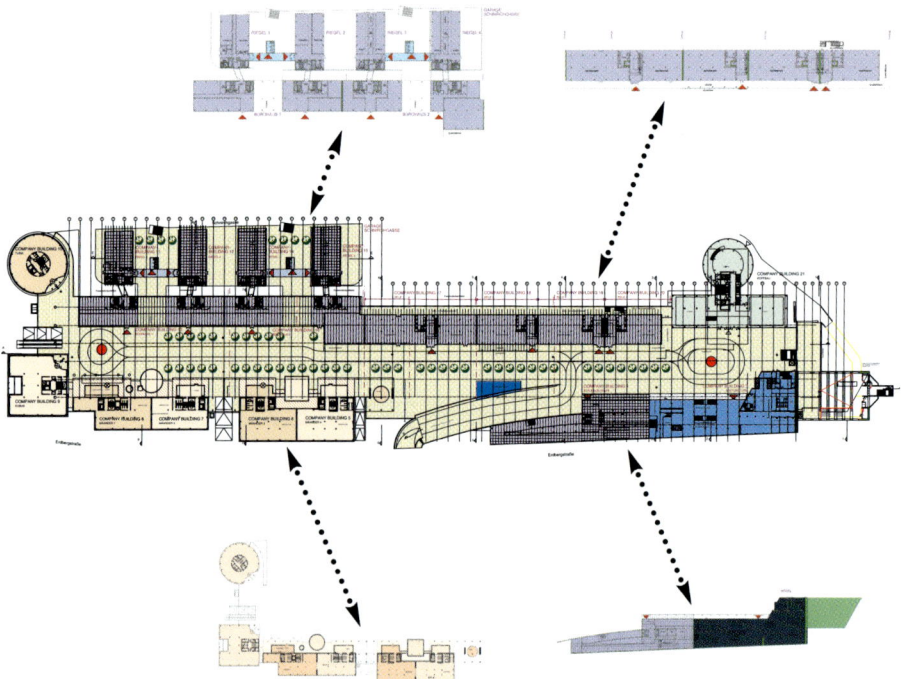

When a new planning level arrives, it is simply copied into the corresponding floor before deleting the older information. Floor management is used prudently in this complex planning environment. In order to guarantee ideal control of the overlapping fields, sections in the building structure were saved as separate ArchiCAD project files stacked on top of each other as floors, instead of inserting the portions in section windows. Both longitudinal and cross sections as well as exterior views can be superimposed over

the transparent floor and examined for consistency purposes making use of the level management function. The floor management is based on the so-called "Wiener Null"-Niveau (Viennese Zero Level) and the "Gauss-Krueger Coordinates" – this makes clear positioning possible and reduces potential sources of error.

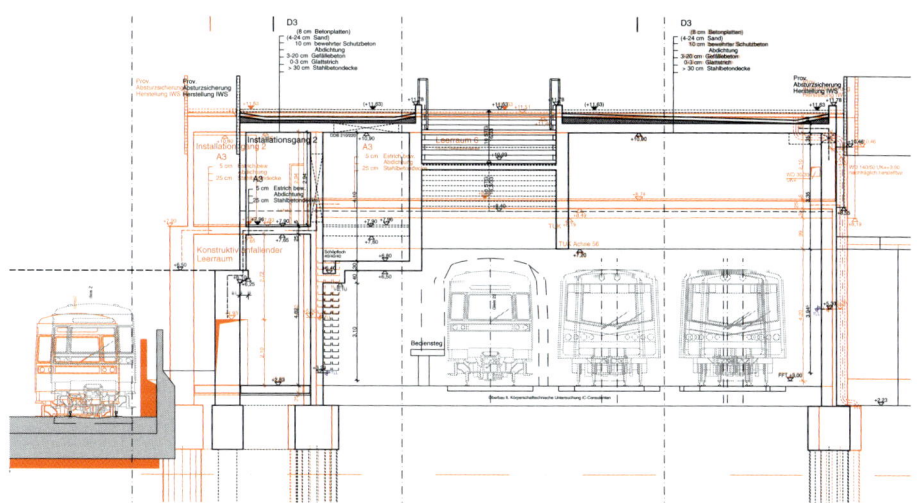

■ Urban Projects for Boston, Detroit, London and New York (USA/UK) | Urban Strategies, Toronto (CAN)

During the course of the *Greater Downtown Reinvestment Strategy* the administration of Detroit supported urban strategies in its endeavor to trigger a physical regeneration process after a period of neglect and decay that lasted a number of decades. The area affected by this development covered approx. 10 km² of the city. One of the objectives was to revitalize the connection between downtown Detroit and the port area and bring new life to the pedestrian area.

The implementation of a development plan for the last undeveloped site on the London Docklands represents the continuation of the international *Silvertown Quays* (Docklands) competition. The planning comprises commercial and cultural agendas and also includes the construction of a residential environment surrounding a large water basin.

The *Brooklyn Bridge Park* serves both as an access facility and recreational zone for pedestrians, cyclists, rollerbladers etc. and creates a link to the surrounding urban areas. The intention was generate sustained development in the areas formerly belonging to the New York City port facilities.

An extensive exchange of views with the area's residents and others concerned took place with an interactive Website. A master plan was created for the former *Fan Pier* industrial site in a prominent location in Boston Harbor. The goal was to incorporate a number of urban functions and a generous amount of open, multifunctional urban spaces along the waterfront. The project concept is based on nine compact building blocks that extend along the existing street grid and allow for a mix of various functions including retail spaces, residential and office spaces as well as hotel and cultural structures.

Using CAD software can be considered a challenge in situations in which a degree of detail and precision is necessary that is difficult to reconcile with the creation of a visualization. Even though it seemed difficult to avoid succumbing to the restrictions of photo-realistic renderings, it was possible to experiment with a technique in which three-dimensional renderings are traced manually. This means that the result won't necessarily look like an ArchiCAD product, but it can be viewed as a fundamental component in terms of production.

- Hamburg Digital 3D City Land Hamburg map | Office of Geographic Information and Surveying of Hamburg (GER)

In the year 1999, a resolution was passed to create a comprehensive 3D surface model for the entire Hamburg urban area. The basic data consisted of a digital city land map (known as "DSGK," scale=1:1000). This makes constantly updated three-dimensional data permanently available and allows for improved steering of urban planning for industrial, port and facility development. Architecture-related tasks require a high degree of detail and precision for city modeling, even if different users have varying demands in these respects.

Building structures were initially rendered as rough blocks in the first, completed development level. A realistic approach, including the roofline is taken during the second stage. A three-dimensional building model consists of individual wall and roof surfaces. All surfaces can be expanded and modified and every building can be clearly addressed via object designations. The integration of windows, doors and other building elements is basically possible, but third parties should complete the corresponding data inputs during the course of project work.

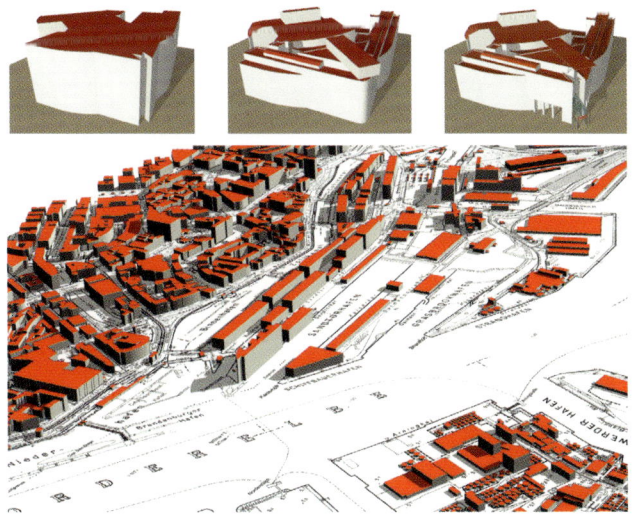

ArchiCAD made a major contribution to the three-dimensional modeling of this 755 square kilometer city area. The digital city land map (DSGK), aerial views of the city, façade photographs and construction records from the respective district office provided the basis for the model. However, ArchiCAD had to be expanded to accelerate the automatic integration of such complex surfaces.

A special Add-On was created specifically for this purpose, i.e. for the conversion of so-called "3D-face" surfaces and und poly-lines on walls and roofs. Additional routines that contained information on the contents of all existing data base entries were also programmed, which allowed automated ArchiCAD data processing (e.g. location and geometry information, type of use, street, house number, date of update and the amount of floors). By taking these steps, it was possible to enter 320,000 building blocks with their extended ID numbers, which consist of street and building data.

The project data that was generated in this work phase covers 245 lots, each one measuring 4 square kilometers. The following phase concentrated on the detailing of a central area (size: approx. 170 km^2) with a level of precision that included all roofs (including smaller roof structures and projections) and data on the terrain.

■ Berlin Digital 3D City Model (GER) | Senate Administration for City Development, Berlin (GER)

In 1995, the Berlin Senate Administration approved the creation of a urban construction planning model that would reflect future Berlin inner city development possibilities. A digital model of the inner city was created on the basis of the digital land register map for this purpose, the so-called "automated real estate map" (known as the "ALK," scale =1:1000). This digital city model makes the continuous visualization of urban planning concepts possible along with

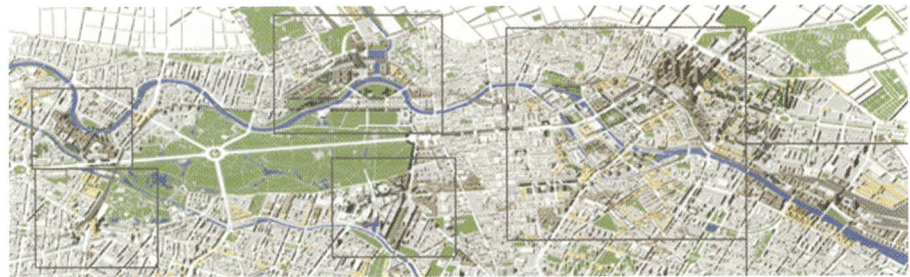

renderings of buildings that are already under construction or projected for construction. The section of the city that the land map was generated for was compiled on 200 ALK map pages. The accumulated information includes the house numbers, the street names and the borders of the respective lots. The computer model shows the area between Ernst-Reuter-Platz to the west and the Ostbahnhof (Eastern Railway Station) to the east. The neighbouring Westkreuz and Ostkreuz areas are depicted only as blocks.

First, three-dimensional models of individual "islands" such as Spittelmarkt or Breidscheidplatz were created. These were then linked to one another, meaning that the areas in between were also processed. Some of the buildings in the Spittelmarkt area of central Berlin even feature precise heights and façade structures. The roof shapes of the buildings were not taken into consideration, except for those of characteristic buildings. This provides a decisive degree of abstraction for urban planning assessment purposes (structural mass model), while ensuring a reasonable balance between expended effort and usefulness. The project data consists of a 50 MB ArchiCAD file.

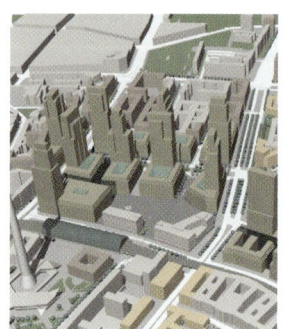

The next goal is to link the ArchiCAD project data file to the ALK. The objective is to link all the objects with the corresponding data. This approach facilitates the entering of all required parameters and guarantees the automatic synchronization of any changes made (e.g. demolition of a new building or construction of a new building). This makes it possible to transfer all ALK information (such as building type, height, use).

■ Dresden-Neumarkt digital city model (GER) I digital electronic kühn gmbh, Dresden (GER)

The model of the city acts as an independent, or "open" platform for architects, clients, planners and/or institutions that would like to visualize their designs in the corresponding surroundings. This creates a basis for a broad public discussion. So far, buildings were modeled whose façades affect the Dresden Neumarkt. Publicly available planning documentation files were consulted and images were studied in certain cases to determine the exact elevation. The material available in the archives is inadequate in some cases. Little source information was available, especially in terms of colors. A continuation of this modeling process is planned for the bordering streets of the "Neumarktgebiet" (New Market Area).

A scanned city map was used as the basis and then manually rectified and vectored. Data was entered according to the construction components, including the façades, cornices and ornaments. The inner workings of the structure were also modeled to avoid depicting hollow façades. It took around 4 to 8 hours to process each building, including the degree of detail shown here.

Current designs were imported according to the data material provided. The use of data isn't only reduced to a pure ArchiCAD environment, since it is possible to export data in common interface formats.

■ Auckland Digital Cuty Model (NZ) I Cadimage, Auckland (New Zealand)

The local New Zealand ArchiCAD distributor realized this city model in order to be able to depict projected high-rise structures within the existing surrounding buildings. Comprehensive additional development wasn't pursued intensively since the amount of projected high-rise buildings is limited thus far.

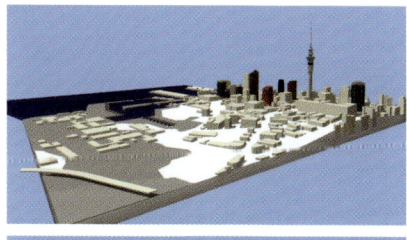
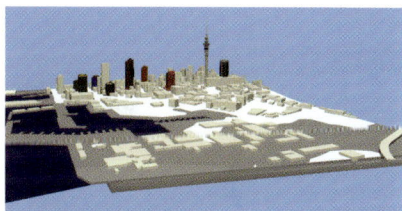

The basic data file consisted of measurement data that had been gleaned from aerial views. The conversion process was complicated in this case, but was finally completed successfully. A 3D DXF file with block-like renderings of XYZ points was also available. An ArchiCAD object was created based on this data.

This made it possible to create a list that included all XYZ points. The data that was generated was then transferred to a terrain model using ArchiSITE. Since this DXF data file included building outlines (top view), it was possible to create the individual building blocks using the roof tool. A few buildings show a higher degree of detail.

■ Laaerberg – "Monte Laa," Vienna (A) I Porr Immoprojekt GmbH, Vienna (A)

A new segment of Favoriten, the 10th district of Vienna, is being built on the 220 meter-long slab covering the Vienna Südost-Tangente (southeastern traffic route). This will lead to the construction of an extensive park area consisting of green belts next to the office, commercial and residential areas. Two towers were conceived as the visible landmark of the area. The form of development chosen should be viewed within the context of international trends: complete service providers offer all services, ranging from project development to project planning and the construction of a building. Hence everything stems from one source, beginning with the vacant site and including various project studies, the planning, execution and the marketing of the entire completed project and the site.

An analysis of the construction surveys was completed during and early stage of the project. ArchiCAD supports the "sketch-like" processing of volumes (building blocks) in this case. Impressions from varying perspectives can be generated in no time at all. The next step is the allocation of textures that help create the illusion of building structures. The constantly updated cost calculation tables make it possible to assess the effect on pricing of the individual construction variants. TeamWork also offers a major planning aid: it is possible for a number of staff members to work on one central file at the same time. Work overlaps and misunderstandings are basically impossible with this approach. The linking of ArchiCAD with PowerPoint has proven to be a reliable approach to presentations. It is possible to integrate planning files and building models of good graphical quality effortlessly via the clipboard. The addition of project data to the execution planning and detail planning information is accompanied by a frequent exchange of data between the project group and the specialized planners. The merge engine data exchange functions and XREF technology are used in these cases.

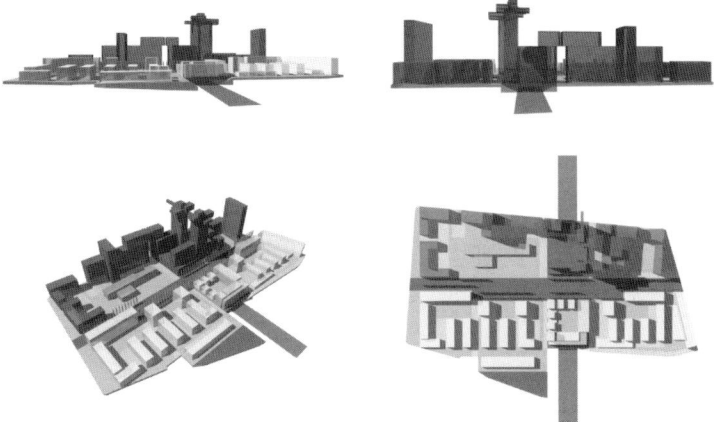

Another focal point in ArchiCAD usage in this context is user-generated textures. Based on this project, it can be seen clearly how images depicting abstract, structures projected on a building or a fa ade can give a quick first

impression of the future tectonics of the building shell. It is then a matter of course to collect these user-generated textures in a texture library.

■ Aussee Wellness Park, Bad Aussee (AUT) | Werner Nußmüller, Graz (AUT)

When locating three building models consisting of a Regional Hospital, a Center for Holistic Medicine and a home for the elderly, the main concerns were the possible views to the south into the valley and the appropriate imbedding of the cubes in the corresponding topography. All of the building modules are linked via an internal distribution ring located under the ground floor level. This subterranean segment also houses the complete technical infrastructure of the building. Access on foot is possible via the common middle ground, or so-called "Village Square".

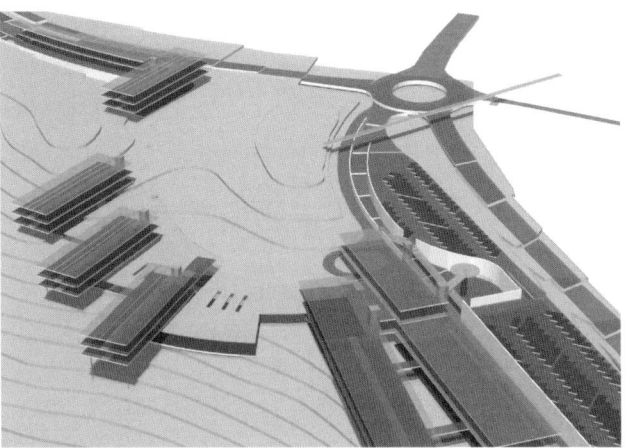

The terrain model section allows for specific testing of structural effects on the cubes used. A global assessment of the spatial program takes places as early as this phase. The effect of this on the Sun City project was the architectural remodeling of the housing rows, which is already complete in this stage. A glance at the organization structure shows that the four building type provide an ideal basis for the use of referenced module technology. Every house grounds plan (ground level and upper level) can be saved as a Hotlink Module, these can then be linked to form a row of housing as required. No additional work is necessary for changes within a type of house. The simultaneous visualization of the entire complex is also possible with the corresponding composition.

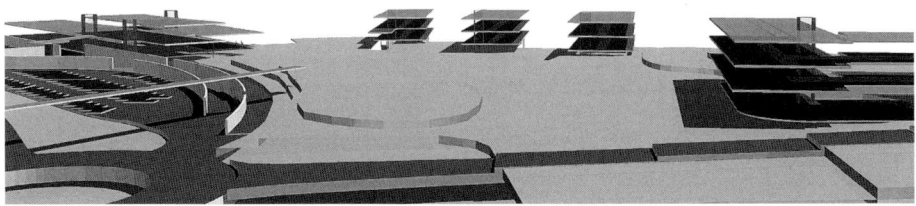

3.1.2 High-Rise Buildings as a Vertical Challenge

It is clear that thorough data structuring within an ArchiCAD project file has a major influence on the smooth processing of high-rise buildings. Not merely because of the large amount of (sometimes almost) identical stories. A "regular story" that is drafted once and used a number of times in the building makes "automated" steps possible.

As well as considering the internal organization of a high-rise building its effects on its urban environment should also be taken into account. The relation between a high-rise and its urban surroundings often causes political disputes and requires extensive preliminary work in terms of project development. Today, this is generally addressed with computer-aided visualizations of the urban environment. Sun and shadow simulations are standard procedures in many cities already. It is therefore hardly possible to realize a high-rise project without such aids anymore. The aim of supported work methods in high-rise construction projects is to automate the use of components that are employed a number of times in a building. Hotlink Module technology is definitely an appropriate supporting feature in designing floor plans, since every change to the "standard floor" can be updated on all similar floors immediately without any extra effort. Using GDL objects and/or Hotlink Modules can also help make the production of planning documents easier for façade planning. After all, files 40-50 MB in size aren't a rarity.

■ PZU Tower and Inter-Continental Hotel, Warsaw (PL)
Tadeusz Spychala, Vienna (A)

The PZU Tower was built at a crossroads in the Srodmiescie district of Warsaw. It load-bearing structure consist of ferroconcrete cores, slabs and piers. A special feature of the façade is its "Twin Face" two-layer glazing. This solution offered the best insulation, and sound proofing as well as ideal protection from the sun. Natural ventilation in the office and conference rooms is guaranteed without being affected by the weather conditions outside. The garage, technical rooms and ancillary facilities are all located in the basements, while the entrance hall, information and monitoring rooms are on the ground floor. The standard floors are primarily used as office and conference spaces.

Careful preparation was important in relation to the vertical arrangements of this building, which features a total of 34 floors. Some floors were created as standard floors and only have to be processed once. Theoretically, all standard floors can be referenced via Hotlink Modules.

In this case, they were simply copied vertically. An interesting work method was developed, or gleaned from the basic ArchiCAD structure in terms of façade detailing: The standard detailing of the exterior façade was generated as a 2D GDL object and used as often as required in the section of the building. This means that only one GDL object has to be changed in the case of a change of connection. The same process was applied to the façade elements in the other perspectives. The exact distribution of the façade elements with all their joints and spaces is exposed to a process of constant change that was optimized with this form of referenced planning support.

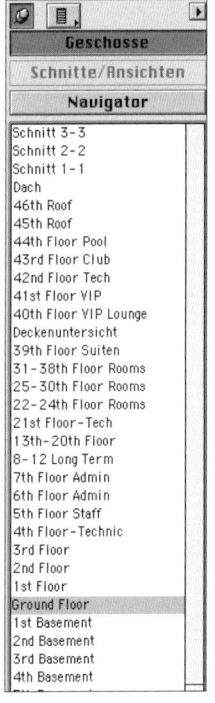  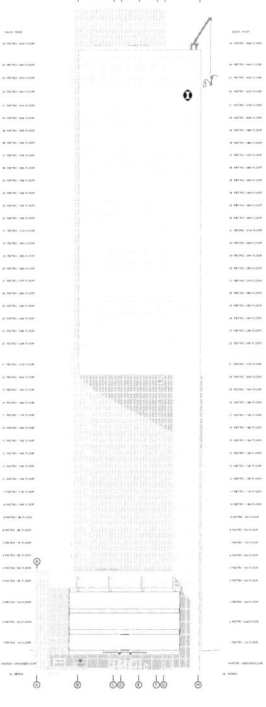

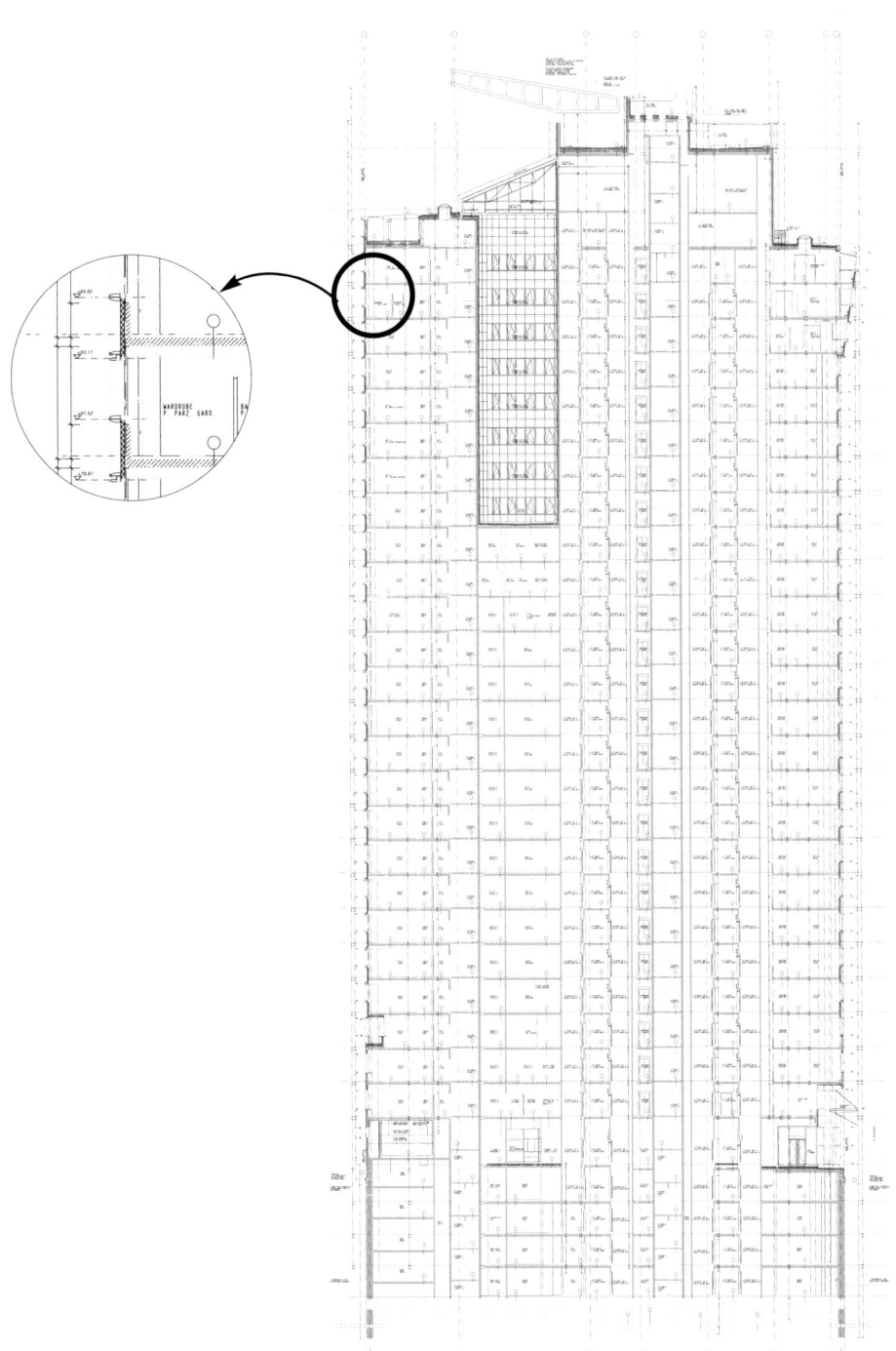

- Eureka Tower, Melbourne (AUS) | Fender Katsalidis Architects, Sydney, Melbourne (AUS)

The Eureka Tower is being built in the immediate vicinity of the Yarra River, the Southbank Promenade, the artists' quarter and the Crown Entertainment Center in the Southgate district of Melbourne. After the end of the construction phase, the residential building with its 90 floors and overall height of around 300 meters will tower over Melbourne. The construction of two higher buildings along the main road had been approved at the time the site was purchased. Instead of building two structures next to each other, the volumes were simply stacked on top of each other. This led to a slender building that is twice as high as originally planned, although it creates much less shadow on the surrounding street spaces.

The Eureka Tower project is characterized by a sophisticated and comprehensive organization of data. PlotMaker was used to generate two-dimensional drawings that reflected the required weights of line, filling colors and printout types. "Hotlinks" between PlotMaker and ArchiCAD allow for the automatic updating of changes. The printing of these drawings is completed via automated batch processing. Around 1,500 sorted drawings have so far been administered in the database to date. This model supports automated coordination procedures and contains error control mechanisms, which can be of great importance, especially in terms of crossfloor technical installations. The project team consisted of an average of 25 to 30 people. These were organized in smaller teams that concentrated on related

building components. The control and coordination of inbound and outbound information was the responsibility of the respective project architect.

Every team was in charge of one sub-model (ArchiCAD-Jargon: Module). All sub-models were then united in the complete virtual model. The decision to use the Team-Work features in this project was made on the basis of existing computer hardware capabilities and the available network connection bandwidths. After all, this project requires roughly 350 MB of space. Any other processing and handling method would have been much more unwiedly, which is why the project was broken down into ArchiCAD modules. The entire CAD model was not often required for the actual production of documents, since segment packages were made. These were generated using the modules. This type of de-centralized approach makes it possible for small teams to communicate more efficiently and reduces the amount of redundant information. But it is still necessary to coordinate the individual modules by comparing their data with that of the entire model. This seems to make the position of a model manager indispensable to insure data accuracy and coordination.

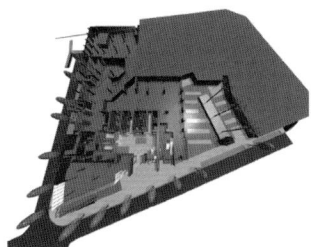

■ Business Tower Nuremberg, (GER) | Dürschinger & Biefang, Germany (GER)

Seven-story office complexes built along the edges of a block are grouped around a large interior courtyard. The courtyard is almost completely occupied by a water basin. Bavaria's tallest building, which was built using a concrete skeleton structure, is located on the corner of the courtyard. With a height of 135 meters and 34 floors the office building (Business Tower) of the Nürnberger Versicherungsgruppe (insurance company) towers over the city of Nuremberg as a new landmark.

This project is characterized by the use of virtual models made using the roof tool; blocks are generated in the (virtual) mass model during an early planning phase. ArchiCAD is mainly used for the creation of two-dimensional construction documents (construction data entries, work and detail planning) during the first construction segment. The third dimension is added during the second construction segment to study individual portions (entrance hall) and the constructions measures required overall. Comprehensive surface and cubature calculations were completed with the aid of the roomzone features in both phases.

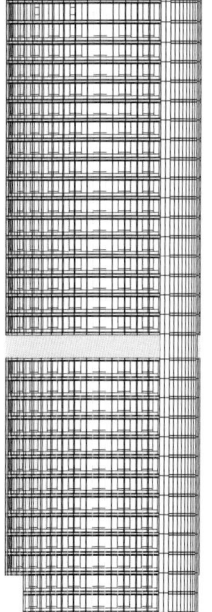

3.1.3 Hospital Construction: Organizing Time and Space

Hospital buildings are the result of highly complex organization and represent a major planning challenge for architects and builders. This pertains to the structuring of individual areas and the synchronization of a number of specialized planners as well as the simultaneous development and documentation of the planning process. These steps make considerable demands on the staff and the CAD software product. Due to the need for external consultant information, the data model has to be kept as "open" as possible. This means that is advisable to use Hotlink Modules and external references in the TeamWork mode to be able to perform fast updates with the highest degree of safety. The use of Hotlink Modules provides perfect support for rapidly changing planning situations. It can also be considered a given that the rough conception of the building is not completed as a digital plan, normally it is the result of a space and function program established in a space reference book. Modular sample rooms can be used for conception purposes here as well, since it is possible to process the relevant space reference book information in these samples at the same time. Another factor that merits attention is the fact that hospital projects are normally planned and built over a long period of time.

Three to five years of planning and construction also mean that ArchiCAD users will be processing the data model with a number of different program versions. The integration and further processing of existing data has to proceed smoothly in these cases. Practical examples show that this is possible with ArchiCAD if the staff are immediately trained to use the new functions and possibilities that become available. The extensive development ArchiCAD has undergone has made it easier to complete data exchanges and integrate specialized planning data as required by individual users. An important aspect of employing ArchiCAD in this context is the integration and use of building data for later user operation (facility management) purposes, which can be performed in conjunction with ArchiFM.

■ University Clinic – Anichstraße Medical Center, Innsbruck (A) | Paul Katzberger and Michael Loudon, Vienna (A)

The new building integrates a considerable volume of construction in the heterogeneous historical center of Innsbruck. The hospital had to include an emergency area, a surgery unit, operation rooms, a research facility and medical care stations. A rectangular building built facing east-west with two interior courtyards was designed to accommodate these requirements. The courtyard structures and special design of the double-loaded wings allow for the highest possible degree of natural light and ventilation in all building sections. Two large, two-story openings put the interior world of the block in close contact with the surrounding city space.

The remarkable expanse of the hospital complex and the extraordinary sophistication of the floor plan documentation required an ingenious layer management system that allowed for rapid access to all necessary information. This case study is characterized by an exemplary use of the level management possibilities that makes it possible to separate the architect's planning contents from specialized planning items at all times. The layer designations with letter prefixes ("A" for architect, "C" for civil engineer, "H" for HVAC etc.) makes it possible to delete files with "outside" prefixes from the project without any fear of data loss in the various layers. However, external planning data can be re-integrated in the user's planning environment via external references (XREFs) or Hotlink Modules at any time.

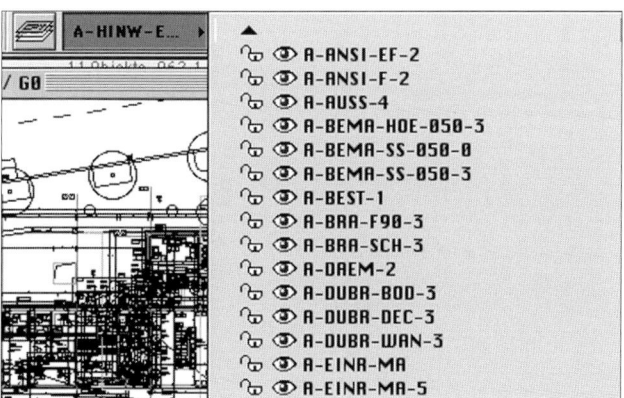

The separation of the sections and views from the floor plan and the integration of a second project file that is also organized as a system of levels makes it possible to both incorporate basic virtual building structures and process their sections and views with all standard tools (including the wall tool, for example). This approach is

advantageous when multi-layer construction components are used. Another feature that deserves mention is the possibility of creating and using your own GDL objects which can then be used productively for façade detailing.

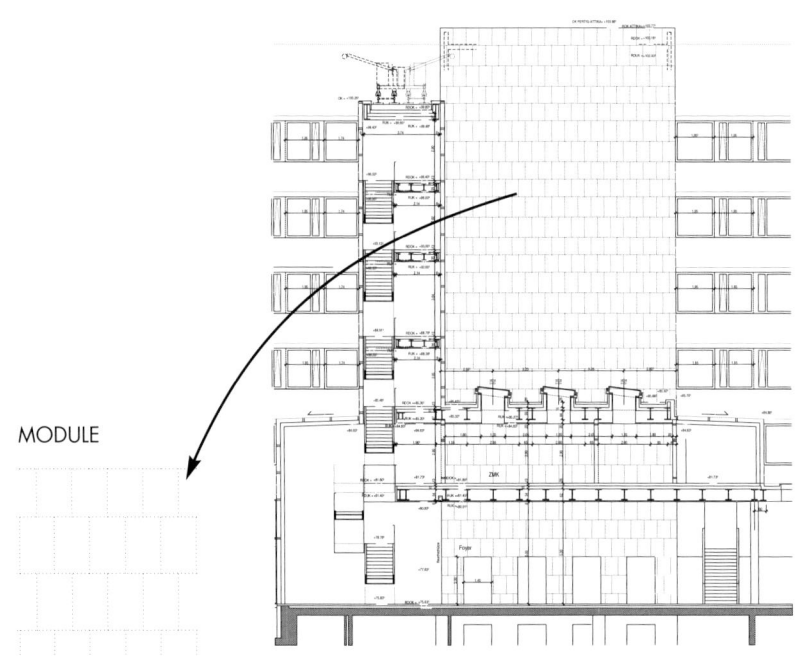

MODULE

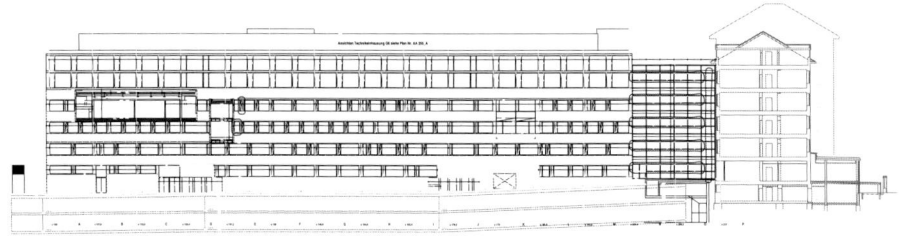

■ Refurbishment and Expansion of the Böblingen Regional Hospital (GER) I Drees & Sommer GmbH, Stuttgart (GER)

The objective of the construction measures was to increase the amount of space offered and optimize exterior internal and external circulation. The Munich architects Freudenfeld+Krausen+Will won the competition supervised by Drees & Sommer. The guiding principle is the separation of the care areas from the examination and treatment rooms. The design features an annex for the main building and the refurbishment of the existing building. This will also include adding new floors to the existing two-story building.

One of the main points of ArchiCAD use is the Construction Progress Simulation (CPS). This makes it possible to coordinate complex time planning schemes. Since the construction work will take place while the hospital is in operation, some access routes have been changed temporarily. Reliable planning files have to be created with CPS for these cases. CPS is a major component in scheduling issues. Clients or their representatives, have been most receptive to this kind of simulation. This makes faster decision-making processes possible with regard to scheduling matters.

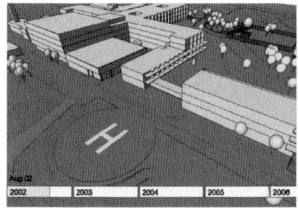 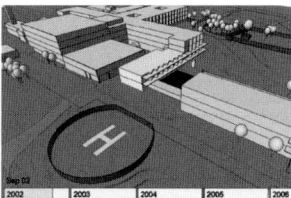 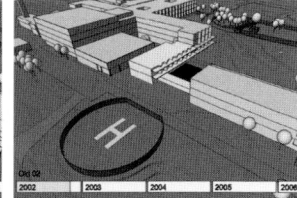

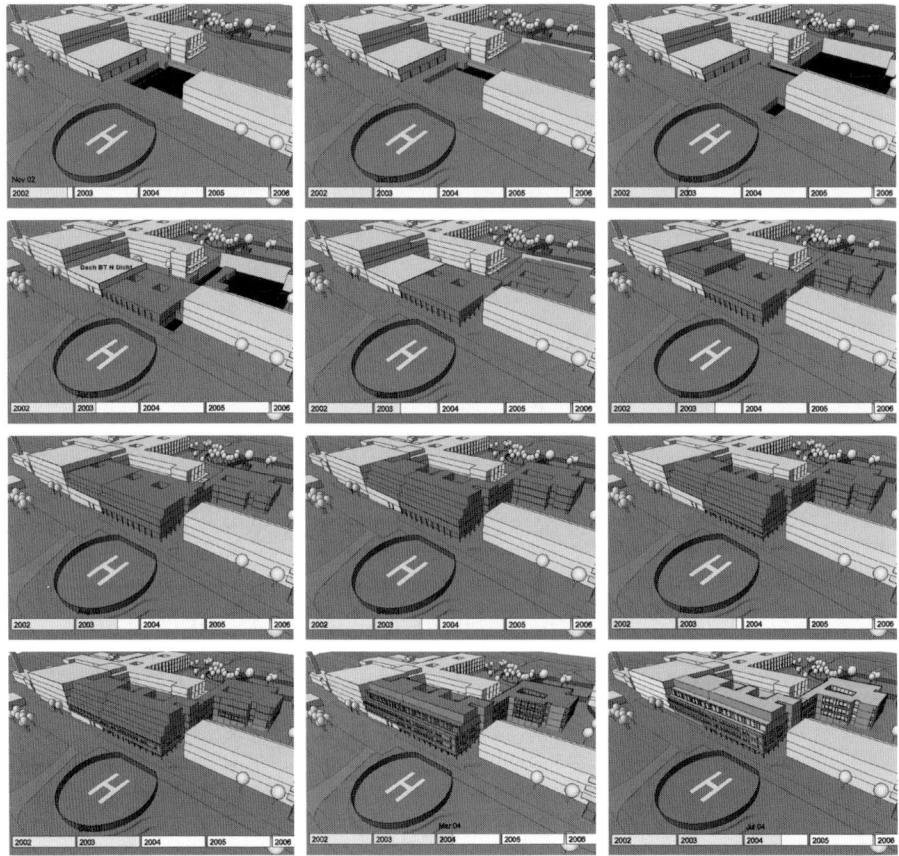

The CPS is based on ArchiCAD data. It is composed with 3D GDL objects that are maintained in an Excel file. This refers to both schedules and the structural progress. The results are presented in common data formats (plans, animations, presentations etc.). Although the possibility of building by section is considered a particular strength, model detailing generally has lower priority. The final points discussed are the reactions to scheduling and planning changes.

- Expansion of Reutte District Hospital, Reutte (A) | Werner Wiedermann, Innsbruck (A)

The existing building dates back to 1968, although it has been expanded a number of times (children's ward, dialysis facilities, etc). Required work space was to be added to the individual areas in the course of the adaptation. The requirements made it necessary to keep the segments added ten years ago on the northeastern end in operation (children's ward, the dialysis facilites and the internal medicine ward).

Therefore, it was realistic to add new structures only on the eastern side of the building. This is also the entrance to the building now. A hall-like segment with covered by a partial barrel roof that also incorporates the cafeteria.

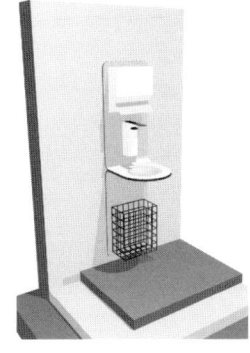

This project is characterized by extensive use TeamWork features and a story management system that was structured according to a special key. Identification numbers were assigned according to subject matter in the execution planning documents. Since the project was worked on over a longer period of time with a number of different ArchiCAD versions, library management also represented a major challenge. Those GDL objects that were used for

hospital planning purposes were all collected in the so-called "project library". Depending on the ArchiCAD version – aside from the project library – it is only necessary to load the standard library to have GDL objects available that are even more up to date. Another feature worth mentioning is the programming of an individual space stamp that was more suitable for the requirements of a hospital than the standard space stamp. Since the project file already needed 100 MB of harddisk space when execution planning began, processing in the TeamWork mode would make the file twice as large and it would require 200 MB of harddisk space. The system administrator should keep in mind that processing speed comes at the expense of harddisk access speeds.

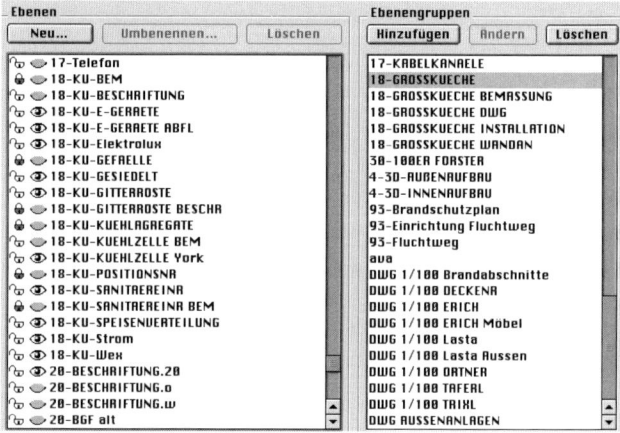

■ Triemli City Hospital, Zurich (SUI) | Architektengemeinschaft Triemli, Zurich/Brugg (SUI)

The contract was for the refurbishment and expansion of the treatment wing (Neubau Süd). At the same time public spaces such as the cafeteria, the reception and admission area were renovated as well and the zone in front of the main building (ward high-rise) was re-designed to fit a new emergency driveway. The new three-story building with a penthouse level and a basementlevel six bays long is linked almost seamlessly to the existing wing. A staircase was added on the east and west sides of the building to complete the connection to the older building. Other areas that required renovation work were not included in this project. This multi-stage construction project required detailed planning and a logistically well thought-out moving and transfer management system. What is remarkable is the fact that the project, work and detailed planning phases were processed at different office locations.

All the planning documentation of the existing hospital block was transferred into an ArchiCAD project file (Version 4.55) for project processing purposes. The goal was to create a 1:200 scale rendering. The building model was built with predefined story heights. These were measured from the floor to the ceiling. Slabs and façades were not entered at this point. The demand for a complete 3D model wasn't an issue at this point. Sections and views were created as separate files since it did not seem prudent to calculate sections directly in the building model due to hardware and software limitations. Due to the long planning and realization phase, it soon became important to find an organizational tool that possible to administrate CAD data flexibly and without redundant contents. In 1999, after a few difficulties in the beginning and a number of version changes it became possible to work with the TeamWork function. What seemed advantageous was the fact that certain basic settings (pens, levels, renderings, PlotMaker etc.) could not – not even by mistake – be changed. This creates additional safety, even when the project file is being used by a number of people at the same time. TeamWork notes are only useful when employed regularly to verify major individual steps. The flowchart shows how the "core plans" of the new annex surrounding the treatment wing are structured. It also shows how grounds plans can be generated from the central building model in varying scales and. Parts of this file have been in use for over six years, although a number of changes were made in terms of program versions, operating systems and users.

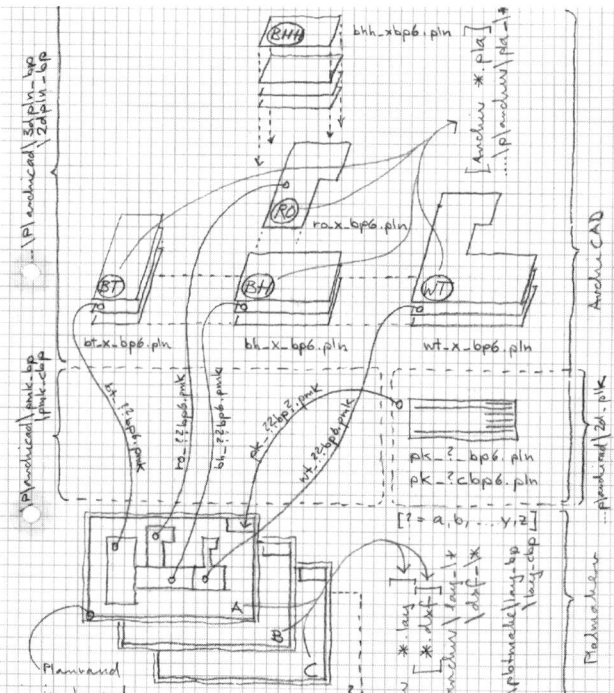

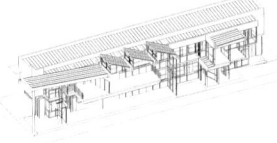

■ Consultorio Baeza Goñi, Santiago (CL) | Hombo & Bañados Arquitectos, Santiago de Chile (CL)

This project comprises a compact health facility within a problematic social environment. A restricted budget and a very small construction site for the required structure volumes were core parameters that had to be reflected in the design.

A "space usage sketch" was created as a first step. The next step was the creation of diagrams of different colors and of the corresponding documentation. The varying designation of individual areas made it possible to make a direct comparison between the original spatial program and the suggested adjustments. The linking of ArchiCAD reports with the Spanish "Presto" software for cost analysis purposes was an important part of this project. This made it possible to maintain detailed records of a number of entries. It was possible to transfer around two thirds of the required information directly from the "calculate" menu. The possibility of creating precise designations and exact level allocations for all construction elements was a prerequisite for this approach.

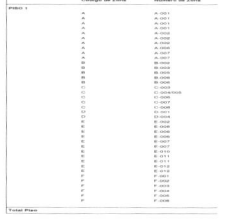
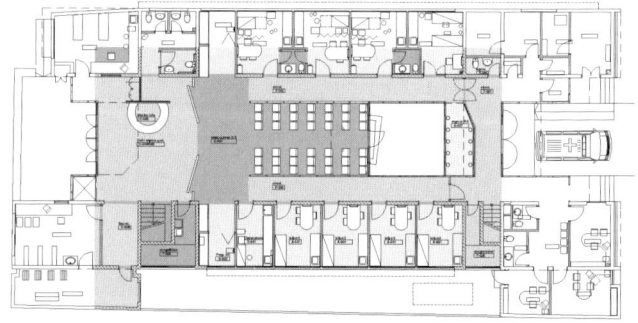

3.1.4 Residential, Hotel and Office Spaces: Recurring Unit Variations

There are obvious similarities between the processing of residential, hotel and office space projects. Floor administration is based on standard floors, and recurring units such as a "kitchen", "hotel room" or "office space" are used regularly. The use of modules also refers to more than one single type within a project. It is therefore useful to create a reasonable structure according to recurring, inter-related fields. If something changes within a module – for whatever reasons – the changes are updated with the "click of a button". But using modules should not be merely reduced to "rubber stamping". The objective here is to encourage variation in serial production.

GDL object technology is mainly used for interior planning in this context. These are primarily standard interiors including technical equipment such as radiators, lighting outlets, switches and sockets. Later use of the building model data for FM purposes would seem wise here. It is also possible to use this form of early spatial reference book for housing subsidy applications.

■ Gentzgasse Residential Project, Vienna (A) | Eduard Widmann, Salzburg (A)

The two building structures aligned in an "L" shape on a closed site that rises steeply to the north create a two-level interior courtyard. The entrance level is also the first garage level. It stretches from Gentzgasse towards the incline without a change in elevation. The garage roof was built with a grassed area on top and acts as part of the interior courtyard before vanishing into the incline. The two residential structures are therefore raised over the garage level by an entire floor and dispose of three (or two in the garden wing) base courses. Bay window-like extensions allow for a view down the length of Gentzgasse. Another major design feature is the form of the continuous terraces on the upper floors. Green islands with trees facing the interior courtyard define the individual terrace areas and create "hanging gardens". The terrace floors are designed in a manner similar to ship structures.

The organization of the individual construction components is of special importance in this project example, since these can be bundled in level groups. This makes it possible to release the various planning drawings quickly and make project information regarding calculations

(competition requirements) or simple gross surface calculations for both building segments (in)visible. The "automatically" generated sections and perspectives from the Virtual Building Model are transferred to an independent document. This step is justified by the fact that the saving of sections and perspectives in individual floors ideally supports the verification of installed horizontal elements (e.g. ventilation ducts, electric cables, etc.) via the transparent floor renderings. A considerable amount of composite structures (calculation elements) were used during detail planning. This permitted the automatic calculation of building masses by means of a special layer group. This makes a rough calculation of expenses for the most important mass positions possible.

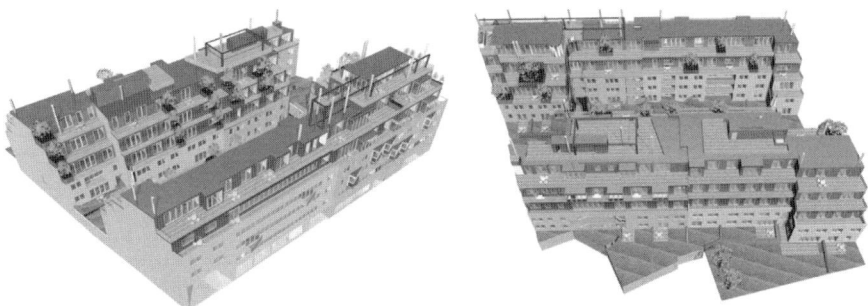

WALLS BY BUILDING MATERIALS						
BILL OF MATERIALS	STORY	WALL TYPE	COMPOSITE THICKNESS	HEIGHT		VOLUME
	1.st +280/+322	W3	0.35 m	2.60 m		4.83 m3
	1.st +280/+322	W3	0.35 m	2.60 m		9.60 m3
W1 /30+5	1.st +280/+322 total					19.12 m3
W1 /30+5	all stories total:					19.12 m3
	1.st +280/+322	Concrete 53	0.25 m	2.50 m		0.56 m3
	1.st +280/+322	W3	0.25 m	2.60 m		0.71 m3
W10/DOOR	1.st +280/+322 total					1.47 m3
W10/DOOR	all stories total:					1.47 m3
	1.st +280/+322	Concrete 55	0.13 m	2.60 m		0.11 m3
W11/SMALL	1.st +280/+322 total					0.11 m3
W11/SMALL	all stories total:					0.11 m3

■ Mutterstraße Residential Project, Feldkirch (A) | Gohm-Hiessberger, Hohenems (A)

This project represents an attempt to use a steep plot of land on Ardetzenberg for a terraced housing project. The question of the appropriate development for such a site had to be settled in cooperation with the authorities. The project has not been built to date.

The administration of all the significant plan documentation is completed in one single project file. The floor management function, which also contains the floor plans and perspectives is used for the separation of the various planning contents. Hence the staff members involved in the project have ready access to a project planning status overview via one single project file.

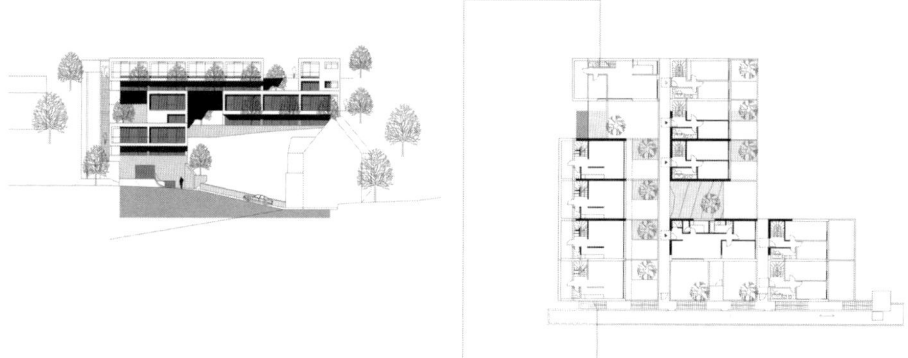

■ Hammarby and Sjostadsporten Residential Project, Stockholm (S) | Lund & Valentin, Stockholm (S)

The design for the Hammarby Waterfront City Gate is part of a larger Stockholm city expansion plan (Sjostad area) that will create space for around 20,000 inhabitants. The project planned on a site at the crossroads of two major access routes play a major role in the existent urban context. The project comprises apartments, commercial spaces as well as office spaces and an underground garage.

The use of ArchiCAD made it possible for the project manager in charge to be deeply involved in all CAD work. The CAD software was used as a form of 3D sketch pad from an early stage of the project onwards. Thus the generation of three-dimensional renderings served for both the creation of presentation images and the monitoring of the current project status during the design process. In-depth talks and discussions were held with the future residents as well, which made it useful to be able to generate alternatives quickly without great additional effort.

■ Lehtovuori Residential Project, Helsinki (FIN) | A-Konsultit, Helsinki (FIN)

The 90-unit residential project composed mainly of single-family houses was the winning entry in an open competition. The objective was to give an area with fundamentally uniform construction a sense of variety. This was achieved with the clever use of structural variants and a broad range of different colors.

The design process was completed using two ArchiCAD project files. One file contains all house types and the respective variants. The second contains a site plan in which the individual buildings are inserted as parametric GDL objects according to the type of terrain. Levels and level groups are used to generate floor plans, section renderings and perspectives of all building variants. Internal fragments within the GDL objects are used to create the various grounds plans renderings of the floors in the site plan (model) via a parameter control.

■ Hotel IMC Krems, Krems (A) | Walter Hoffelner, Vienna (A)

The medical focus of the IMC private clinic ("Innovative Medical Care") is on specialized areas that have barely been explored in Eastern Europe and countries in the Arab world. Since these patients generally travel in the company of one or more family members rather than alone, the plan includes the construction of a hotel complex with a connecting conference center on the clinic grounds in cooperation with IMC. The project segment depicted here is related to the hotel complex.

"Quick and dirty" flip chart images were created as early as the preliminary design stage for the future operator. These images were based on a quickly generated virtual mass model that demonstrated the interplay of the individual areas within the hotel complex. Important characteristics

such as colors, light design and material features are already recognizable at this early stage. However, the main use – aside from client presentation purposes – is the evaluation of the various surface categories that results in a rough calculation of expenses for the project via a table of costs. The use of Hotlink Modules was helpful in detailing the building model, since it was possible to make adjustments in terms of room arrangement and equipment. The project document remained a central ArchiCAD file that was also processed in TeamWork mode; in some cases until the plans to be filed were completed. The next step was the copying of sections and perspectives into the floor plans before being documented as two-dimensional drawings. A bill of quantities was prepared for room reference book documentation purposes during the implementation phase. The structuring was completed with ArchiFM in a manner allowing for later use by the operator.

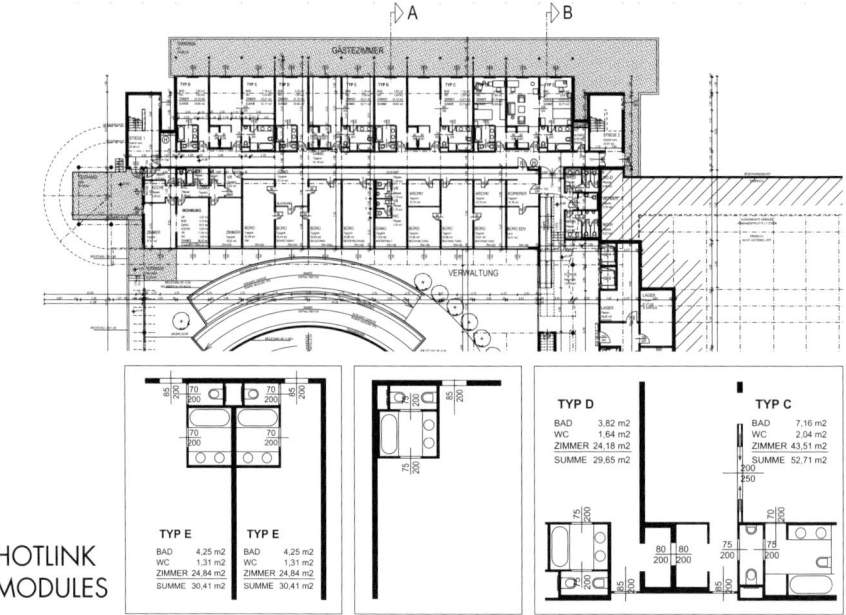

HOTLINK MODULES

■ Hotel National, Moscow (RUS) | Walter Hoffelner, Vienna (A)

The oldest portion of the Hotel National, which is still the main building today, is located in the historical and economic center of Moscow. The old structure is grouped around a large, rectangular interior courtyard. Due to the condition of the building, a general restoration was completed giving particular attention to the external and internal Jugendstil elements. A re-organization of the hotel function was aimed at achieving an ideal symbiosis between preservation (landmark), restoration and expansion. The installation of modern building technology was particularly problematic. The functional structure was largely preserved, only the public spaces were expanded with annexes and outbuildings.

The exchange of data between the surveyor and the architect was of central importance to the data organization of this project. The building coordinates delivered by the surveyor's office were transferred step-by-step via DXF and integrated in the floor plans. It was only possible to print plans for the authorities and implementation plans after assembling this information. At the time, it was decided to use the roof tool to visualize irregular and polygonal walls using ArchiCAD versions 4.1 and 4.55; these shapes are not difficult to create today.

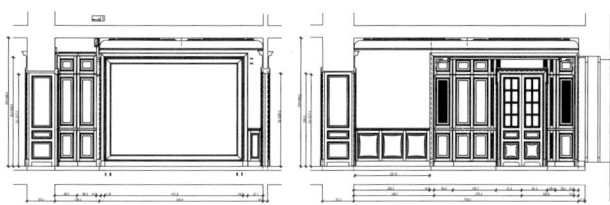

However, it was possible to always use a single wall with parallel sides in locations where windows and doors where were placed. The creation of windows and doors required a separate GDL object collection that allowed for connections to the surrounding building elements. The Virtual Building Model remained intact apart from the internal walls of individual rooms. The varying renderings required for the different consultants made it necessary to copy the central file in some cases, to be able to exchange planning data effortlessly.

■ Austrian Airlines Group: Training Center, Schwechat (A)
Tadayon Gilani with AXIS Engineering, Vienna (A)

Various Austrian Airlines training facilities were to be consolidated in the Training Center. The complex consists of an eight-floor administration and access wing, a three-floor, L-shaped lecture hall wing and a mock-up hall. Large surfaces remain unused in a rectangular hangar. A two-story pavilion was added on one of these "leftover spaces".

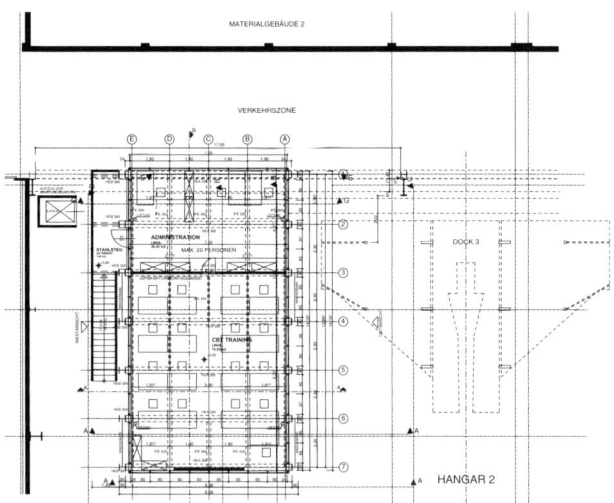

This representational project contains planning documentation that begins with the preliminary study (via simple 3D building visualization) and ends with detailed planning information. The project also includes the second construction segment, which has not been built yet. The existing hall with the flight simulator and the neighboring multi-level structure with lecture halls show how it is possible to create a floor management system for neighboring buildings with components of varying heights. Three-dimensional depictions of the sections and perspectives were used up to the implementation planning phase. Consultants then continued planning based on the delivered DXF/DWG material.

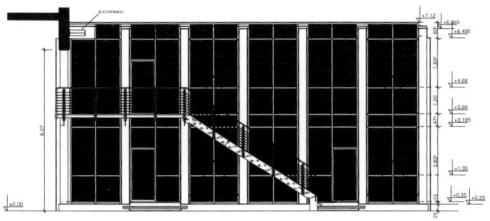
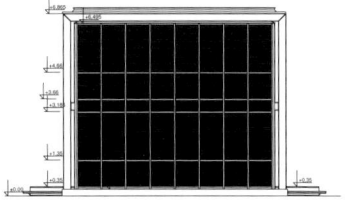

■ Körösistraße Administration Building, Graz (A) I Werner Nußmüller, Graz (A)

The purpose of the design was to emphasize the building's function as a service facility for the population with an inviting gesture and the legitbility of the individual offices with alternating patterns and projections. The objective of the spatial concept is to link the economy of a middle-access structure with a glass-roofed, five-floor hall. The concrete skeleton structure also made it possible to realize the curving of the upper floors as intended in the design. The highly frequented areas are located on the ground floor, less frequented office are on the upper floors.

The use of ArchiCAD within the framework of a competition is often defined by a tight schedule. The construction of presentation and design models is largely replaced by the use of a virtual building. Section perspectives and the visualization of important key architectural statements in the design are the main characteristics of ArchiCAD usage in this project. It offers an insight into thoughts behind a concept in any segment of the project without any additional time loss. An additional layer group makes the load-bearing structure visible, which offers a view of the vertical and horizontal development of the individual building segments. The usage of ghost story options in this example allows for permanent control towards complex overlaps between individual story areas during the design process.

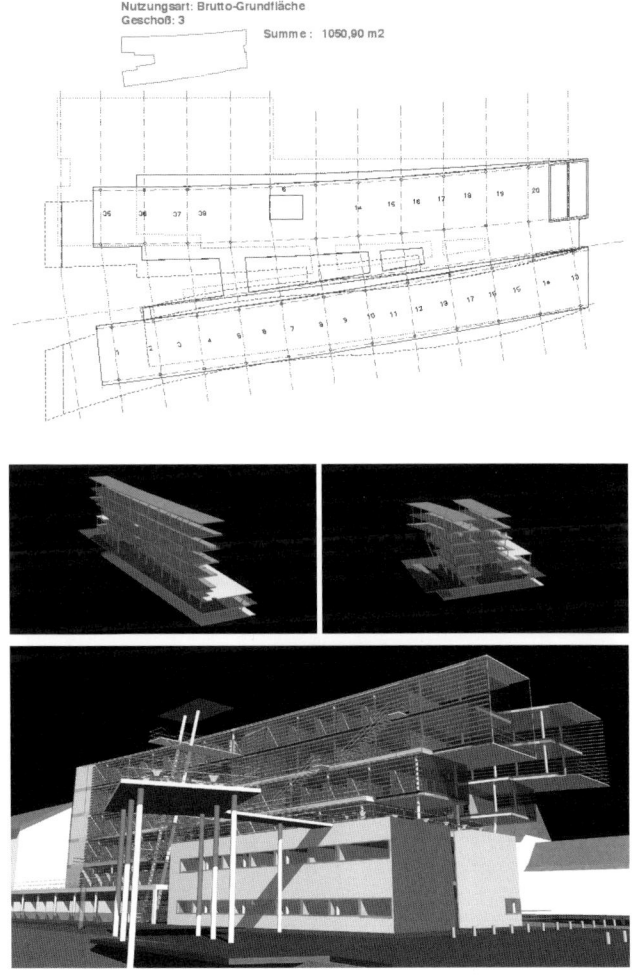

- Office Building and Showroom – Armellini Carpentry, Hard (A) | Wimmer-Armellini, Bregenz (A)

The existing workshop was refurbished, the floor plan was "cleaned up", and a new spray-painting and drying facility were added. A two-floor administration and personnel building is the "head" of the entire complex; the upper level consists of a showroom that features a large, window flush with the façade that seems to watch over the frequented pedestrian area and cycling route along the Ache River in Dornbirn. All the other windows are aligned along the inside of the external walls. A horizontal strip of windows runs across the building on three sides and expands close to the entrance area. The sculpted finish of this structure was achieved with a combination of load-bearing concrete ceilings on steel columns and self-supporting lightweight timber external walls.

The existing buildings and the new structure were administrated separately in individual level groups. The project file contains all the required plan renderings (grounds plans, sections, perspectives...). A separate plan was generated during the course of the project presentation that represents the graphical depiction desired by the architecture office. This file focuses on the planning composition in combination with photographs of the completed project.

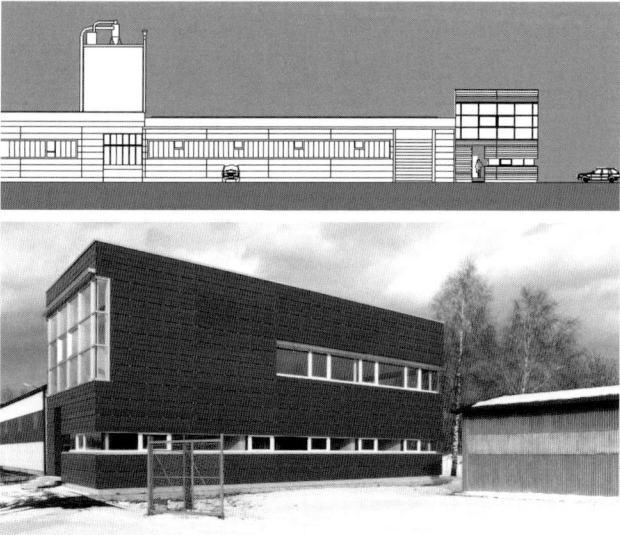

■ Biotechnology House, Göteborg/Änggården (Sweden) I
Liljewall Arkitekter, Stockholm (Sweden)

The function of this building is as a main source of medical research and training in Göteborg. The building itself consists of laboratories and offices as well as an atrium, park areas and a variety of service facilities. The four-part structure is located on an incline and follows the terrain with the central atrium acting as a connecting element. The rather exposed location allows for generous views of the surrounding landscape and also guarantees a striking visual presence.

This is the first project the planning office processed completely with ArchiCAD. The range of tasks includes volume sketches, 3D illustrations, planning documentation and drawings. Both 2D and 3D GDL objects were used in this project. ArchiCAD was also useful in grappling with the complexities of the terrain and developing the great variety of three-dimensional building element intersections and detailed connections required.

■ Commerzbank Expansion, Munich (D) | Dietzel und Partner, Munich (D)

The entire project consists of two buildings. The shifting of the customer area made a portico necessary. The expansion included the design planning (room occupancy and furnishings) as well as the operational plans (ceiling and lighting plans).

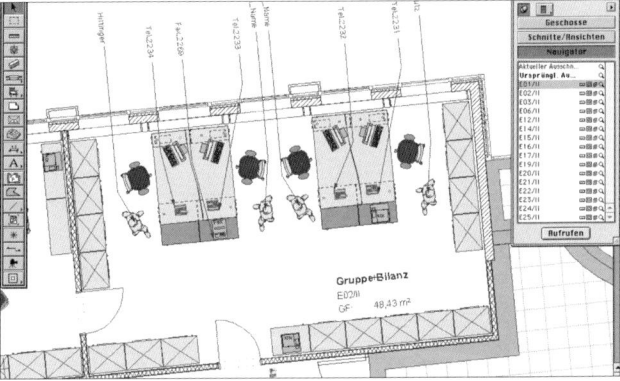

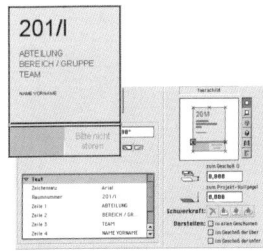

The ideal use of story management and layer structuring are the salient points of this project. Every individual room was defined as a planning segment with the aid of the navigator and an ingenious surface allocation system was also created for the project. A double click brings all the key room information to the screen in the right scale. It is remarkable that real-life objects were used, even for the doors (Novoferm steel doors in this case). This helps to show the characteristics of the actual door in the building model for later use (Facility Management). The programming of a separate "door sign" GDL object with all the important information on the room's condition (e.g. occupied/vacant) also facilitates ideal data use between the ArchiCAD project file and a database (e.g. use in ArchiFM).

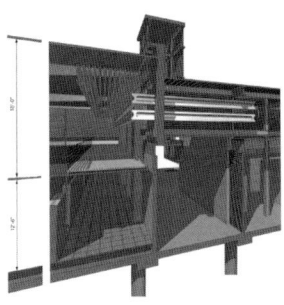  

3.1.5 Revitalization or Handling Old and New Simultaneously

The broader the base of digital documentation becomes, the greater the desire to be able to use CAAD model data for other purposes instead of just creating "drawings" by pushing a button. Digital plans of the existing buildings are available for most revitalization and refurbishment projects. These then become the basis for project planning. A factor that is often ignored is that the data structure of the plans of an existing building are very different to those required by the authorities or for an implementation plan. This mainly refers to level management, which is structured to allow for the consolidation of varying planning contents if so required. It is therefore advisable to use data on the existing buildings as referenced information and create a separate building model for new planning purposes. The advantage of being able to use information from the building model justifies this step in many cases. This point should be kept in mind when beginning a revitalization based on available 2D plans of existing buildings. There are also situations in which no digital information is available. The question in such cases is how much of the existing or computer-aided vectors of hand-drawn plans can be used.

A general recommendation cannot be made here. However, the dimensional stability of the sample should be tested before new design work begins. Scanning often leads to visual distortions of planning material on paper that become a source of error during later processing due to drawing and measurement discrepancies. It is only possible to avoid such errors by creating a new building model according to existing documentation on paper using the measurement figures recorded on it for orientation.

■ SOS Kinderdorf Children's Village – Expansion of the Administration Building, Innsbruck (A) | maaars architecture, Innsbruck (A)

SOS Kinderdorf is a social charity for all religions. The project comprises the expansion of the main office and the improvement of its structural appearance without losing sight of an intrinsic sense of "adequacy" with regard to the design measures. An upright angle, consisting of a tower and a block above it, should house the required functions and also have a calming effect on the heterogeneous nature of the existing structures.

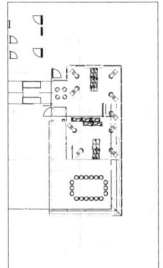 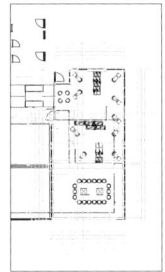 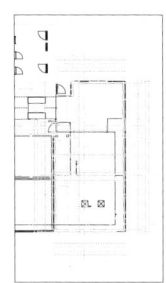

The simultaneous use of the existing older building and new building data was an important challenge during this project. It can be considered an exemplary case in terms of working within the technical framework of one project file. The existing building was entered as a three-dimensional element and made accessible with a clever layer generation and layer group structure. The "submission plans" layer represents the construction entries, while the "lighting plan" or "floor finishes" layer group already documents the implementation and detail planning.

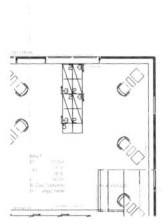 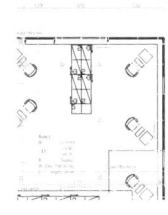 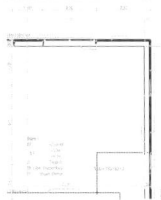

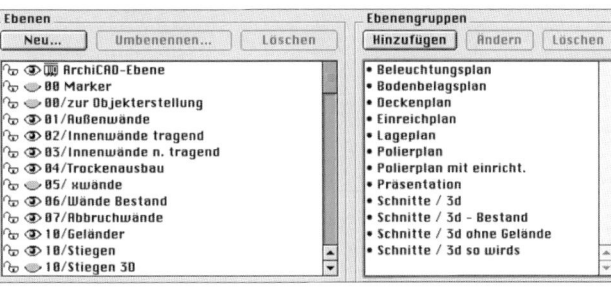

■ Revitalization of the Sparkasse Niederösterreich (Savings and Loan Bank) Head Office Building, St. Pölten (A) | Arge Beneder-Fischer, Vienna (A)

The Sparkasse building (1886) was remodeled as a customer and competence center. The lowering of the mezzanine to the ground floor level put the hall on a new plane and extended the main circulation road to the Herrengasse entrance. This change also led to a generous expansion of the cellar rooms, since the site formerly had an interior courtyard in the center.

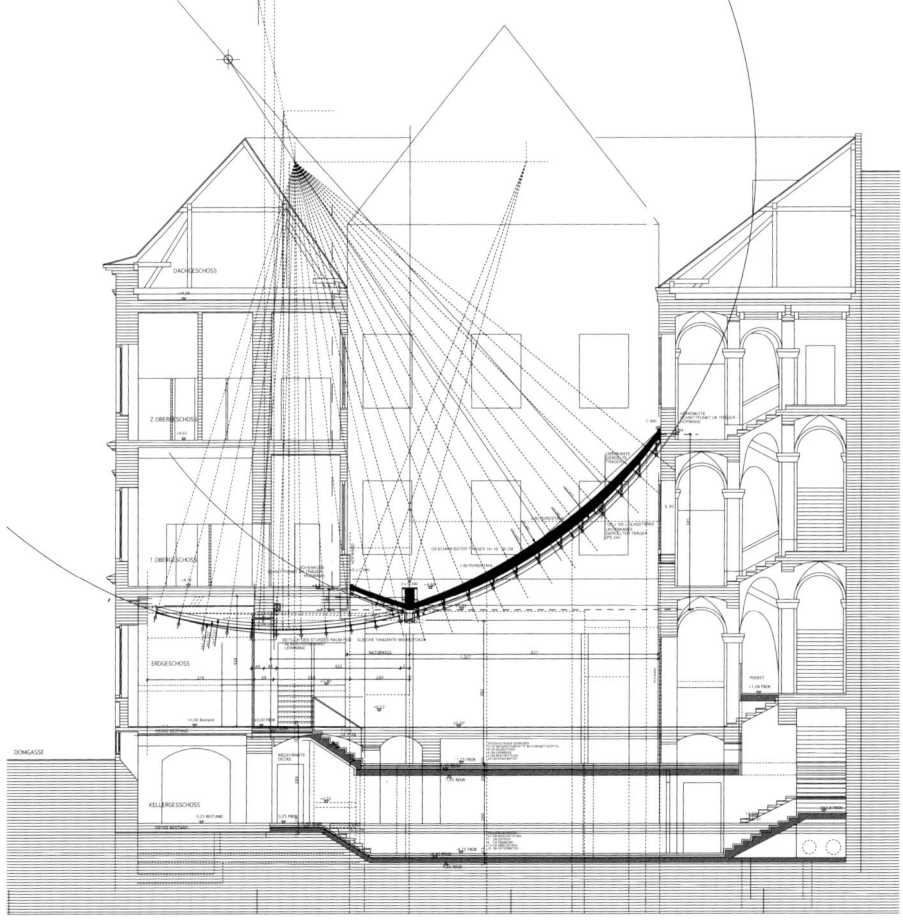

The interior courtyard is covered by a curved steel/glass construction. At its high end the old formal stairs is incorporated in the space's overall effect. It swings outward as a back-lit ceiling on the lower end, connecting the customer care units with the hall.

The spatial development of the planned refurbishment could be monitored and relayed to the client at an early stage via a virtual mass model. This design monitoring possibility is advantage that allows for the early detection of weaknesses in a planning concept. ArchiCAD is of great use as a constructive sketching tool for the conception of technical details (e.g. segmenting arcs).

3.1.6 Industrial, Commerical and Engineering Construction: Making Elements out of Construction Components

The following list of a number of building types is based on the use of building components as elements in a broad range of different structure types. These elements aren't necessarily limited to prefabricated components. The spectrum includes pre-cast concrete industrial halls and even complex production lines. The element as the basis of planning is a particularity of ArchiCAD. All are the same, whether it is a component that was created with standard tools, or a GDL object. The logic of the connection between the individual elements and their alignment is the key to success. The organization of the Virtual Building Model of a structure built with construction elements requires careful consideration. If a four-story office building with standard story heights is erected next to a 10 m high, single-story production hall the visibility issues and the required graphical planning renderings on the individual floors should be established in advance. For example, should a wall surface extending over four floors be entered? Using real building techniques as reference (e.g. how tall are prefabricated columns really?) can be helpful here. The feature of ghost story renderings or of Hotlink

Modules and the extensive use of (user-generated) GDL objects are effective aids in the planning process. Visualizations and embellished photo collages are often used to compensate for the lack of architectural sophistication in prefabricated industrial construction. However, the intelligent use of visualizations for structural and production processes can also have a major influence on the decisions to be made in industrial construction.

■ Molding and Press Works – Welser Profile AG, Gresten (A)
AXIS Engineering, Vienna (A)

This production site expansion was designed for a customized metal profiles refining and processing plant. Seven halls, a three-floor office building as well as railway and truck loading stations were built for this project. Logistical sequences were of central importance during planning. An exploration of the possible variants led to the final configuration of the production, warehouse and disposition areas.

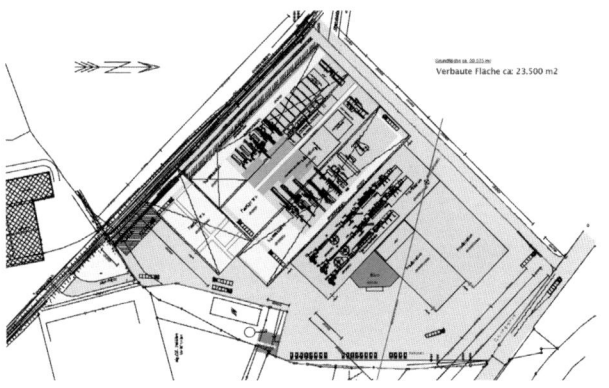

The use of GDL objects made it possible to simulate the loation, position and alignment of production units over a num-

ber of planning steps. These insights led to simplified updating of the changing surface requirements via database enquiries. Before submission for approval by the authorities the project was presented on an aerial photomontage to inform the public on the effects of the building measures.

■ Traunsteg, Wels-Thalheim (A) I Herbert Moser and Klaus Hagenauer, Linz (A)

The design of a wooden bridge follows the idea of creating a place for communication. User-friendliness in the sense of eliminating unnecessary inclines and terrain projections are the result of this priority. The design follows the forces acting on the site and is intended to eliminate additional costs, which might ensue from building foundations in the water. Hence the structure is restrained and helps incorporate the route in the surrounding areas.

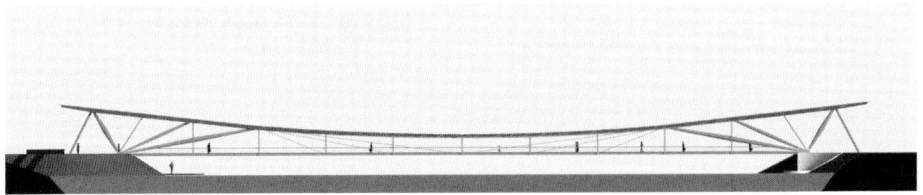

The story administration option that allows for the rendering of vertical or box-in-box elements as separate floors was used often on this project. This helps improve legibility and planning efficiency. Therefore, the ArchiCAD project document consisted of five floors (roof, bridge/ walkway, terrain, data import and object creation). The possibility of working on and/or rendering construction segments without needing to turn on layers created a clear overview during the construction phase. The distribution of model elements on various layers seems useful here.

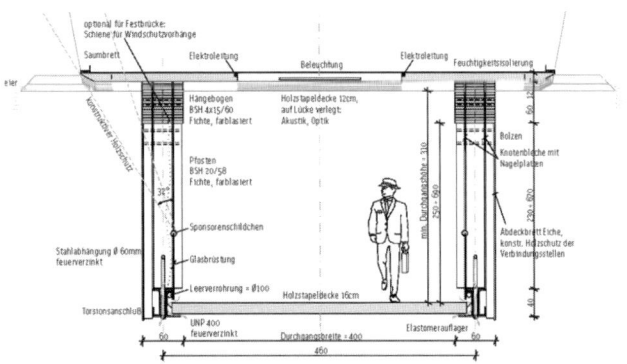

■ Funicular Station, Göstling am Hochkar (A) I Wimmer-Armellini, Bregenz (A)

The massive components of the summit station at an altitude of 1800 m create a sculpture with tectonic dynamics that is in dialogue with the transparent body of the glass cube in the same manner as the base station. The base station consists of the funicular cable drive, the return area housing and a basement train station with a green area. These individual buildings are consolidated in one ensemble and positioned to overlap with the striking roof of the existing building. The ancillary cable drive and service buildings were built using exposed concrete. The funicular return area housing hovers suspended between these two lateral buildings.

The preliminary design resembles an exact drawing that can be entered without undue effort. Although the project consists of two separate buildings, one central ArchiCAD document was used to create the planning documentation. Even the presentation layout for both buildings including two different groups of rendering scales was generated using this single file. The user can switch between the separate level groups of the implementation plan (S=1:50) and the presentation plan (S=1:500).

■ Bay Bridge West Span Bicycle/Pedestrian Pathway, San-Francisco (USA) | Donald McDonald, San Francisco (USA)

This feasibility study represents an endeavor to create a bay crossing for both cyclists and pedestrians with the partcipation of the population. A number of different design variants were conceived for the project. A ramp rising around the site creates a small park ("Plaza") and the design integrates the existing bridge with the railing elements and lighting systems.

Photo-realistic depictions are used to illustrate the extension of a historical bridge to include a pedestrian walkway. Since no additional technical plans were required, the task was to consider design possibilities and create visualizations. A PLN-file was created during the modeling process that created different layers, each for an individual design proposal. Most of the individual components were implemented as GDL objects, some were user-generated and others were created using the different ArchiCAD tools.

3.1.7 Educational and Public Service Buildings

The size of the material to be handled should be kept in mind when discussing large-scale projects. Where are the limits to reasonable ArchiCAD use? This is less dependent on hard and software performance than it is on the qualifications and organizational skills of the project team, although a 1 GB project file might bring some computers to their (virtual) knees. It is only possible to work sensibly with the project-supporting ArchiCAD work techniques if the planning team is working with a clear structure within the project. Office standards are important here in terms of identical basic project settings (layer management, line types, building element hatching, etc.). Large planning teams combine the use of (user-generated) GDL objects, Hotlink Modules and XREF technology. A TeamWork structure should be created for teams with three planners or more. The "2D or 3D" question is also an important aspect. Should one begin with a 2D input – meaning less initial effort – or should the third dimension be added at a later date? It is also tempting to use only two dimensions for certain buildings, especially if "simple" geometries are being used, that is at those places where simple extrusion is enough.

However, that isn't the case with carpenter-finished roof constructions. ArchiCAD favors 3D modeling from the beginning. But the 2D derivative can still be "correct" if the 3D model contains "faulty" solutions. Virtual Building Model use is interrupted or continued in a reduced form in some project sitiuations. This is often due to the large amount of incoming information that is required for a correct three-dimensional work, which often arrives in irregular intervals. However, it is still possible to use ArchiCAD effectively to administrate all perspectives and sections within a project file and take advantage of the floor structuring possibilities (e.g. as a transparent floor).

■ Donaucity Elementary School, Vienna (Austria) | Hans Hollein with AXIS Engineering Services, Vienna (Austria)

Complex structures characterize this composition, which consists of a number of structures elements with loosely staggered heights. The building houses a nine-class elementary school and after school care center for four groups as well as a creche. A projecting structure in the middle of the northwestern façade is completely glazing, accentuating the impression of a "gate to the Donaucity". The placement of the entrance hall behind the building line of the main wing on struts made it possible to create a protected open space immediately in front of the school building. The circular entrée serves as a distribution ring.

The main focus was on the organizational structure: A well-devised file management system based on the project num-

ber, planning theme and planning status was used for this project. This example also shows how participating architecture offices are able to work on the project without giving administrative duties too much importance. The data of various consultants (mainly in DWG and DXF formats) was also integrated in the project data structure.

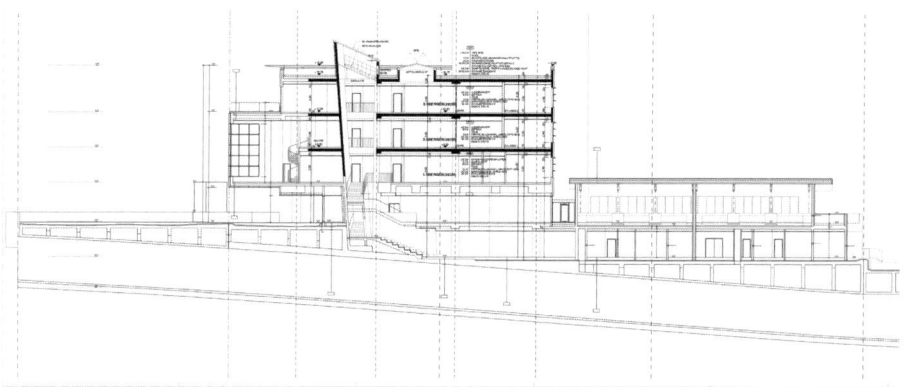

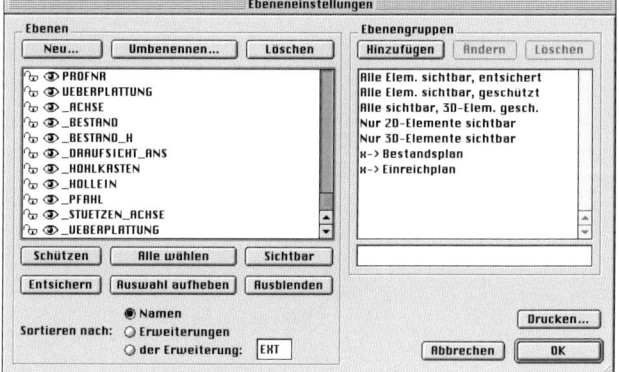

■ School with After School Care Center "VS/HS Morre", Graz (Austria) | Werner Nußmüller, Graz (Austria)

This school project contains eight classes and was built as a two-floor prefabricated timber structure. The basic approach: to create a "hovering block", that establishes a sense of permeability on the ground floor level. Large cubes such as the gymnasium and the gymnastics room were located under the classrooms as colored cubes. The appearance of the after school care center group and activity rooms is characterized by an upper grass surface that serves as a roof and play area.

The project was completed with a simple data structure. It is remarkable that the internal organization of the project required the creation and use of only 20 layers. A large part of this information is based on imported surveyor data, which were integrated at the beginning of the design phase (site plan). The existing parts of the school building were implemented in the 2D data structure, while the planned new building made use of the Virtual Building Model.

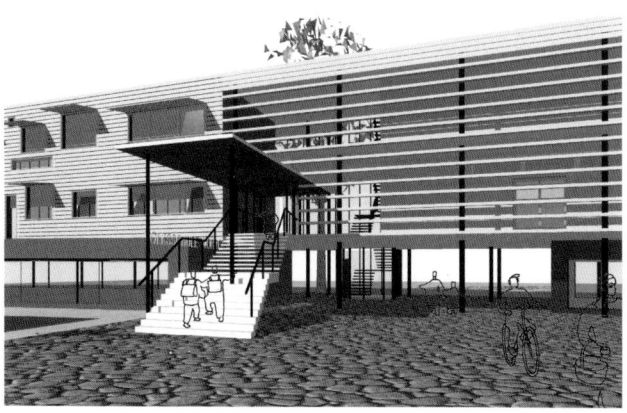

■ Georgia Perimeter College, Clarckston, Georgia (USA)
Richard+Wittschiebe Architects, Atlanta (USA)

The expansion of the existing school mainly concerned classrooms and the creation of a computer room, as well as a lobby and reception area. The new classrooms have floor-to-ceiling windows and lead directly outdoors (terrace access). This helps to create a visual link to the lobby.

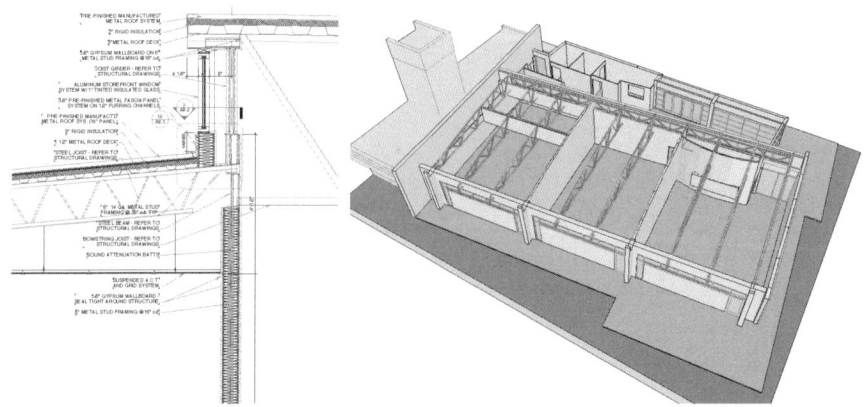

Detailed three-dimensional elements were modeled as they became necessary for reasons of understanding or for presentation purposes as the project progressed. Hence only a rough structure was used in areas of secondary importance. The TeamWork function was also used, which ansured that the users operated within the internal office CAD standards.

■ TKK Hall 600, Otaniemi (FI) | A-Konsultit, Helsinki (FI)

Alvar Aalto designed the main building of Helsinki Technical University (HUT) in the early sixties. The brief for this renewal entailed the construction of an auditorium seating 600 that would be integrated into the existing structure.

The IFC data exchange format was used in this project for the first time. This guaranteed the reliable transportation of comprehensive, structured 3D information between designers and consultants. The model created by the architects was used for presentation purposes and to supply data on the costs, life cycle assessments, acoustics and construction.

The extensive use of GDL objects as design tools is another remarkable feature. Instead of conventionally drawn structures that would have required re-working during processing, floors, walls and windows were created as GDL objects to facilitate and verify decision making with regard to geometry, material selection and structural requirements.

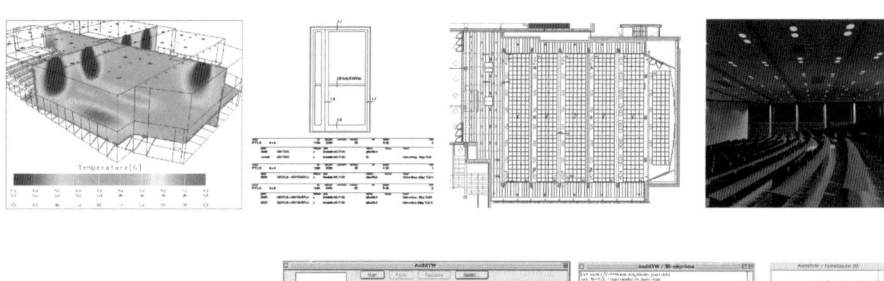
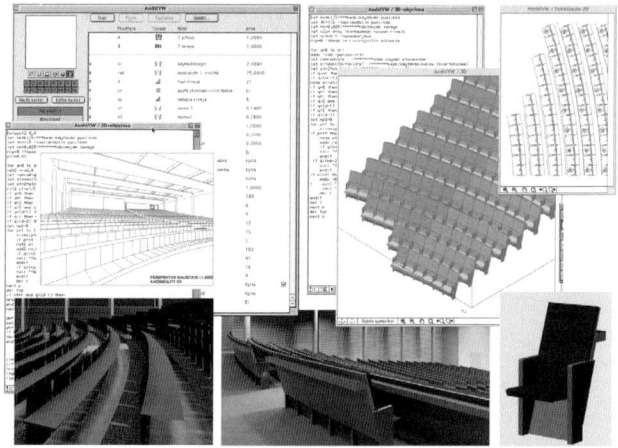

■ Science Center, Norrköping (Sweden) I Lund & Valentin Arkitekter, Göteborg (Sweden)

The goal of this project was to re-design an existing building and create a center for the sciences under the motto "Sky and Ocean" within an area lined with historical industrial structures A self-supporting reinforced concrete structure was used to achieve this objective. It creates a "building within the building" with a gap between it and the surrounding floors and walls. The complex building technical equipment is located in this gap, among other things. The building shell was restored and expanded in certain areas.

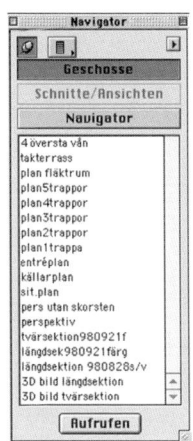
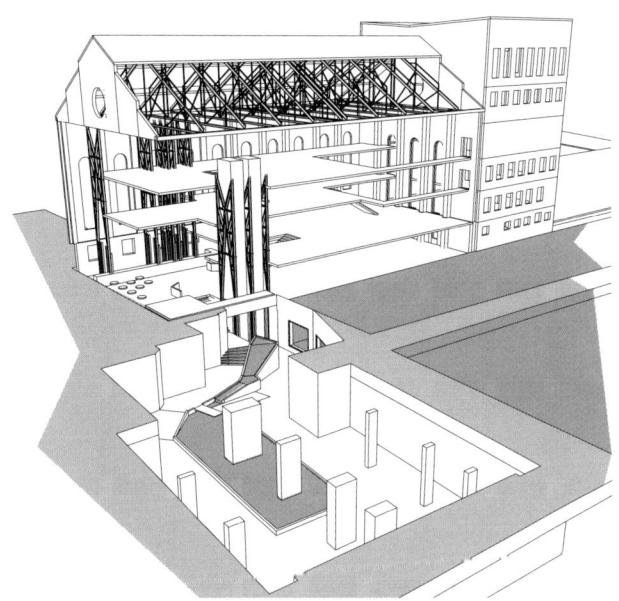

This example shows clearly how the differing requirements of presentation and communication mesh. It is important to address both the engineer's need for floor plans and the wishes of other persons who are involved in the project who may need entirely different display and explanation materials. Additional stories were created for the storage of display images and axonometric renderings along with the standard project renderings. The user can switch between the stories during a presentation and provide the required information.

■ Liefering Children and Youth Home, Salzburg (A) | Thomas Forsthuber, Salzburg (A)

A self-contained city, without hall and stairway structure. The largest volume is the community room, which acts as a large lung next to the dormitory buildings and also adds horizontally layered depth to the site. Every age group has a cell of space that can be opened to the community rooms to create a larger space. The spatial structure creates tension with levels and spaces used for a variety of purposes. An exposed concrete retaining wall and boundary encompasses the layers of the structure's borders.

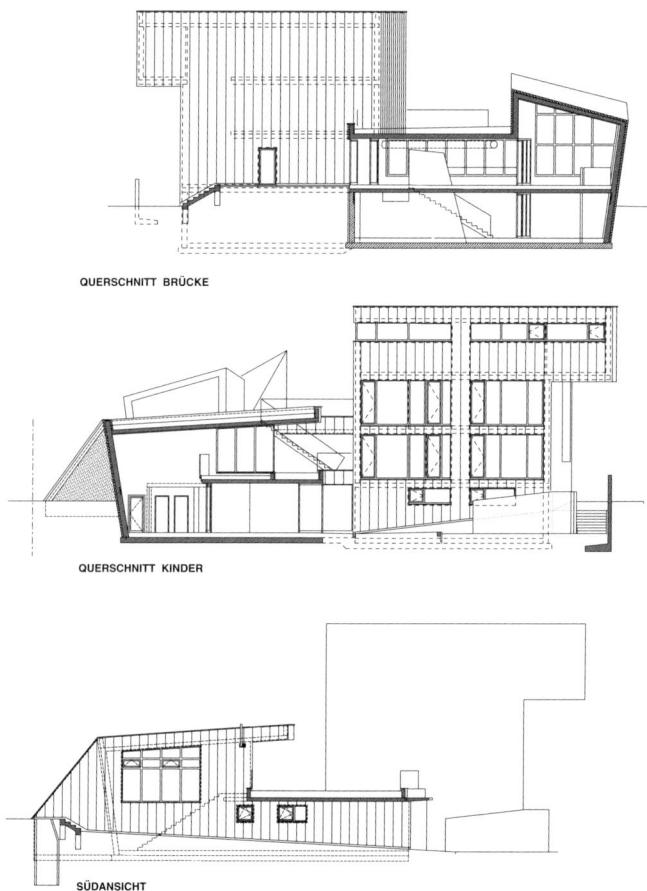

QUERSCHNITT BRÜCKE

QUERSCHNITT KINDER

SÜDANSICHT

Work continued in two dimensions based on carcass perspectives in the implementation and detailing phase, without creating complex 3D renderings in the virtual model. But the Virtual Building Model remained important in terms of the floor management. A number of individual ArchiCAD files were created that were nonetheless grouped in one folder (directory) for detailed planning purposes. Technical drawings provided by the manufacturer were also used to compile planning details (e.g. window sections). This information was integrated in the plan using DXF/DWG formats. The ability to present transparent floors is definitely an advantage when working on this type of project. This function makes it possible to monitor the alignment of vertical structures on superimposed floors.

■ U-Bahn/Subway Stations – U2 Extension, Vienna (A) | Paul Katzberger, Vienna (A)

Eight elevated subway stations will be built as part of the extension of the U2 Subway line. The project is an attempt to create a presence defined by light and brightness. The elements that will be close to the user are treated specially in terms of material and surface quality. However, parts such as the concrete structure are mostly left untouched by design. The appearance should be utilitarian and also be usable and easily cleanable.

The digital city map of the city of Vienna provided the basis for the design of the surroundings. The data from this so-called "multi-purpose" map (MZK) were referenced with Hotlink Modules in this project. The ArchiCAD project file requires around 45 MB. The possibility of using XREFs to integrate planning basics was discarded due to the expected storage requirements (around 128 MB in this case). Using Hotlink Modules also makes it possible to make the contents of individual 500 x 500 m fields invisible by fading out a single level. This option would not have been available using XREF technology.

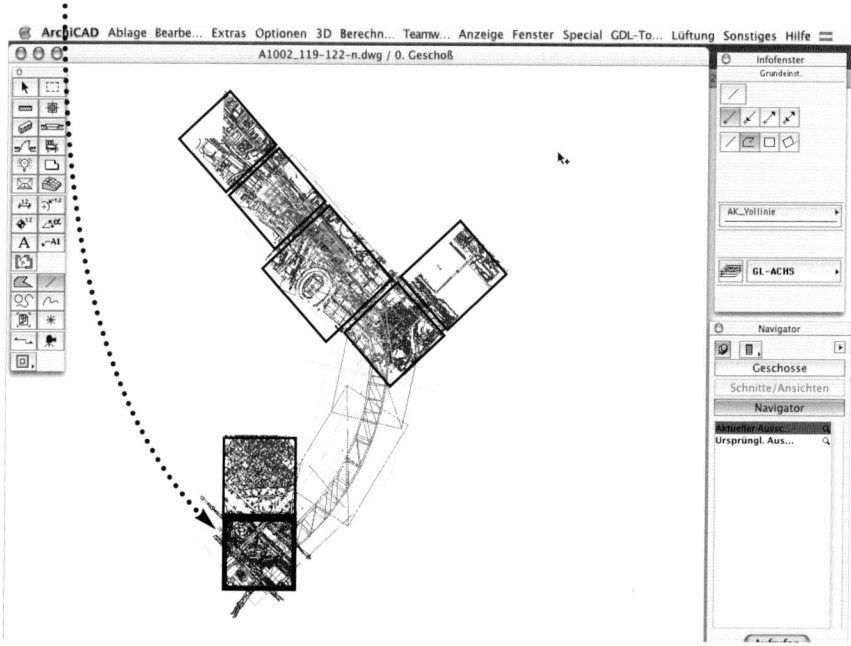

- Eurogate Zurich Main Railway Station (SUI) | Ralph Baenzinger - RBAG, Zurich (SUI)

This project was the winning entry in a multi-stage competition for the commission to expand the western segment of Zurich main station. The most important architectural elements of the track roofing are the large transit area with the adjacent train station approach and the service center that features a large glass-roofed central hall and six light wells. The city square, train station hotel and entrance pavilion act as a hub in this arrangement. RBAG was responsible for all project planning and coordinated the work of all expert planners, specialists and the authorities.

Basic structural preparations were necessary to complete a task as complex as this. A comprehensive CAD manual covers everything, from data organization (document management) to internal layer structures, line- and hatchtypes. Basically, a project is organized in work areas which contain individual levels of drawings. These are consolidated in a "masterfile", although the parts remain individually linkable via layer groups. A planning management coding system was also used according to a pre-defined scheme.

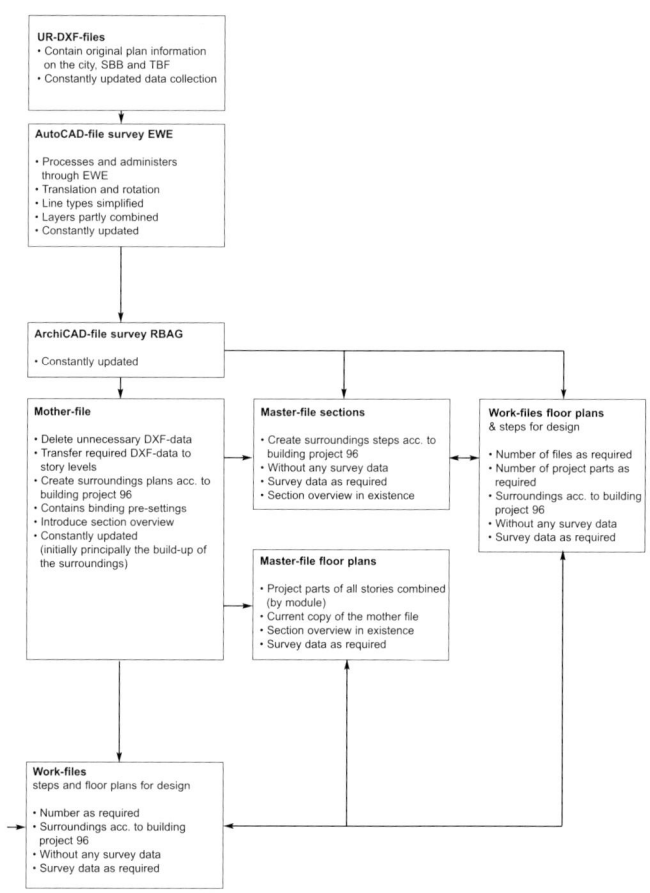

Example: HOT-00.06.15-CR-GR-Var.2b.PLN

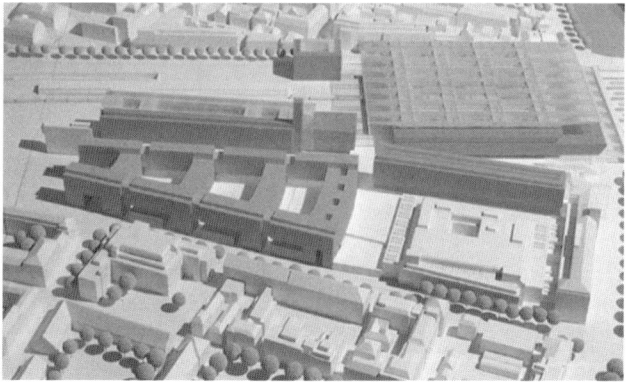

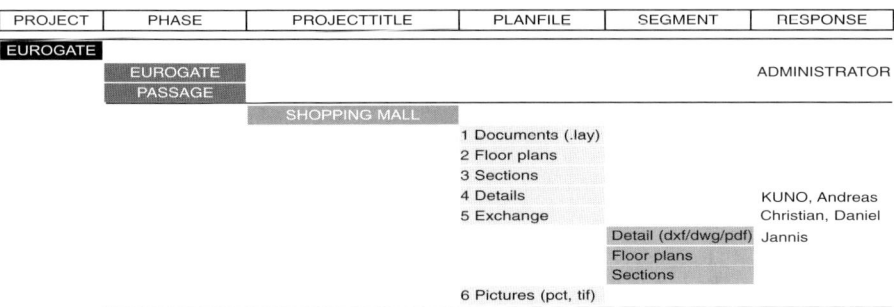

■ Rosenberger Highway Station, Hohenems (Austria) maaars architecture, Innsbruck (Austria)

The object of this project was to integrate a filling station with a shop and restaurant in one building. The floor plan reflects this need and the height of the restaurant area creates the intended sense of breadth and openness. Four dominating timber and steel struts support the roof load and define the broad restaurant space.

The use of the Virtual Building Model didn't end with the design process, it was also used during the implementation phase. Even sections and perspectives were linked to the three-dimensional data model. The rough 3D model renderings are complemented with 2D drawings. The increased use of layer groups that permit the switching on and of various special planning documents is another remarkable feature. The thorough integration of external planning information (HVAC, interior design, quantity surveyor...) that was available in form of 2D-DXF/DWG-Format was responsible for the 32 MB ArchiCAD project file size.

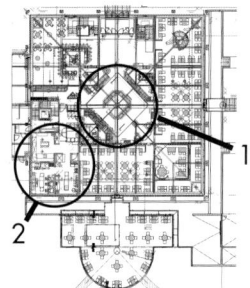

Due to the large building dimensions the possible size of a drawing segment on a computer screen is very limited. This allows only a limited overview of the project. A number of navigator segments were defined during planning that facilitate on-screen navigation.

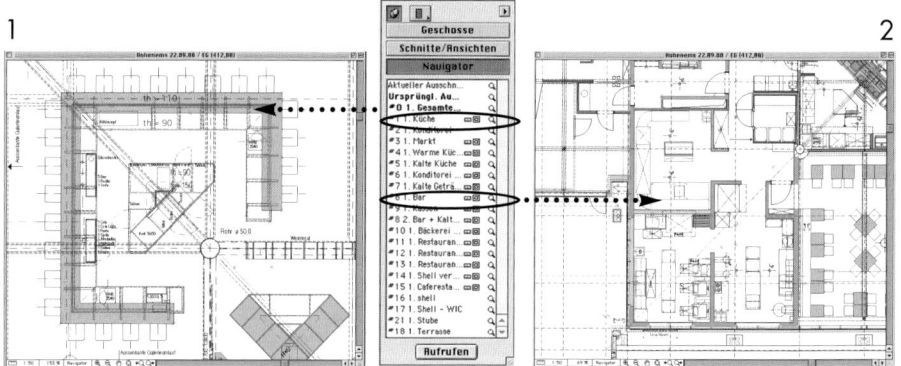

■ Centro Cívico San Joaquín, Santiago de Chile (CL) Hombo & Bañados Arquitectos, Santiago (CL)

The San Joaquín project covered the construction of both public and private service facilities. The center located in a poorly developed area of town is symbolic of "democratic" public spaces. A dominating façade structure wasn't the priority here. Instead, the design focuses on the central square. The partly lowered seating was placed in the middle of this elliptical Piazza. Service functions were located in the triangular building segment. The higher building portion creates a landmark and bears testament to the continuing development of this part of town.

The use of ArchiCAD in this project was based on module technology applied in small, managable units. Each of these units contains an identifiable part of the project. This makes it possible for the participating staff members to work on various elements without conflicts and synchronize them periodically with the master plan. The development of the tower was a special case: 12 floors were required as well as two independent volumes for access and connecting areas. Both also functioned as modules of the "C" module. A few versions were generated. Another interesting aspect of both projects is the effortless space/zone management, since a large amount of reports were required. Spreadsheet analyses were completed with a directly integrated ArchiCAD database (space reference book lists, etc.). A coded zone designation system made it possible to generate different report types.

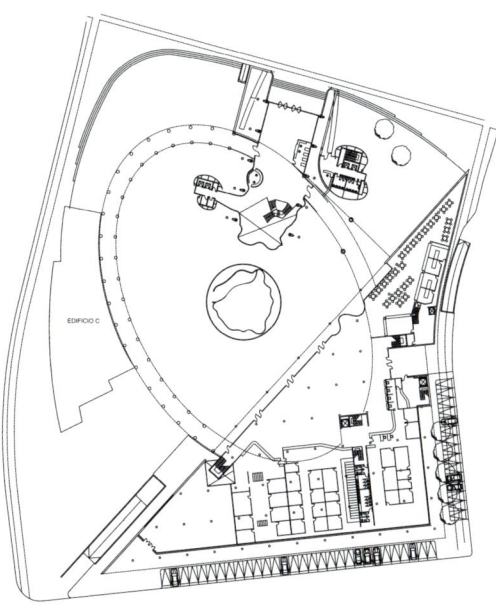
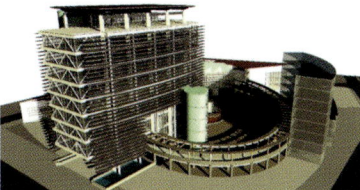
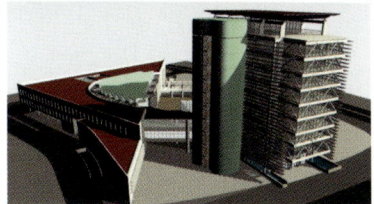

■ Municipal Building, Lake Havasu City, AZ (USA) | Orcutt WinslowPartnership, Phoenix, AZ (USA)

The administration building in Havasu (Arizona) was designed to create space for all the city authorities in one building. The design team developed a structure that incorporates the existing building and reflects features in the surroundings. A special shadow system defines the appearance of the building.

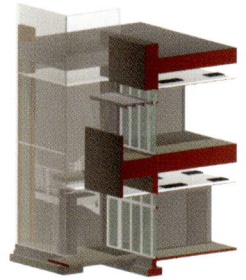  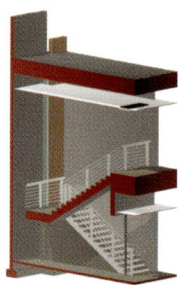

Three-dimensional "panels" were removed from the model at characteristic places and represent section and perspective details – after dimensioning. The integrated database works in the background, provding information for bids, areas, etc. when needed.

The 3D model is useful, even when a project such as this one is already being built. Combined questions from contracting companies can be answered using three-dimensional segment renderings (one model perspective). A snapshot can be produced quickly and sent via Email. This is an effective way of providing up-to-date detail solution information.

3.1.8 Interior Space Studies and Realistic Renderings

Interior design projections require comprehensive renderings with a relatively high degree of detail. A rough sense of the spatial volume might suffice for a first impression, but the interior furnishings play a decisive role in the next stage. Designing spaces requires the interplay of materials, colors, shapes and light. It is therefore advisable to avoid building a large-scale physical model (1:20) since it would require a geater amount of work. Individual objects are created as GDL objects and used a number of times in later stages. It is also possible to re-use models of segments again – for a chain of shops, for instance.

Another argument in favor of 3D modeling is the fact that interior spaces aren't all shaped as simply as a shoe box. Wall drawings are only of limited use to laymen. Axonometric sections are much better demonstration tools for spatial constellations and they can be generated easily from the 3D model. However, visualization via ArchiCAD alone isn't enough if a great degree of photo-realism is needed.

■ Palmers Shop Design, Wiener Neudorf (A) | Baudenkstatt Michael Alteneder, Vienna (A)

The re-conception of the interiors of all Palmers branches shows how many interior furnishing variants and configurations have to be developed before the newly developed corporate design can be applied in all stores. The first step was the creation of detailed interior furnishings and their integration in a visualization. The configurations developed in this way, including the lighting concept, create the framework for the mandatory Palmers store interior look.

The main point of ArchiCAD use in this series of projects lies in the ability to create images to illustrate the implementation of a design quickly and show variables in terms of materials, colors and lighting. Individual objects and varying scenes for the final high-end presentation were created with Art•lantis Render. The generated perspective views of a furniture element (3D window) were copied into the drawing (2D window) along with the plan and issued. The furnishings were modeled with default ArchiCAD tools.

■ Shoe Fashion Group Fair Stand, Taufkirchen / Yume Japanese Restaurant, Vienna / Rigler Electric, Waidhofen/Ybbs I B.E.H.F, Vienna (A)

The shopping mall principle was applied to the Shoe Fashion Group fair stand design. The objective was stress the individuality of the brands presented while creating a central point of reference. The separate subsidiaries were integrated as individual bodies of space under one large roof. The remaining surfaces were used for ancillary rooms, technical equipment and infrastructure requirements. The overlapping sections of the spaces serve as entrance areas. The skylight slits surrounding the stand create a horizon for the presentation of the collection.

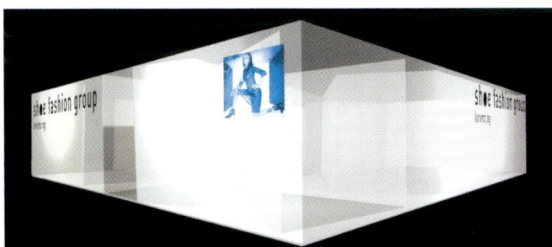 

The Yume Japanese restaurant uses the contrast between black and white to create a striking design. Clean interior and exterior perspectives, clearly cut spaces and the use of a reduced spectrum of materials help make the process of cooking and eating the central point of interest.

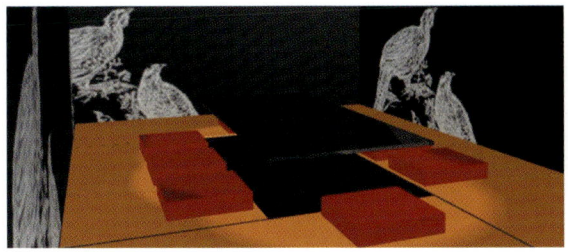 

An exciting shape and the consistent use of materials and light define the new building for the main office of *Rigler Electric*. The structure follows the bordering train and road line before closing as it reaches the traffic areas. The interior concept emphasizes functional separation and spatial crossover areas.

A more-or-less finished design of the future building offers the first opportunity for the visual presentation and communication of the concept. This approach is supported by the examples of "digital sketches" shown here. The use of ArchiCAD was limited to the creation of abstract renderings that provide information on the surrounding construction in this phase of the project. The sparing use of material textures helps accentuate the key features. The comparison between photo-realistic images and photos of the completed project and the comparison of the same sites show the advantages of this method.

■ Peak Fair Stand | maaars architecture, Innsbruck (Austria)

The project comprised the design of a fair stand for a television station. The company logo colors and materials were design pointers for the project. One of the priorities was weight reduction since the fair stand had to be transported to Amsterdam after the fair via air freight. Therefore, the support structure was based on a locally available scaffolding system that was put together using the required awnings, chipboard panels and connecting elements.

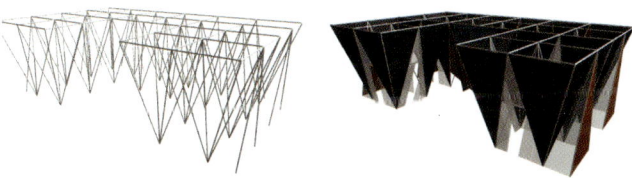

The use of ArchiCAD was limited to a few elements. The only items used except for the GDL objects for structural purposes and the stand interiors were the free shape surfaces for the design of the stand's awning. Project rendering variants were available via the layer groups. The structure of the layer is also interesting, since they were separated according to similar construction elements (e.g. stand awning).

■ Deloitte Consulting, New York (USA) | Suben/Dougherty Partnership, New York (USA)

The goal was to transform an 82-year old building with an irregular floor plan into a high tech office for Deloitte Consulting. Glass steps mark the end of a catwalk that acts as a backbone for the structure. Two skybox conference rooms crown the multi-purpose hall and the range of materials includes perforated wood panels, glass elements and a metal mesh ceiling.

The existing office standard was applied to the internal organization of this project. This makes work on the project, even by those staff members who joined later, easily verifiable at any time. Since this project focused on conversions, a separate layer group was created for the original existing building. This layer group was complemented by a number of standardized groups that contained the various informations for consultants (available via layer group selection and project navigator).

 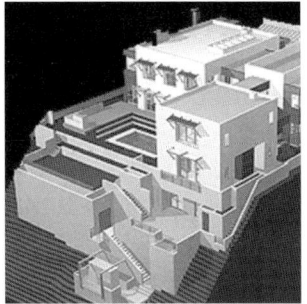 

3.1.9 Single Family Houses: Everything from One Source

A single-family house is a classical architectural task for which ArchiCAD can be used comprehensively as a tool. It defines an interesting option for small offices. The main feature is the ability to work in three dimensions from the very beginning. Is complete processing worth it? Generally, it isn't easy to be paid for all the required effort. The main point that should be emphasized here is easier communication with the client, since the construction of a physical model isn't necessary in some cases.

Although few explanations are required to discuss simple designs ("shoe box"), the opposite is the case with complicated spatial sections (e.g. penthouse structures). ArchiCAD makes it possible to create QuickTimeVR scenes directly. These scenes help encourage a "playful" approach. A horizontal section that casts a one-meter tall shadow can be used as the basis for a planning rendering that is legible for a layman. Axonometric section renderings can be created in a similar way and it is possible to cut the building structure at any point. This is much more complex with a cardboard model and has to be taken into consideration in advance. It is hardly possible to disassemble it after construction. However, it is possible to break the virtual model down into individual parts or component groups with a few rudimentary preliminary preparations. It is also important to stress the usefulness of information segments at a later date. This doesn't mean that a specific project is simply reproduced – no matter what the context, since detail development is very useful in this field (keyword: "productivity").

■ Roosevelt Way, Drucker Browstein and Grandview Residence | House+House Architects, San Francisco (USA)

The *Roosevelt Way Residence* is located on the Twin Peaks in San Franciscos on a site that slopes down from the back to the front. Generous openings contrast with the closed façade surfaces and give the structure a sculpted air. A surrounding pool is anchored in the slope at one end and opens on the other, far above the road. Recessed façades provide generous views of the surroundings from all rooms.

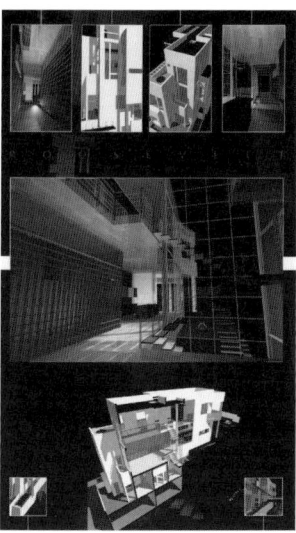

This project is one hour's drive away from San Francisco. It is located on a gentle incline between boulders and tall oak trees. The lateral wings of the *Drucker Brownstein Residence* contain the private rooms and reception areas. A two-floor cylinder that houses the dining area with an upper master bedroom "deck" acts as the connecting element.

The design of the *Grandview Residence* strives to create a house that can be understood as a retreat. Entry of sunlight and the wind and view directions were studied very carefully. Energy flow considerations and spirituality were conceptual components for some of the spaces in the house. Curved walls, deeply cut windows, the comprehensive use of colors and the proportions of the individual rooms accentuate the design objectives.

ArchiCAD was integrated in the design process to allow for a thorough exploration of the house's complex connecting shapes. Three-dimensional modeling was used from the very beginning. A number of different perspective renderings were created before selecting the images that provided the most imformation on a given context. The retouching with Photoshop serves to emphasize specific structural elements and make corrections.

■ 561 Grand Residence, Venice (USA) | Rockefeller/Hricak Architects, Venice (USA)

The *561 Grand Residence* project concentrated on the remodeling of an existing balloon frame construction. A self-supporting steel construction was built into the existing building in view of the circumstances. This structure supports both the new residential level and the new energy supply system. The sophisticated heating and cooling system is therefore closely linked to the bearing structure.

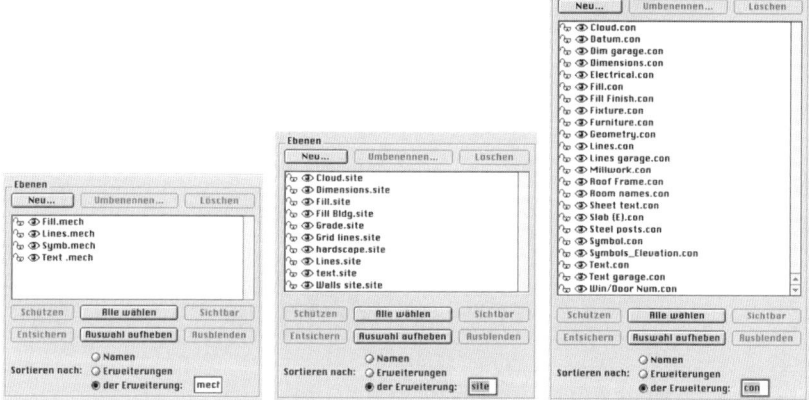

Well-organized layer groups define the backbone of project organization. Planning contents allocated to individual layers are made immediately available by using "layer extensions" (updating and depiction of a specific layer group). The story management also shows an intelligent use of a vertical administration structure. The various contents (mainly technical equipment) installed in spaces between floors that would be irritating in an architectural design are separated, but they remain visible in the layer organization as a 3D rendering.

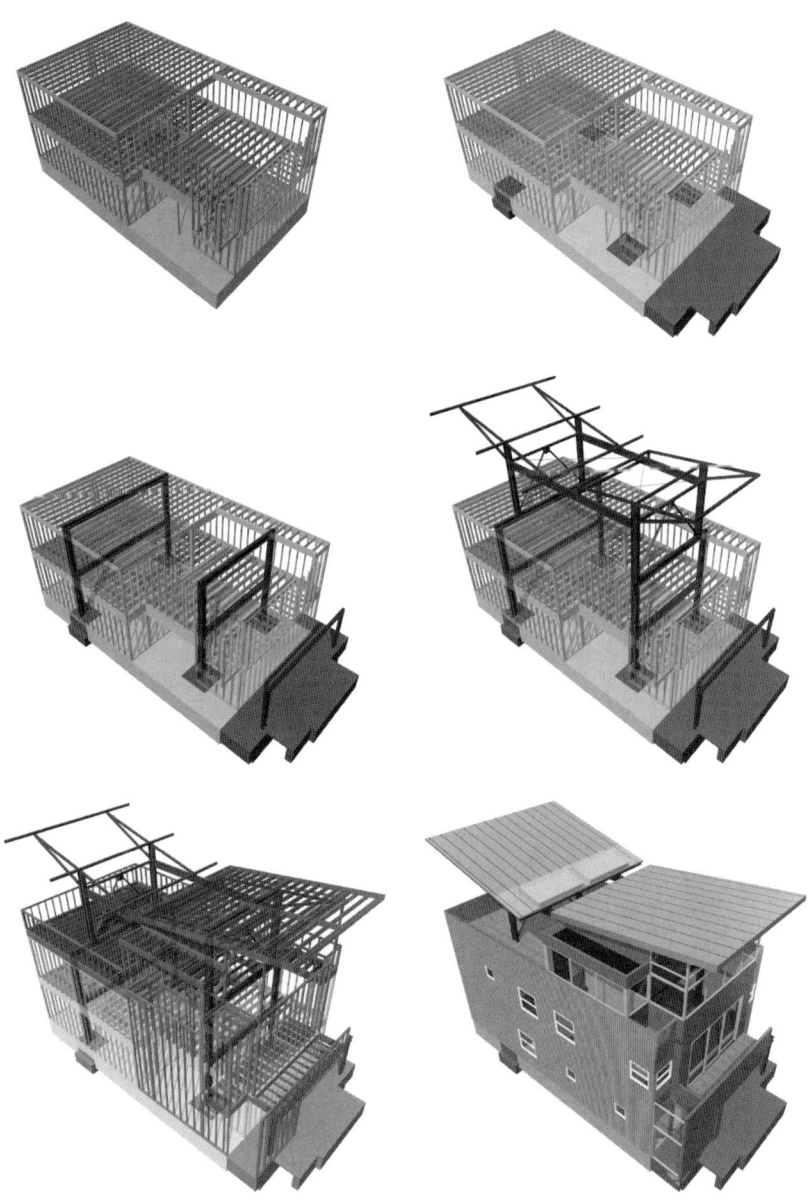

■ König Single-Family House, Feldkirch/Nofels (A) I Gohm-Hiesberger, Hohenems (A)

A swimming pond and a forecourt extend from the house to the borders of the site. The garage was positioned facing the street so that the garage door acts as an additional shield for the pond when opened. External curtains contrast sharply with the hardness of the building.

The small size of this project made it possible to complete both the construction entries and the implementation planning within one single ArchiCAD file. The story management was used as the organization structure for all project documentation. It was also possible to switch between the planning contents and the implementation plan via two layer groups for rendering purposes.

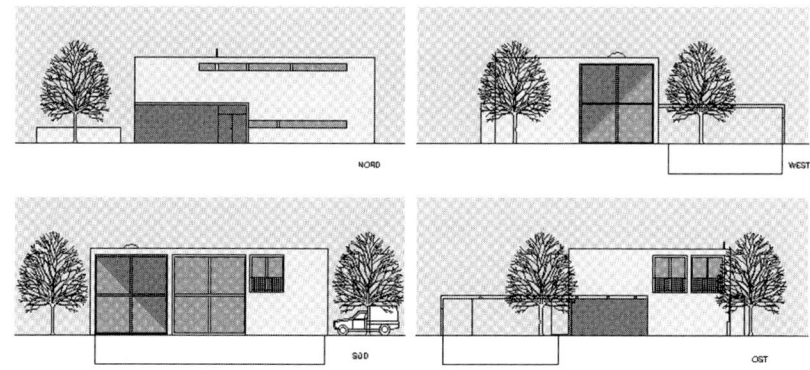

■ Stonehouse, Steindorf (A) | Günther Domenig, Graz (A)

Stonehouse lies on Ossiach Lake. It remains uncompleted to this day. The rough, geometrically stringent poured concrete bodies, some of which are hollow, reflect the remarkable landscape configurations of the surrounding mountains. The object that was built therefore seems to be a landfill with boulders striving to break free from it.

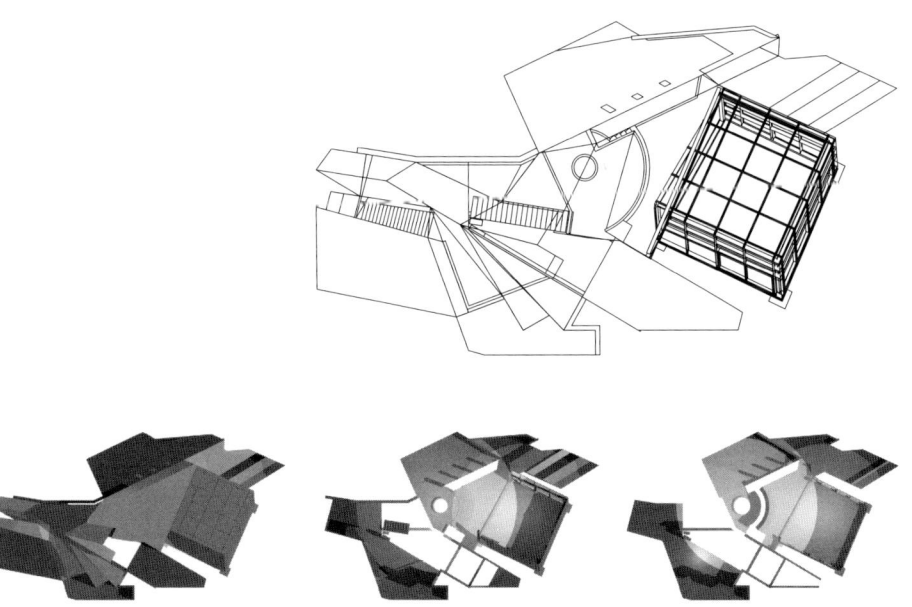

CAD was only used at a relatively late stage of this project. The building entries were based on surveyor information that was used for three-dimensional modeling. The building itself offers the possibility of generating a section or perspective at any time and in any place due the three-dimensional rendering. This documents the complex inter-linking of building components for the implementation phase.

3.1.10 Small-Scale Applications, Individuality and Variety

ArchiCAD makes effortless modeling of small-scale objects – especially those used in everyday life – possible. There is an analogy to urban construction planning here since we are now at the other end of the scale (large vs. small scale). This means that the same "standard parameters" that apply to the creation of walls, ceilings and roofs apply when a chair is modeled with the standard tools. A thin ceiling with a density of 0.9 mm can be used as a furniture slab. The parameter entries allows for this option, even if this is not the usual dimension range in which ArchiCAD-users operate. After all, the motto is: anything can be modeled. This is especially the case for user furniture designs and interiors, which can be developed with ArchiCAD support. This approach is intended to address the completion of an interior and less as a production-oriented tool. This makes it possible to show the room and the items a room normally contains. It is useful to show space needs and the user also has the option of creating his own GDL object collection if the default and additional object libraries aren't enough. It is also worth considering the generation of real objects in the form of available (construction) products that are depicted geometrically as GDL objects. This involves the creation of a specialized digital model as opposed to designing the structure.

■ Table Design, Vienna (A) | Helmut Heistinger, Vienna (A)

All the furnishings and interior elements were designed and produced in the course of a penthouse re-modeling project. Each one is a unique piece that was custom-made to fit its specific space in the penthouse.

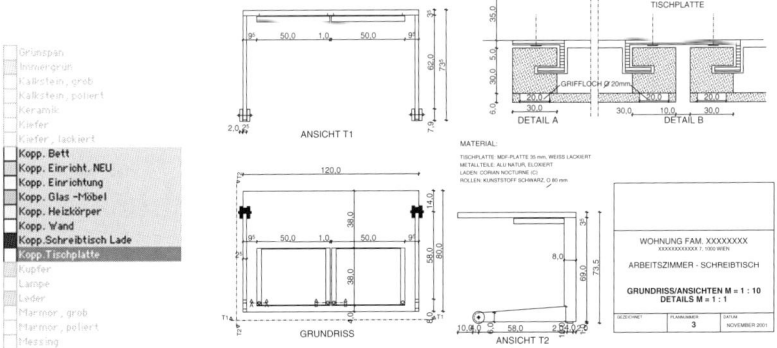

Design drawings were duplicated in one single project file and then compiled for detailed presentation. The automatic section and perspective generation modes were also used on this project. The results were copied into the floor plan renderings and then used to create a detailed plan for the production of the furniture item. A number of new material colors were added to be able to create realistic visualizations.

■ CAT Furniture Designs | Mikula+Partner, Graz (A)

ArchiCAD was used for the design, production and sale of this furniture system. It is therefore possible to create work plans based on the models and complete interior design suggestions for entire office levels.

 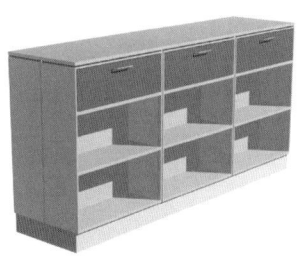 

It should be mentioned that the entire production sequence, including prototype development and the creation of work plans, was exchanged via PLN format files between the hired companies. The elements were developed exclusively with ArchiCAD standard tools. However, the elements were saved as GDL objects once their development was completed and represent a form of furnishings library for more comprehensive interior planning. Separate surface colors and textures are useful here for a preview visualization of complete interior situations.

■ Tiled Stove (A) | Peter Ltd., Waidhofen/Thaya (A)

This example explains the planning and visualization process involved in creating a specifically developed tiled stove. The large amount of possible tile types and colors and special features (equipment) made it necessary to create a separate tiled stove GDL object collection.

Varying shapes as well as available patterns and colors were administrated in this project. This example shows the connection of tiled stove to the kitchen stove that is fuelled from the kitchen side. The example chosen explains the demands that come to bear when planning a specific tiled stove. The customer should be given an image of the planning results in advance. It should contain a quick sketch of the planned stove along with the most important surrounding elements in the desired location. Both GDL and ArchiForma objects were used to create the "ledges". The tiles are special objects that can depict the selected tile pattern. Special elements such as oven doors (for kitchen ovens) or ventilation screens are also illustrated with projected images. The grounds plans and perspectives are also useful for the construction of the stove on-site. The layer structure organizes the stove in different zones that are named after construction criteria, from the base to the cover.

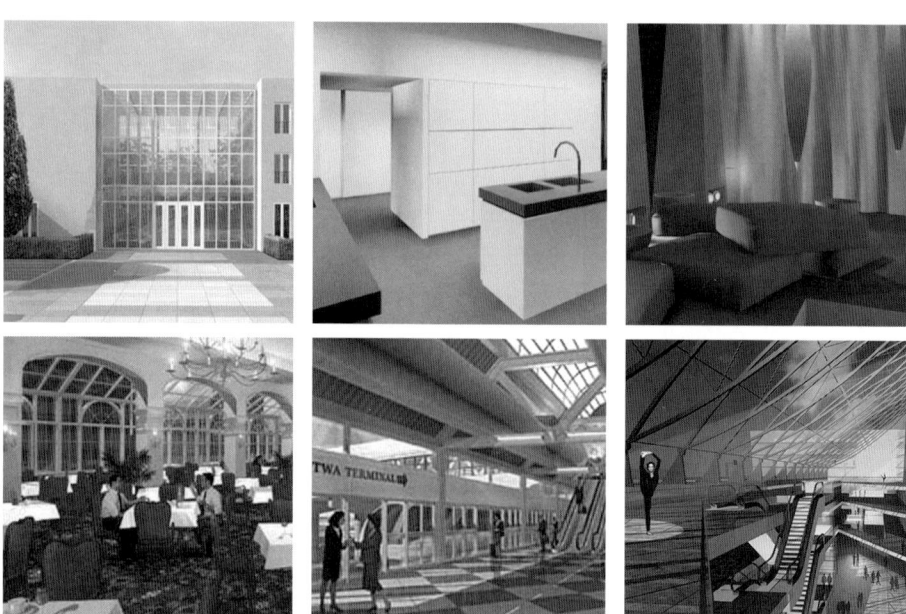

3.2 Visualization Strategies

CAD software product work is often considered equivalent to visualization. What is sometimes ignored is that the actual advantage of using CAD software products is the efficient support of architecture production and the supply of integral information for such projects. Computer-aided planning offers more than just a few advantages for the generation of construction plans (and/or documentation) when users work with the "right tools". It also facilitates communication between those participating in a project. A number of visualization strategies have been developed for presentations as the performance of personal computers has improved. The presentation needs of the respective target group are normally decisive when the use of (photo-realistic) images is considered. Hence there are no merely "good" or "bad" images as long they at least reflect a minimum of technical quality.

Visualization products are used to generate sales. For that reason they cannot be ignored in this book. The temptation to press the "standard visualization" button is great, but more thought is required for effective visualizations. Some visualizations are also unsatisfactory to those who create them, although it is too easy to blame deficiencies on the software product. The basic principle of "less is more" should be applied to the use of material textures and to photo montages, that are sometimes created with insufficient photographic material. Poorly cropped images (e.g. "shiny white edges), persons mounted in the wrong perspective and the unrealistic size of furnishings are a few of the "irritants" that can make a computer image seem "unreal" or even fake. An improvement can often be achieved by simply changing the view point and the angle from which the object is viewed. This is similar to photography: the choice of subject (cropped image) is the photographer's, not the camera's.

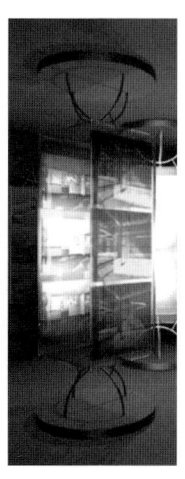

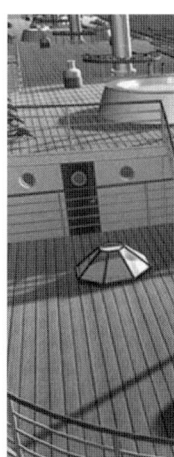

3.2.1 Conveying a message with visualization

CAD can be used to sketch in a manner similar to handmade drawings – to a certain degree. The purpose of an architectural sketch is to bring the core statement of the planned form of the architecture to the attention of the viewer. Virtual space renderings offer a broad range of project communications possibilities, from extremely sharp images to exaggerated sharpness. In some cases, a wire model or a quickly generated and shaded rendering makes the desired statement perfectly, while other projects require sophisticated collages based on complex geometric calculations and photographs. The guiding principle could be "show what need to be shown".

■ Studios Architecture, San Francisco (USA)

A glass backbone that follows the terrain serves as the interior access system of a multimedia agency in San Francisco and leads to the landscaped roof of the structure. Visitors are offered a beautiful view of the city from here, while the façade tries to follow the scale of the surrounding buildings.

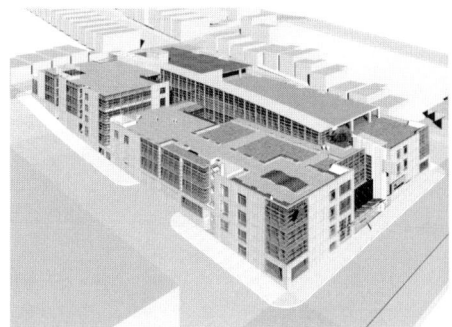 

The *Madstone Theater Project* (Denver) was an attempt to re-model abandoned movie theaters and revitalize them as design and fashion facilities. The calculated use of color and the installation of new projection surfaces in the rooms should bring new life to unprofitable structures.

■ Helin & Co Architects, Helsinki (FIN)

The new 16–floor Baltic Square office tower rises in the middle of a new area of town, Ruoholahti. The use of Corten steel played a central role in the design of the building. According to the master plan it was to be used in the façade areas, but it was also understood here as a link to the existing older industrial buildings built of brick.

The *HP Bazaar* is an innovation center for emerging mobile computing. The projected interiors are intended to support mobile e-services advertising. The bazaar is located in Espoo and is primarily used for communication purposes. It is also the site of marketing events and a variety of presentations.

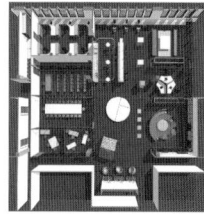 

Form the outside, the Pfizer Office Building formation is a dialogue between a dominating cube and a lower, fan-shaped building that sets the building in the surrounding park.

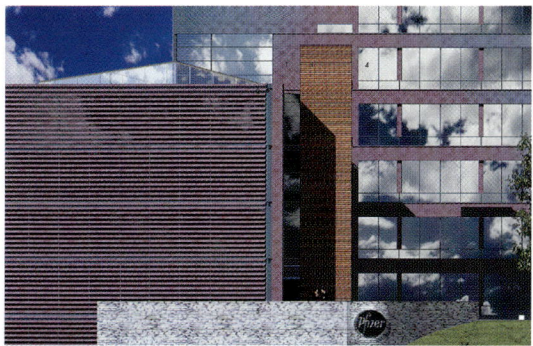 

A multi-functional atrium was built in the space between the two structures. *Nokia's* rapid growth made it necessary to expand the main building. The management chose a design that is defined by a curved structure and a rectangular block. The semi-cylindrical atrium connects the two main bodies and serves for conferences and festivities.

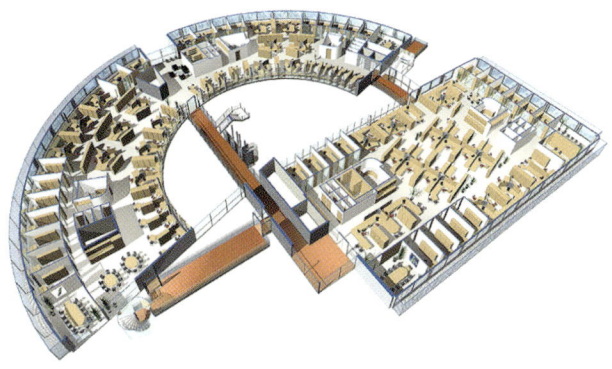

■ Bau I Kultur, Linz (A)

The City of Linz announced the demolition of the two highrises on the Harter Plateau in 2000 (realized in 2003). There was no possibility of preserving the two buildings.

The project design included two multi-purpose buildings with large green "oases" that seem to penetrate them. The goal was to explain a design concept to the public, e.g. to persons without specific training.

■ Liljewall Arkitekter AB, Stockholm (S)

It can be seen clearly that the solution applied to the *Hildedal project* (Hisinge/Jörlanda-Tuvevägen) was concieved using a perspective generated with ArchiCAD as the basis for a hand-drawn image. ArchiCAD was used during this phase to give an urban construction context an individual touch and to convey a natural degree of accuracy and authenticity.

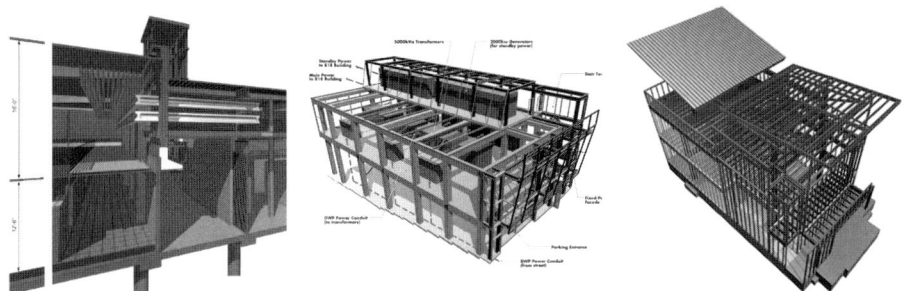

3.2.2 Explaining Connections with Visualizations

Visualizing architectural connections is different from the rendering of technical or construction functions. This fact can be helpful for purely organizational uses, but it can also help with timeframes or the sequence of events during the use of a building. The results used are generally presented in form of one-color (shaded) images that explain functional sequences. A single image is not always enough to convey something effectively. Hence a series of images is used that also takes the time factor into consideration. Designing sun protection elements on a façade is a characteristic application, since it tests and presents the function by means of a documented sunshine study.

■ Helmut Heistinger, Wien (A)

The objective of the restoration of the *Marienheim* (Bruck/Leitha) was to improve the light and shadow situation while performing a general overhaul of the façade. The goal of the study was to create a new architectural design and observe the amount of sunshine that can be expected during the year. The data of the existing building was recorded meticulously before the renovation. This data was used to create a 3D model of the façade. After the design was completed, the sun was studied during a number of key days to be able to calculate the angle at which light entered the rooms and the shadow the new sun protection elements needed to provide. This process was repeated on all four sides of the façade to create a cohesive solution.

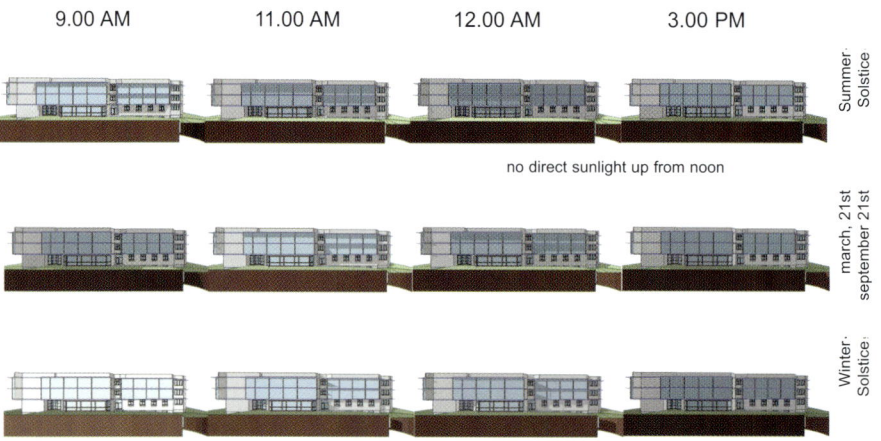

■ Rockefeller/Hricak Architects, Venice (USA)

The *Power Station* project in Los Angeles shows the design and possible urban integration of purely technical infrastructure. The necessary generators and transformers are concealed behind the street façade. Visualizations were created to address landmark preservation issues and shorten the approval procedures with this information.

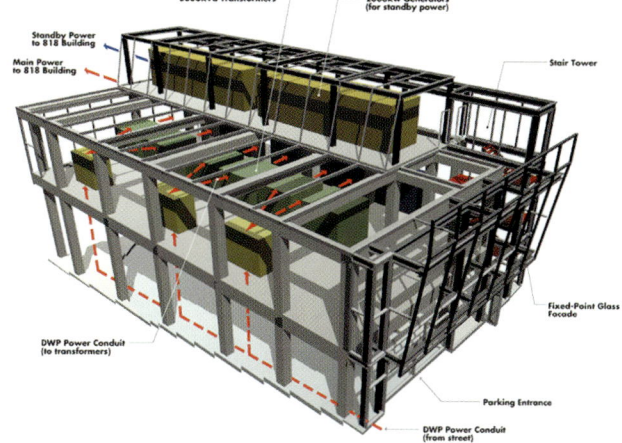

■ Tillberg Design, Fort Lauderdale (USA)

Tillberg plans and designs the complete structure and interiors for *luxury liners*. The renderings show the structure of the individual suites and also give laypersons a clear impression of the space they are renting. The use of detailed modeling makes the plan and the axonometric more readable in relation to the scale.

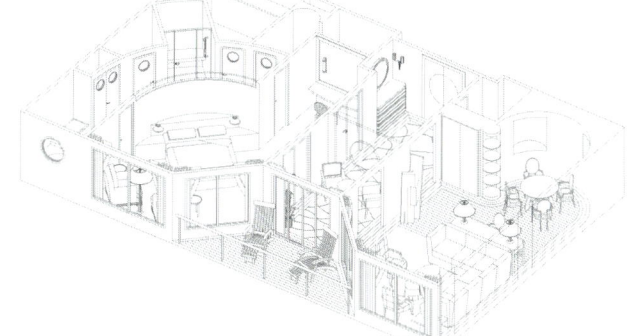
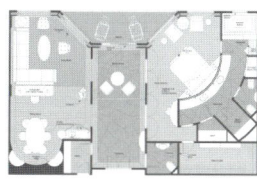

3.2.3 Custom-made Visualizations: contents and technical perfection

A number of specialized companies have been established over the last few years that create "made to measure" visualizations for architects and architecture offices. Generally, these visualizations are of particularly high technical quality. At first glance, the level of perfection of this type of visualization is impressive. However, a second glance shows what target group this type of image is for. High technical quality is often complemented by a lack of clarity as regards the statement the project is supposed to make. Sometimes this kind of rendering is exchangeable and makes no real statement, as far as the actual quality of the architecture for the later user or owner is concerned. It also doesn't really matter whether such as scenario is supposed to depict architect A or architect B's project.

■ LuminetlK, New York (USA)

The interior renderings of *apartments* in New York were used as sales-support documentation. They show the interior design planning that was modeled with ArchiCAD and later finished using Art●lantis.

These visualizations are part a multimedia presentation conceived for the *fair stand of Mark Krueger Designs*. These are segments from an animation created with radiosity. The focus of the presentation was on concepts for the use of theatrical lighting for retail purposes. The animation illustrated the use of lighting, which was demonstrated at the corresponding fair stand.

The intention was to give the newly-renovated *National Newark Building* increased presence in its urban surroundings using a specific lighting concept devised by H.M. Brandston (New York). A number of nocturnal renderings were created for this purpose using Lightscape.

Another project rendering shows a *Southhampton beach house*. The architecture is defined by specific relations with the surrounding garden landscape. The design modeled with ArchiCAD was visualized using Lightscape.

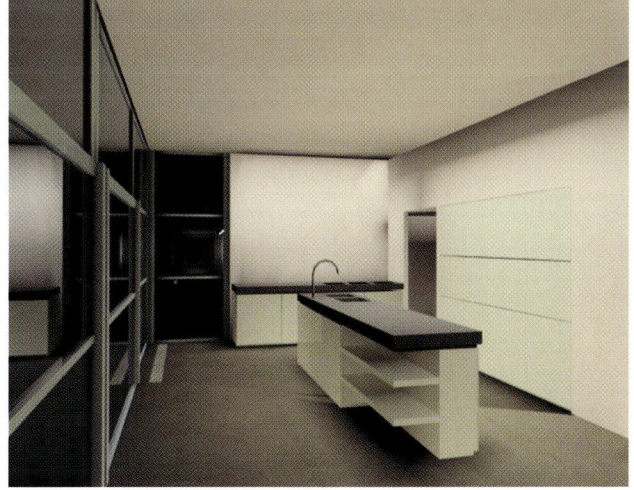

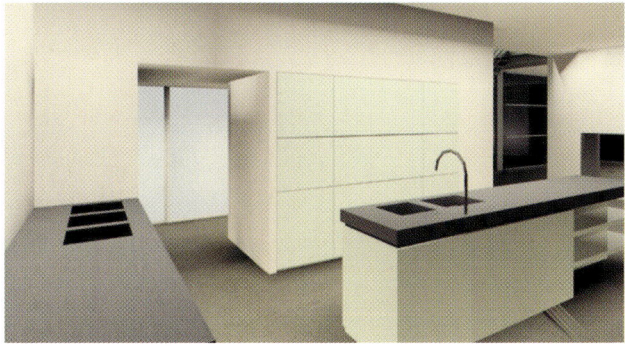

■ LengyelToulouse Architekten, Cologne (GER)

The structure consists of a production hall and administration, which creates a balance between uniformity and differentiation. The façade structure and ribbon of windows along with a ribbon of exposed concrete, grace all four sides of the building, that was constructed for *Korte Einrichtungen* (Kuerten). The ribbon windows at the top and the respective curvature make the entrance and monitoring function of the administration evident, without interrupting the building's coherence. The clear structuring of the building conveys design clarity and precision in the formal and technical excecution.

A glass entrance and access facility was built to complement the existing buildings of the *Göttelborn colliery* (Saarland, Germany) electric workshop. An architecturally designed plateau was added to stress the building's solitary, representational function for the workshop. The larger part of the old building was preserved, the historical segments are recognizable in the planned culture center.

The possibility of moving the *offices of VDI* to Berlin was explored in a feasibility study. The projected new building was conceived as a five-floor complex grouped around an interior courtyard. The structure is dominated by a U-shaped office block. The required lecture halls are located in separate building segment.

■ PAASTUDIO – Ivo Venkov, Santa Monica (USA)

The set-up of the *Biolabs* design follows biomolecular structures and links the requirements of the spatial brief with the terrain. The structures trace the morphology of the site. The garage is below ground level to minimize the building height. A "tropical garden" awaits visitors on the inside.

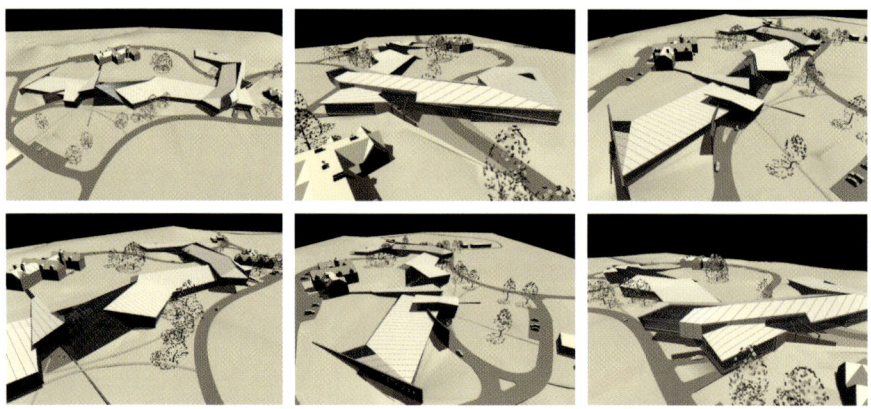

A projected *multi-functional office building* comprises a two and a three-floor complex with a deck on the top. Above it lies a wave-shaped, transparent metal roof.

The *Heritage Welcome Center* project aims to display heritage items and create a symbolioc bridge to the past. A cantilevered bridge dominates the entrance area, it is both a gesture and protection against the weather. The building segment behind it tries to interpret local construction traditions. Pathways leading through the landscape and a number of small service facilities surround the complex.

Located in the center of Sofia, the projected *Municipal Gallery of Art* is intended as an interface for a different art forms. The design follows the principles of versatility and openness. The entrance of the building also acts as a public space that will be the site of performances and sculpture presentations. The purpose of the dominating, curved wall that intersects the building is to create a symbolic bridge.

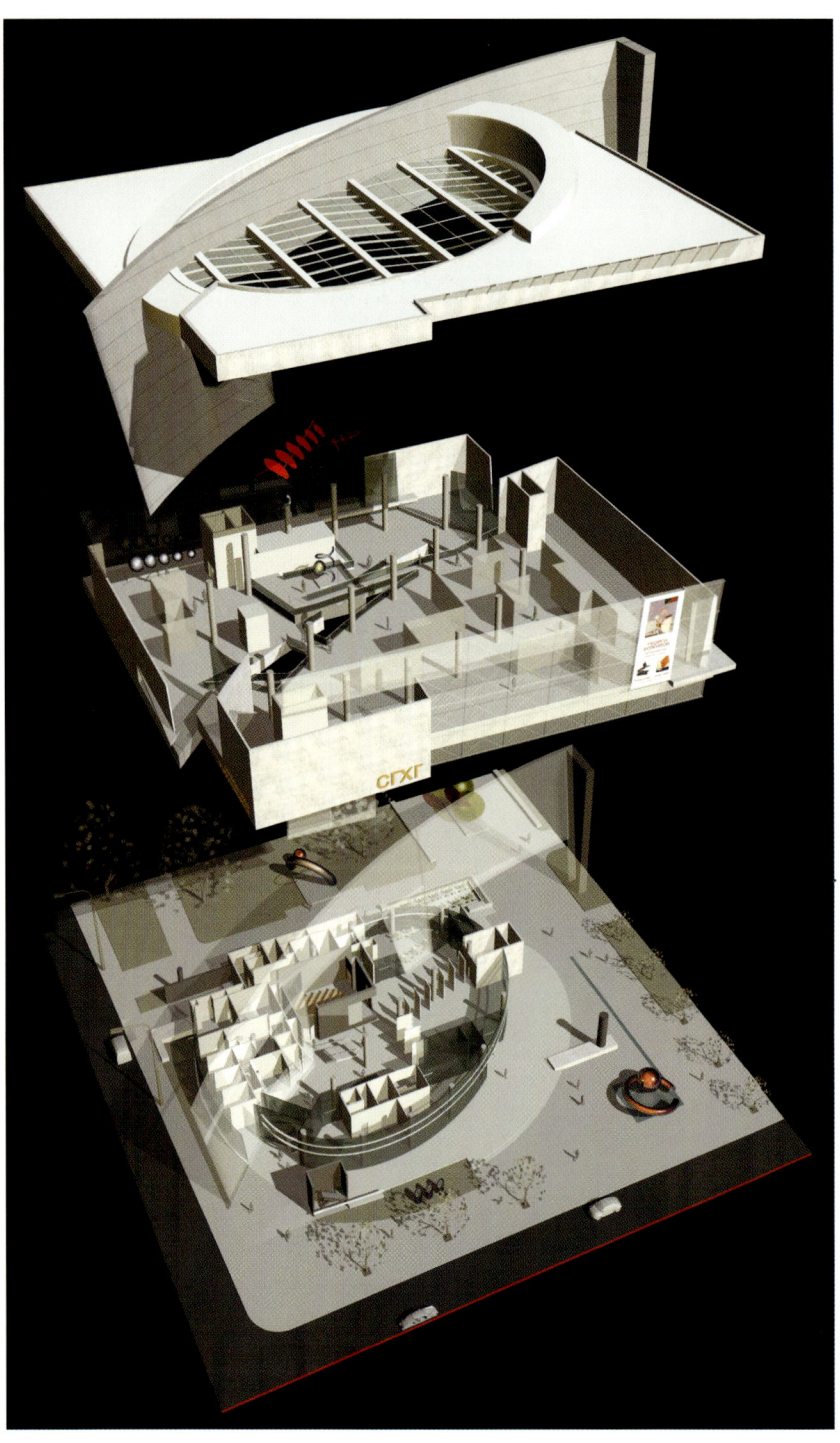

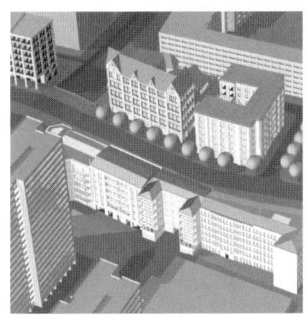 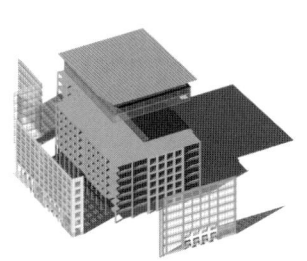 

3.2.4 Visualizing Virtual Mass Models

It is possible to model building concepts with ArchiCAD much the same way it is possible to create a "quick sketch" with a pencil and paper. The use of slabs, panels, slanted and free shapes in a composition often creates the first impression of the sequence of spaces in a building or a group of buildings. It is also possible to create visualizations of shadow areas and perform rough surface and volume calculations. This leads to both architectural development and an approach to cost calculations. The rendering methods are often simple: the so-called "Phong Shadows" without reflections or abstract façade textures and patterns can be used to represent the tectonics of a building.

■ Kimon Onuma, Tokio and Pasadena (JP/USA)

The *Tokyo City Model* was created to explain varying approaches to city design. It served as the basis for a range of GDL objects and for the conception of large-scale urban planning measures. The *Atlanta City Model* and the Tokyo model are used in many different ways.

The Atlanta City Model was also used in a number of advertisements during the 1996 Olympic Games.

■ Gasparin & Meier, Villach (A)

A shopping, residential, recreational and cultural complex was designed for the 10 hectare *Brachmühle area* in Vienna according to the needs defined in a certification process based on comprehensive traffic research and center studies. A number of theme, relaxation, commercial and office spaces and the corresponding green areas were also required. The project proves that is possible to develop and realize urban planning sequences with scale models. The continuation of construction on the "Wagramer Strasse" axis will be undertaken while keeping an eye on the extensive longitudinal development.

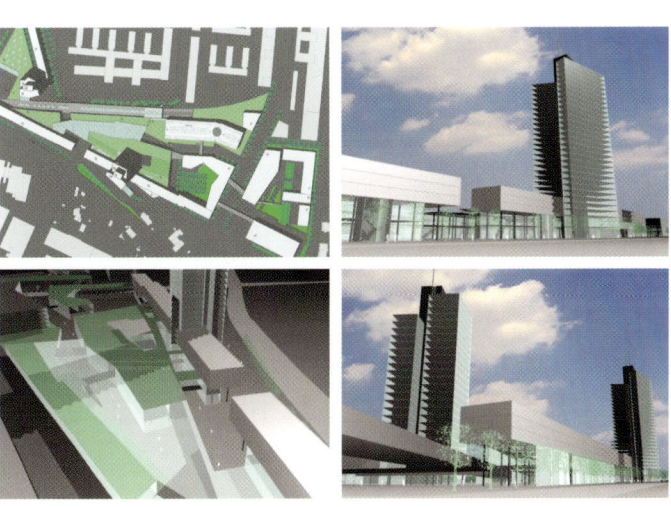

This project is an example of the use of a digital work model that conveys a rudimentary sense of detail. Floors are suggested, for example. Transparency is also used. This makes it possible to convey more information and show approaches to architectural implementation.

■ STUDIOS Architecture, San Francisco (USA)

A master plan had to be developed for a "multi-block solution" south of the San Francisco Foundry Square market area. The project consists of four-building complex. The buildings have varying heights and configurations as well as ample space – for the needs of technology and multimedia companies.

ArchiCAD was used at an early stage in this project, in the schematic design phase, when the future development was studied with a simple building mass model. Fine-tuning took place in the following work steps, including a study of the shadow cycles.

3.3 Examples of Non-Commercial ArchiCAD Applications

The adjective "non-commercial" may irritate a little at first glance. We do not mean to say that the main aspect of the examples shown here is their non-binding character. On the contrary: since we have now entered primarily into the domain of university instruction and research, the economic tight spots – as they exist in every-day building work – are situated differently. The main goal here is not the presentation of a building project situation oriented around profit. For this reason, the general constellation of a building including life cycle (design, erection, operation, demolition, ...) hardly still exists, particularly since we deal with limited subsections such as the design phase. In the case of a reconstruction, the process direction is even reversed. This means that the use of the ArchiCAD database plays a different role in this context. The main interest is much more focused on the possibility of three-dimensional modeling. In addition, the advantage of 3D models is clear: it is their location-independent availability – at several places at the same time – with the option of error-free selection of individual components or component groups.

The EDU version was created for students at educational institutions; it is available to them for only a fraction of the cost of a full version but uses a data format that is incompatible with the commercial ArchiCAD license. However, the working options are not reduced and the tools have not been limited. Limitations do exist in the area of data exchange for understandable reasons (e.g. DXF export). If we now consider the situation of higher education in more detail, it must be emphasized that CAAD knowledge is viewed today as an opportunity par excellence for increasing one's personal market value. Classical, passive instruction has only limited value, however, as significant differences in individual knowledge are more the rule than the exception. Simply demonstrating the innumerable functions and commands achieves at best a basic understanding, but the motto "training on the job" still applies. In fact, the average ArchiCAD novice will quickly experience some success, but ongoing education and further training remains indispensable. This experience of success is also based on the requirements of the user interface. Dealing with or freeing oneself from the user interface is difficult. Only then could the title "experimental" be given. In fact, the coming generation of ArchiCAD users has a different relationship to computer equipment than their predecessors. If one has grown up with widely available electronic media and can use it without difficulty, this cannot be without consequences for the practical use of ArchiCAD.

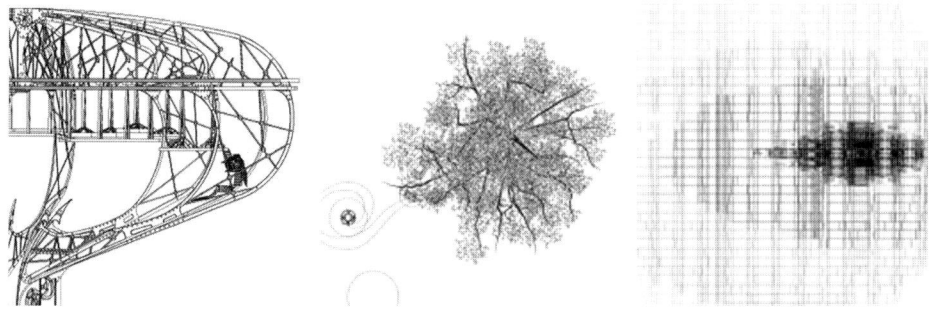

3.3.1 Competitive Results of a Virtual Architecture

The "Graphisoft prize" (http://www.gsprize.com) was created to promote the development of a virtual architecture. The name refers to the software company that created ArchiCAD and continues to develop it. Participation in this global competition is free, but is primarily directed toward participants from the disciplines of (landscape) architecture, city planning and related disciplines. An invitation for submissions was issued every year, which has shown a particular interest in literary topics. The goal of the competition is to demonstrate and stimulate the potential of computer-aided generation of architecture. The evaluation is performed by a jury that consists of recognized experts. A selection of winning projects from previous submissions for the Graphisoft prize and a regional competition in Finland (http://www.mad.fi) is presented below.

■ Competition hosted by M.A.D., Helsinki (FIN)

The rules for this competitive event were simple: ArchiCAD student versions are provided at no charge, however, all graphical material created with it must be submitted. In conclusion, a jury decides on the best submissions, which are given awards and rewarded with material prizes. The results include a wide range of interesting, playful and simple, sometimes even scurrilous, entries.

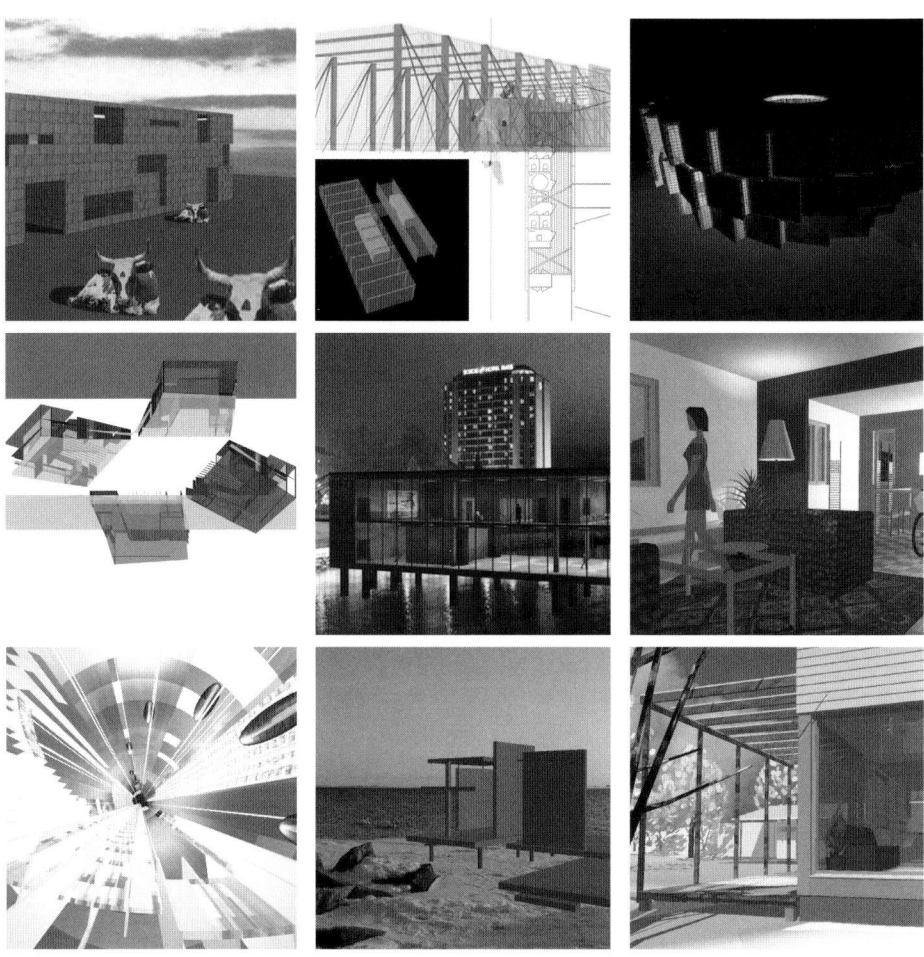

■ Graphisoft Prize 1997 – 1st Place | Ginder Akos Ignac University of Belgrade (YUG)

The project *Asgard* leads the observer into Nordic mythology. In a world beyond this one rules a virtual Valhalla.

The modeling attempts to give form to the history and the spaces its contains. The light towers, the exaggerated stairs and spiral ramps without handrails indicate the presence of transcendental beings.

■ Graphisoft Prize 1997 – 3rd Place | Bogdan Ristivijevic and Zoran L. Pantelic / University of Belgrade (YUG)

Based on Italo Calvino's *Invisible Cities*, this project leads into the "City of Memory". A real city experienced by the creators of the project is subjected to a transformation through a conscious process of remembrance. The locations, streets and squares thus developed convey the examined essence of this city in their memory.

■ Graphisoft Prize 1998 – 1st Place (Student Category) A. Maynard, S. Mess et al. / University of Tasmania (AUS)

Based on Bulgakov's novel *The Master and Margarita*, the design leads into the "Ballroom of the Devil". The supporting structure transforms into a mysterious shape of steel. The treatment of the subject is handled extremely playfully and with high perfection in the technical application of ArchiCAD.

■ Graphisoft Prize 1998 – 2nd Place (Professional Category) Branislav Drgon, Trnava (SK)

Also based on Bulgakov's novel, this project, *Hell Memory*, attempts to visualize the term "hell" and pursues the basic concept of conceptualizing the unimaginable location as an apparatus operating in infinite space. The individual vessels are interpreted as a fully enclosed microcosm.

 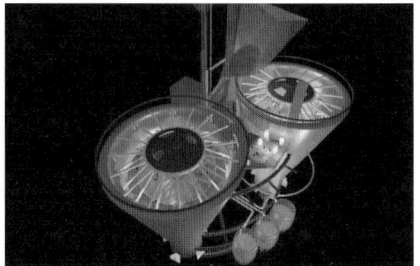

- **Graphisoft Prize 1999 – 1st Place (Professional Category)**
  P. Bach & P. Hadadi / Technical University Budapest, (HU)

The project *The Cheap Hotel* takes its theme from the novel *Neuromancer* by William Gibson. It provides entry into a spatially perceivable matrix. A mysterious city is crossed with no apparent gravity. The structure mutates into an insane garden with no exit; the thoughtful use of light and mist dramatically amplify its suggestive effect.

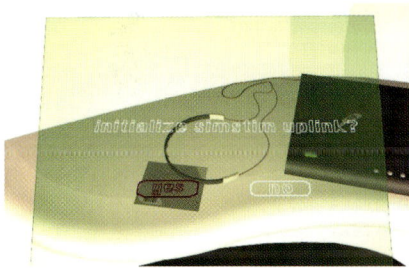 

- **Graphisoft Prize 1999 – 2nd Place (Professional Category)**
  I. Pölös and M. Illyes / NANA Architects, Budapest (HU)

Based on Thomas Mann's *Joseph and his Brothers*, the project attempts to visualize stations of the novel. The main emphasis is placed here on *Pharaoh's Palace*. Because only rudimentary information about the rooms was available, numerous details had to be creatively added with the ultimate goal of creating an image to convey a feeling.

- **Graphisoft Prize 2000 – 1st Place | Sam Rajamanickam, Design Collective Inc. (USA)**

The design of a virtual world based on Francis Ford Coppola's *Cotton Club* provides a view into the world of inner imprisonment. Only by moving the variously formulated volumes can the space required for existence be revealed. The configuration of these alternating constellations is based on the three main characters of this cinematic tale.

- **Graphisoft Prize 2001 – 1st Place | Hartmut Liebster and Bergit Hillner / HTWK Leipzig, Leipzig (GER)**

The translation of Borge's *Library of Babel* is dedicated to the topic of unlimited possibilities that arise from the combination of various information sources. From this diversity comes the question of the limit between knowledge and utopia. Grids of various densities create a spatial fabric that makes the imaginary library visible.

■ Graphisoft Prize 2001 – 2nd Place I Andrei Radu / Technical University, Asachi (ROM)

The architectonic figuration of this project also refers to the *Library of Babel*. The structure transformed into graphical worlds attempts to give shape to the verbally expressed infinity. Repetition, transparence in dialog with opacity as well as motion and motionlessness generate the basic ingredients of this limitless, imaginary library.

■ Graphisoft Prize 2001 – 3rd Place I S. Oeltjen, W.H. Chun and L.S. Wei / University Tasmania (AUS)

The project is an attempt to reconstruct a long-lost world based on the novel *The Geisha* by Arthur Golden. The visualizations lead the observer into the beautiful designed Japan of the twenties.

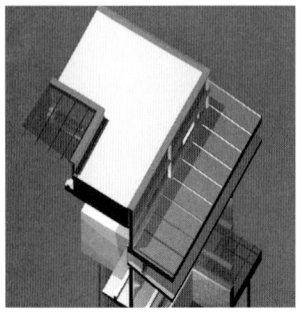 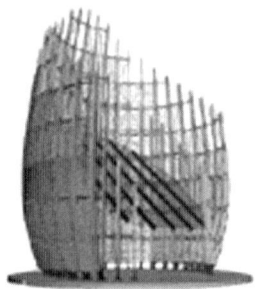 

3.3.2 Application Examples from Architecture Education

Teachers of architecture with large numbers of students are confronted with the question of how CAAD knowledge can be most effectively taught without relying exclusively on dry swimming exercises. Here it appears initially useful to convey the horizon of CAAD with compressed information and take the first steps in modeling and visualization of spatial forms. This is supplemented by considerations of abstraction during input as well as the age-old "form-content dilemma": is CAAD used for reasons of illustration or is it about exploration (discovery)? Students who have never dealt with a computer before have practically "died out". In the mean time, powerful hardware and software has become widely available and is it is becoming more common for students to purchase or finance it themselves. Then the results of exercises and graduation projects are presented.

- Exercise Work: Elective Subject CAD 111B I Students of the University of Adelaide – Advisor: Susan Pietsch (AUS)

The purpose of this educational course for students in the third year of training is to transform a known object from the physical reality within a virtual context. During a two-week course, the examples shown are created. The goal of the exercise was to learn competent use of the software as a communications medium and to develop an understanding of how a CAD program changes the drafting process.

The specific structure of the floor administration permits a differentiation of the building elements, which is used in an innovative way in combination with the floors created.

■ Exercise Work: Whangarei Airport Terminal | Steve Johnson, Unitec Institute of Technology (NZ)

Within the scope of a design studio, the task was to design an airport building. A lightweight roof structure rises over the pre-fabricated transport containers and dispatching rooms.

During the studio, a series of GDL objects were programmed, whereby specific requirements were implemented via the GDL scripting. These referred to a simple transport container, container support structures, curved walls and sliding doors.

■ Exercise Work: Judenplatz in Vienna | Students at the TU-Vienna – Advisors: Peter Bleier, Bob Martens, Jay Potts (A)

Within the scope of an exercise, a group of students considered possible perspectives for the historically significant square. For this reason, detailed modeling was performed first, whereby individual properties were each handled by a single person. Then the individually created buildings were combined so that a complete model could be presented.

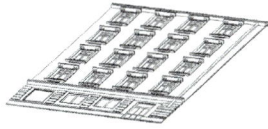

To be able to perform the intended modeling task effectively, the façades were subjected to a 90° rotation, as if they were "laying on the ground" and the external form could be created with the ceiling tool. The planned openings could then be cut into the plane thus created. Additional ornamentation was also created with the ceiling tool and "laid" onto the base plane. Because openings can be multiplied, complete window axes were duplicated in this way.

■ Graduation Project: Revitalization and Expansion of the University Hospital Meilahti in Helsinki | Tom Cederqvist, Helsinki University of Technology (FIN)

The functional and technical service spectrum of an existing hospital complex was to be improved. To this end, a fundamental revitalization and expansion was required, which comprised eleven service levels, a new main entrance, a relaxation area, a winter garden, a technical floor and a roof terrace. The expansion is connected to the existing building via bridges. In this way, a permeable second shell was developed in front of the existing building.

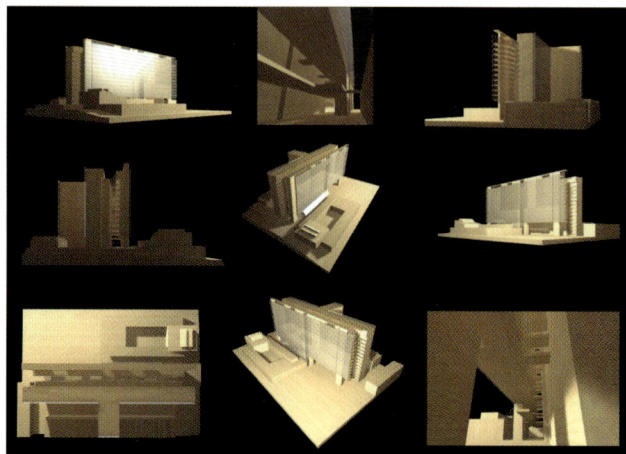

A particular point about the visualized model is that it was treated as a physical model. It was therefore provided with a "wood mapping" for the modeled examination. Even the cutout of the floor slab matches that of a physical model. The selected black background also neutralizes the depiction.

- Graduation Project: Open-air / Indoor swimming pool, Salzburg | Wolfgang Kurz, TU-Vienna (A)

The task was the development of a vision for this specific site as well as the implementation of the use of an existing environment for recreation and wellness.

Because an open-air pool previously stood at the same location, a usage in the direction of an open-air/hall swimming pool was included in the general considerations. The design of a hall pool opens into an open-air pool combines the idea of a modern adventure pool with an increased recreational value in the surrounding grounds.

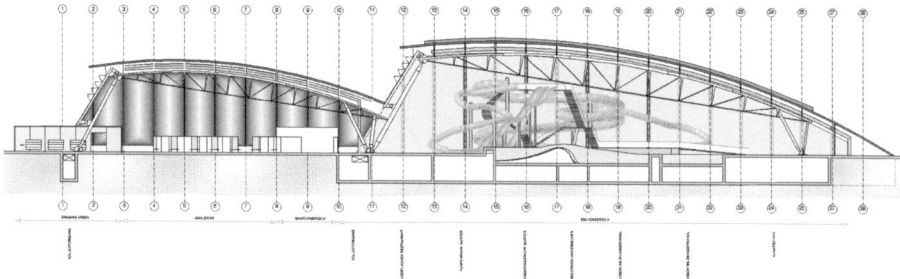

The emphasis in the use of ArchiCAD was initially on the visualization of the planned building volume and the associated recreational offerings. The required special geometrical shapes were created as GDL objects, whereby the GDL toolbox was also used as a modeling tool (e.g. for the creation of the water slide in the hall area). The three-dimensional building model served as the basis for all plan documents; however, the drafting of the above ground details was done within the scope of 2D detailed drawings.

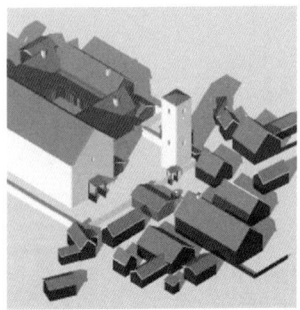  

3.3.3 Reconstruction of the Past as a Research Topic

The visualization of (architectural) objects that no longer exist and the worlds surrounding them is similar to a "virtual comeback". Irreversible destruction that has removed identity-defining structures from city areas over time provides the impetus for an attempt to re-imagine spaces. In addressing this reconstruction, the problem arises of the reliability of the available documentation to be used as a basis. Photographs – if available – supply only limited information about the object under observation. It is only all too clear that the missing part must be supplemented or substituted by additional sources. Within the process of assembling and superimposing multiple data sets, the method of handling these fragments enters the focus of consideration. The elementary information regarding the perception of three-dimensional objects also includes the effect created by color and material. In this regard, black and white photographs are not very informative. Without a doubt, the three-dimensionally entered object offers substantially more opportunities within the subsequent working process than a "cardboard model with taped on façade photographs". Only the completely depicted model structure offers a lasting visualization of the sculpted appearance of an architecture. In addition, a virtual model can be turned into a partial model without this "disassembly" requiring a destructive process. The virtual model also permits the generation of various reconstruction variants with regard to color and material. Moreover, architecture models of physical nature are bound to a specific location.

■ Tron Church, Edinburgh (UK) | Tina Mikrou, University of Edinburgh (UK)

The *Tron Church* in the center of Edinburgh – a three-hundred year old structure – experienced numerous changes over the course of the decades. The building was shortened in some places and parts were entirely removed. Today, the structural fragment is used as a visitor center and exhibition room. The goal of the virtual reconstruction is to achieve an increased understanding of the building's original structure and to develop an extremely precise visualization of the original structure, including the previous roof structure. In addition, the established basis can be expanded into an interactive presentation. In this way, a virtual environment can be created that makes it possible to test out future interventions within the framework of an exhibition program. This refers to operations on both the interior and exterior and includes further options for simulation of various lighting conditions.

The reconstruction of historical structures with a CAD software product often "suffers" from the fact that deformations – i.e. deviations from the orthogonal system – are no rarity.

Ceilings and walls in particular are often not planar surfaces and/or are not situated plumb to each other. Such characteristics cannot be recreated with the ArchiCAD wall tool.

The same might seem to apply to the ceiling tool. It seems remarkable, but this task can be completed with the roof tool because it allows the selection of arbitrary angles. This method was used for the church reconstruction presented here. ArchiForma was also used intensively for modeling of support structure elements and ornaments.

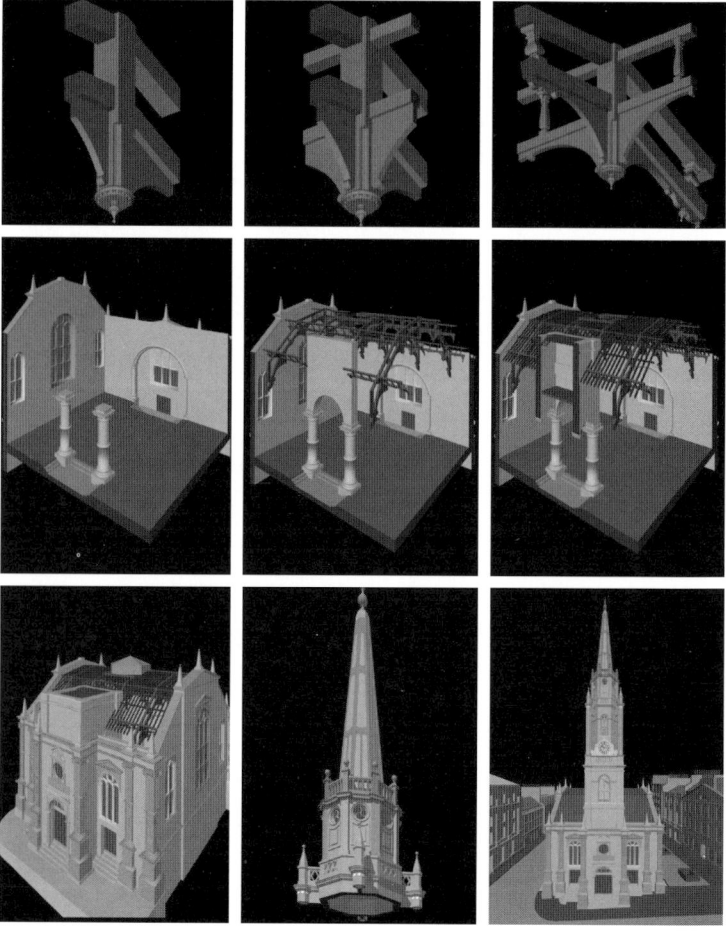

- **Reconstruction of Monasteries Cluny I - II and Carnuntum I**
  ArgeProjekte / TU-Vienna / Multimedia Plan, Vienna (A)

The monasteries Cluny I and II each serve as the basis for a virtual reconstruction. The former Benedictine abbey Cluny in Burgundy, which was torn down shortly after its dissolution in the years 1798 to 1814, exerted a lasting influence on the monastic building arts of the Christian West. Hardly anything is known of the first building phase (Cluny I). Information about the appearance of the larger complex erected a few decades later is also available only via archeological excavations. Despite the sparse source material, however, an attempt was made to virtually reconstruct the history of the structure across its various stages.

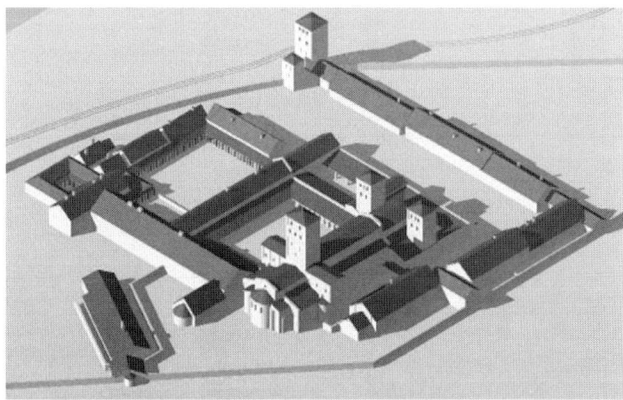

The Carnuntum project pursues the goal of providing a glimpse into the lost world of the Romans. In this case, the city of Carnuntum is being reconstructed. Virtual experiencing of the settlement should permit a broad impression in addition to the archeological finds. During the course of a virtual tour, one gains an impression of the daily life as well as the structure of the city.

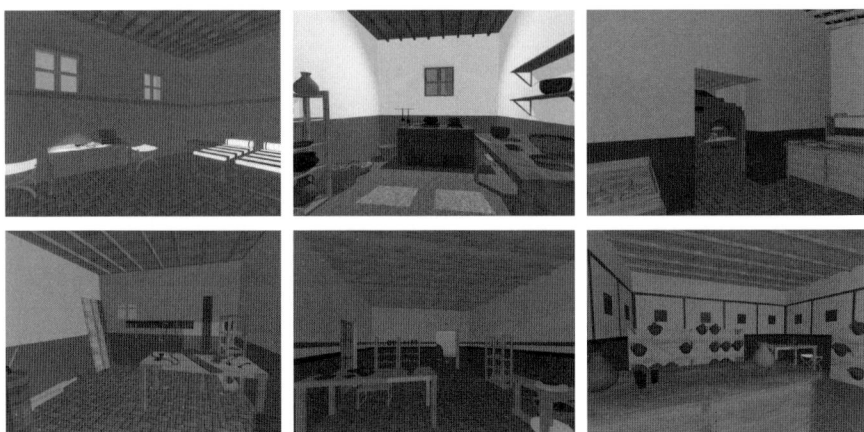

Additional tools such as the Profiler and Roofmaker were used for the scene modeling. Because no complete GDL object libraries are available for the "configuration" of Roman houses, approx. 200 required GDL objects were created. Further programming work was not performed here as only a single use was planned. The scenes were visualized with ArchiCAD for practical reasons because initially only a "technical" reconstruction consisting of projection drawings and diagrams was to be created. Only during the course of this work was the scope of the project expanded.

■ Virtual Reconstruction of Viennese Synagogues I Students of the TU-Vienna – Advisor: Bob Martens (A)

The Viennese synagogues that are the focus of this reconstruction project were almost all destroyed in the year 1938. Because any remains were eliminated shortly thereafter, no immediately accessible information regarding the structural reality is still available. For this reason, the virtual recreation is based on "canned information". During the memorial year 1998 – 60 years later – an initial synagogue reconstruction was begun. The medium-range goal, however, was defined as the reconstruction of at least ten additional synagogues.

The basis for the reconstruction work is researched archive material, which largely determines the validity of the reconstruction. The archived filing and substitution plans (scale 1:100) represent a reliable source. However, these planning documents typically do not contain any information about possible fixtures and furnishings. On the other hand, a large collection of building cross-sections improve the accuracy of the reconstruction. This is also the case when interior photographs are discovered. However, these are almost exclusively black and white images which means the colors can only be guessed at.

First, planning documents of the building to be reconstructed must be organized according to structural criteria. For instance, wall structures are identified according to their various functions (interior or exterior wall) and expanded with supports, floor slabs, intermediate ceilings, stairs, roof structure, roofing, roof truss, façade elements, ornaments, fixtures, etc., to provide the varying users with a view of the data organization. It is important here to document related (geometric) elements on a corresponding level in the form of an independent three-dimensional depiction. The labeling of the layers and the graphical depiction of the respective contents should sufficiently label the building components. The type of depiction of the level content should be shaded where possible.

The project is divided into phases that will stretch over several years. Progressing developments in the area of computer-aided modeling technology and the implementation of knowledge gained from cooperation with art historians result in additional modeling processes. The – sometimes interrupted – modeling is performed by various modelers (individual and group work) and under changing conditions (seminar, degree project, etc.). In such a situation, the data organization quickly becomes complex. Here, the structural principle of separation by building part within a simple story structure does not suffice to provide a view of the overall structure. The aspect of usability at a later point in time represents an important requirement for the subsequent modeling processes. The fluctuations in the area of the project workers therefore demand a legible structure in this regard.

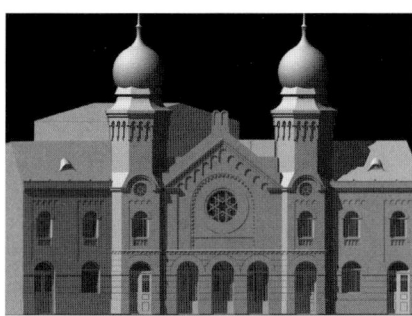

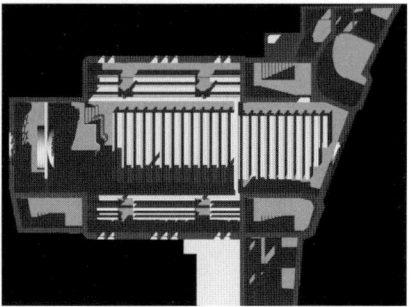

4. Developmental Perspectives: Integrated Building Simulation

In the previous chapters, concepts in working with ArchiCAD were discussed and corresponding practical applications shown. In this way, it was possible to present a "state of the art". The final condition of the future expansion of a CAD software product is and remains difficult to predict. The so-called "update cycle" is based on 15- to 18-month steps. This not only provides feedback to the users ("we are still alive, we are working for you"), it also implements strategic ideas regarding the careful expansion of the range of services. If new versions appear at intervals that are too short and contain major changes, this would overtax many users. Earlier, new ArchiCAD versions were given "arbitrary version numbers", such as 3.42 or 4.55. One could have interpreted this as meaning that 42 or 55 of 100 possible percentage points were implemented. Today, advancing by whole numbers has been adopted. This means that the ArchiCAD version 8 will be followed by 9 and then, presumably, by 10. Version 8 is primarily directed toward the Autocad user. This means that the needs of this CAD user group will be considered more extensively and an "orientation" for those who switch from Autocad to ArchiCAD is being strongly promoted.

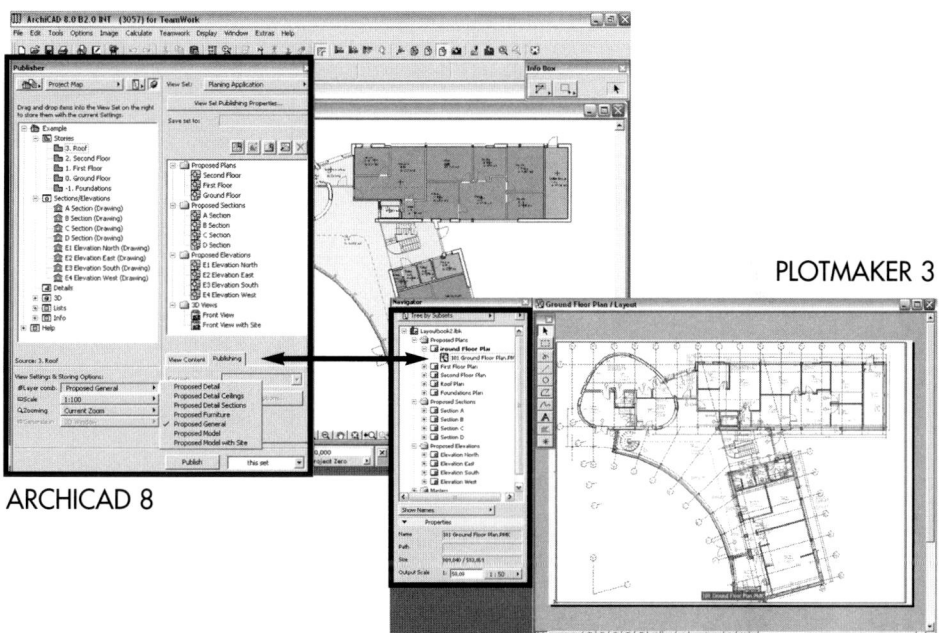

ARCHICAD 8

PLOTMAKER 3

Certainly a long wish list can be found on the desk of the ArchiCAD senior developers, maintained in close contact with the users and their feedback. For instance, Internet compatibility (e.g. publishing of ArchiCAD data in the Web browser) and batch processing (= automated application of one or more menu commands – e.g. "save as DXF" for all or multiple selected levels, sections and views) were implemented in ArchiCAD 7. The long-awaited integration of ArchiCAD and PlotMaker in the form of a plan book will also soon be available. The multi-window technology is undergoing continuous further development and offers in ArchiCAD 8 the option of a separate "detail book" within the project file. ArchiCAD 8 also achieves a milestone in product development in regard to the use of so-called "Boolean operations". The use of object clipping has long been part of the feature set, at least in relation to standard tools. The new feature is that now every element can be clipped with any other element.

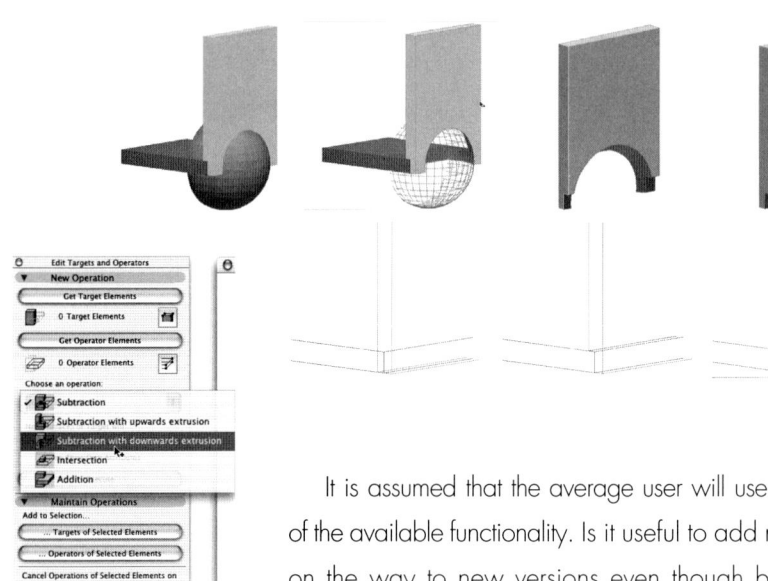

It is assumed that the average user will use "only" a part of the available functionality. Is it useful to add new functions on the way to new versions even though basic working opportunities are not already completely exhausted regardless of whether a new ArchiCAD version is appearing? Outside of the ArchiCAD program structure deficits regarding the naming conventions for (project) files used are on the agenda. If one listens to helpdesk employees, the topic of "printing/plotting" (incl. management of pens and colors) is truly a long-standing issue. With regard to the concrete use of ArchiCAD, occasional deficits in level management and the use of the XREF technology can be seen. "GDL basics" also sometimes form a blind spot. This certainly explains why a high interest in "user-friendly" GDL tool applications exists. This notwithstanding, many users are interested in GDL programming work.

■ Vito Bertin (Chinese University of Hong Kong) investigates possible *interactions of GDL objects* such as melting together of touching wall elements or seamless merging of floor panels and walls. On the other hand, up to Version 7 there are no graphical tools for modifying parameters of GDL objects except for stretching in the x- and y-directions. GDL objects must first be selected, then additional parameters defined in dialog windows and a series of numerical values input or selected. Then the dialog must be closed. Bertin shows with simple examples that the concept of interaction is only used in the initial approach and unexploited potential remains. For instance, the graphical parameters A and B are "misused" to simulate other parameters. A similar situation exists with the so-called "context-sensitivity". For instance, elements and components of a system can configure themselves depending on their location within the system.

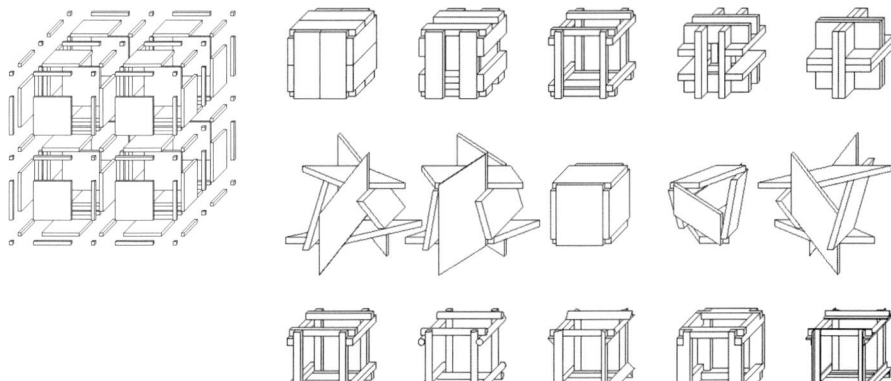

■ Parts of the drawing process can be largely automated through the use of "intelligent" objects. This involves primarily the reduction of repetitive tasks. Bruce Hill has taken up this subject and developed a *drawing document* that imports all project information from an external text file, inserts a north point and takes scales into consideration, whereby the page size changes with the displayed scale.

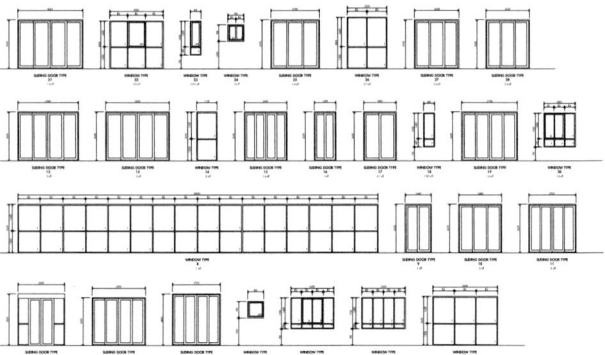

In the evaluation of windows and doors, a GDL object developed by Hill recognizes which window and door types were used in the project, sorts and places them automatically in a separate (dimensioned) plan document. Objects such as wardrobes, cabinets, etc. receive text labels that always retain their horizontal position regardless of any object rotation/mirroring. Different levels of detail are displayed in a scale-dependent fashion. However, the objects possess complete detailed information at all times. This means that this information is actually depicted in the event of a projection view. This means it is not necessary to input the drawing again.

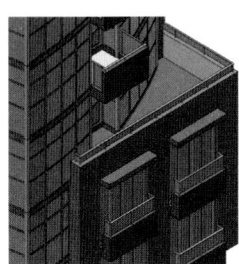

On which hardware platform is ArchiCAD used most often today? Although significant regional differences exist, Macintosh and Windows remain in balance. It should be added that competing CAD software projects have discontinued their Macintosh versions and a large portion of these users migrated to the ArchiCAD environment. Even if it was still believed in the Budapest Graphisoft headquarters at the start of the nineties that the number of Windows versions would grow faster than the Macintosh versions, this is not happening due to the competition situation for CAD software products on Windows PC platforms. Data exchange is still a central topic. While the sharing of paper-based plan drawings results in no immediate loss of data, experience has shown that this is not automatically the case during the integration of imported CAD data into separate project structures. Apparently perfect graphical representations lose all but a minimum of the stored information upon conversion from CAD software package A to B. The motto should be: walls remain walls, ceilings remain ceilings, windows remain windows, etc. For this reason, the IAI (International Alliance for Interoperability) was founded in the year 1995. The purpose of this independent and globally active institution is to define an "intelligent" digital exchange format that is supported by planners, software developers and the construction industry. In addition, the implementation of internationally valid and independent standards means security for all participants from dependance on the arbitrary decisions of individual software developers. After a good nine years of development and implementation, the currently available IFC 2.X2 can be viewed as the standard for data exchange. The combination of Internet-based technologies –

such as XML – is planned for subsequent IFC versions. Northern Europe stands out as exceptionally advanced in the use of IFC as a data exchange format between architects and public customers in recent years. Within the scope of a project financed by the EU, for instance, all "public" construction projects in Finland were shared via IFC.

Facility Management (FM) is a field of activity in which digital utilization of ArchiCAD data appears interesting. A connection to the pertinent FM applications has been planned. This means that reentering of the data is avoided and a significantly higher portion can be transferred directly from the ArchiCAD database. The possibility for direct use of the data from the ArchiCAD project exists in the management of the surfaces, incl. assignment to individual departments or persons. A direct integration of "Virtual Buildings" with database queries permits the modification of assignments at any time via graphical input as well as via database access.

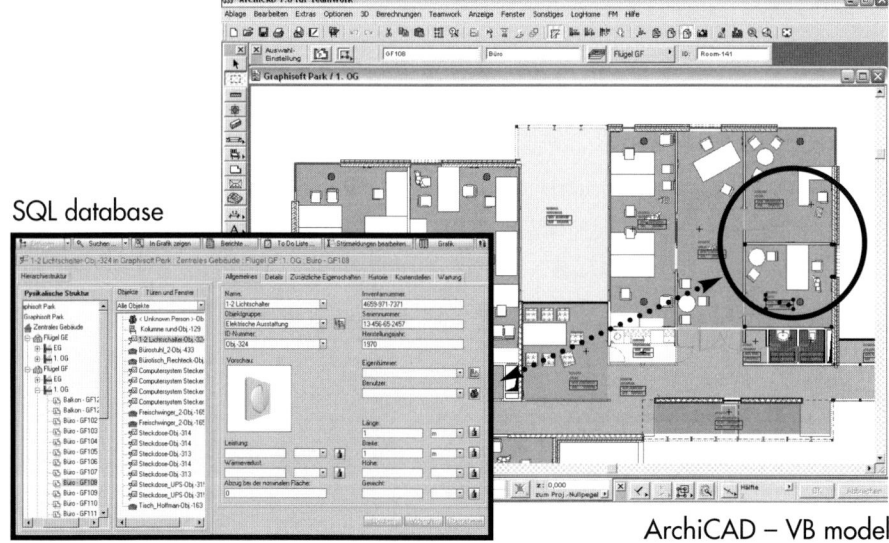

Standardized database interfaces to additional properties managed in a company allow comprehensive evaluation of the costs. Furthermore, "classical" fields of implementation within the scope of facility management include moving and maintenance, tenant-, key- and inventory management, etc. The integration of the "new" media now permits location-independent report queries via the Internet. In this way, decision-makers can access the desired data, cost breakdowns and reports at any time. The attractiveness of a graphical representation of this topic in book form remains limited, however appetizing application examples should definitely be pursued.

The introduction of a CAD software product with the properties of an "egg-laying wool milk pig" is still a current topic, especially since architecture offices would like to reduce the number of applications as much as possible for understandable reasons. As such, the performance of building physics calculations within the scope of building inputs is of significant importance. ArchiPHYSIK accepts all relevant component information (e.g. material, component area, orientation, etc.) from ArchiCAD via an integrated interface and calculates the U-value, vapor diffusion, sound protection, heating load, heating requirements, heating costs and energy balances for solar energy systems. In order to optimize the building performance with regard to thermal energy issues a library of over 3,000 featured building products is supplied. The goal is to check building components as regards their thermal, sound and moisture suitability.

In the field of building services (HVAC, etc.), there is, for example, in the UK a direct link with the software package *CADlink/Cymap*. This covers the areas of electrical, heating, ventilation and climate control installation. Integrated building services planning and calculations are possible here for which the graphical results – for instance in the area of cable paths – can be imported directly into ArchiCAD. In the future, applications such as ArchiPHYSIK and CADLink should be more useful as an integral addition to ArchiCAD and it should be possible to query available information directly from the ArchiCAD database. This means that the architecture creator can estimate the consequences of his actions already during an early stage of the design process – and not only in an aesthetic regard – within a certain margin of error.

In conclusion, it is hoped that ArchiCAD will become the architect's best friend and advisor in the not too distant future, in other words, a CAD software product that not only masters basic design and planning tasks but integrates specialized knowledge and know-how to provide the architecture creator with the freedom that complex architectural tasks doubtlessly demand.

Training Manuals and Reference Materials

- Atkinson, Dwight: Illustration in ArchiCAD. Budapest: Graphisoft R&D Rt., 2002.
- Graphisoft (ed.): IFC Reference Guide. Budapest: Graphisoft R&D Rt., 2001.
- Graphisoft (eg.): ArchiCAD Step by Step. Budapest: Graphisoft R&D Rt., 2001.
- Kulisev, Lubomir: ArchiCAD Training Guide. Budapest: Graphisoft R&D Rt., 2001.
- Langdon, G.M., Byrnes, D. und Grabowski, R.: ArchiCAD for Autocad Users. Budapest: Graphisoft R&D Rt., 2002.
- Nicholson-Cole, David: Object making with ArchiCAD: GDL for Beginners. Budapest: Graphisoft R&D Rt., 2000.
- Nicholson-Cole, David: The GDL Cookbook 3. Nottingham: Marmalade Graphics, 2001.
- Rattenbury, Bill: ArchiCAD Project Framework. Auckland: CADImage ltd., 1998.
- Rattenbury, Bill: Projektgrundlagen für ArchiCAD. Budapest: Graphisoft R&D Rt., 1998-2000.

Internetlinks

ArchiCAD Sales and Hotlines
The international Website: http://www.graphisoft.com leads to all distributors.

GDL-Object Technology
http://www.gdlalliance.com
http://www.gdlcentral.com
http://www.realobjekte.at
http://www.gdltechnology.com

http://www.objectsonline.com
http://www.lasercad.se
http://www.archiforum.de
http://www.archimedia.de
http://www.objectclub.com
http://www.cad-lib.net

Plug-ins (API-technology)
http://www.gdltoolbox.com/
http://www.cigraph.com
http://www.archimage.hu

Data Exchange /Interfaces
http://www.iai-international.org

Communication and training
http://www.archicad.at (ArchiCAD User Association Austria)
http://www.ecaade.org (education in CAAD in Europe)
http://www.acadia.org (Association for Computer Aided Design in Architecture)
http://www.caadria.org (Computer Aided Architectural Design Research In Asia)
http://www.sigradi.org (Iberoamerican Society of Digital Graphics)

Userlinks
This is a list of the users who contributed their project materials to this publiation:

http://www.agu.at (Architektengruppe U-Bahn)
http://www.a-konsultit.fi (Architekturbüro A-Konsultit)
http://www.archconsult.com (Architekturbüro Domenig)
http://www.arching.at/wimmer-armellini (Architekturbüro Wimmer-Armellini)
http://www.architecturcad.de (digital electronic kühn GmbH)
http://www.archrbag.ch (Architekten AG)
http://www.axis.at (Axis Ingenieurleistungen ZT GmbH)
http://www.behf.at (BEHF Architekten)
http://www.cad-am-bau.de (Dietzel & Partner Architekten)
http://www.cadimage.co.nz (CadImage Solutions Ltd.)
http://www.donaldmacdonaldarchitects.com (Donald MacDonald Architects)
http://www.dreso.com (Drees and Sommer)
http://www.gasparinmeier.at (Architekten Gasparin & Meier)
http://www.hba.cl (Hombo & Bañados Arquitectos)
http://www.heistinger.at (Architekturbüro Helmut Heistinger)
http://www.hoffelner.at (Architekturbüro Walter Hoffelner)
http://www.katzberger.at (Atelier Katzberger)
http://www.lengyeltoulouse.com (LengyelToulouse)
http://www.liljewall-arkitekter.se (Liljewall Arkitekter AB)
http://www.luminetik.com (LuminetIK)
http://www.lund-valentin.se (Lund & Valentin Arkitekter)
http://www.maaars.at (maaars architecture)
http://www.mikula.at (Architekturbüro Mikula)
http://www.nussmueller.com (Architekturbüro Nußmüller)
http://www.onuma.com (Onuma & Associates)
http://www.owp.com (Orcutt/Winslow Partnership)
http://www.paastudio.com (Paastudio – Ivo Venkov)
http://www.porr.at (Porr Immoprojekt GmbH)
http://www.rharchitects.com (Rockefeller/Hricak Architects)
http://www.rplusw.com (Richard+Wittschiebe Architects)
http://www.studiosarch.com (STUDIOS Architecture)
http://www.subendougherty.com (Suben/Dougherty)
http://www.urbanstrategies.com (Urban Strategies Inc.)
http://www.webscape.com (Onuma & Associates)
http://www.widmann.at (Architekturbüro Eduard Widmann)

Trademarks

ArchiCAD is a Graphisoft R&D registered trademark.
Autocad is a trademark of Autodesk Inc.
GDL Object Explorer, GDL Object Adapter and GDL Web Plugin are trademarks of GDL Technology R&D
Quicktime /QuicktimeVR – Apple Inc.
Windows is a Microsoft Corp. trademark

All other trademarks are the property of their respective owners

Photo Credits

12:	Stefan Klein, Technische Universität Wien (A)
16:	Graphisoft R&D, Budapest (HU)
19:	Wilhelm Hochenbichler, Technische Universität Wien (A)
24:	Graphisoft R&D, Budapest (HU)
25:	Graphisoft R&D, Budapest (HU)
31:	Graphisoft R&D, Budapest (HU)
34:	Martin Standfest, Technische Universität Wien (A)
35:	Nina, 8 Jahre, Wien (A)
45:	Andreas Muttenthaler, Wien (A)
60:	Gregor Kassl, Thomas Omansiek, Manfred Schnabl, Christian Trügler / Technische Universität Graz (A)
92:	Ganahl/Ifstits/Larch Architekten, Wien (A)
111:	Lengyel/Toulouse Architekten, Köln (A)
112:	Lengyel/Toulouse Architekten, Köln (A)
131-133:	Architektengruppe U-Bahn (Holzbauer/Marschalek/Ladstätter/Gantar; Peichl & Partner; COOP Himmelb(l)au, Wien (A)
133:	Urban Strategies Inc., Toronto (CAN), Michael Trocmé
134:	Urban Strategies Inc., Toronto (CAN), Michael Trocmé
135:	Urban Strategies Inc., Toronto (CAN), Michael Trocmé
136-138:	Amt für Geoinformation und Vermessung der Hansestadt Hamburg (D), Bernhard Cieslik
139-141:	Senatsverwaltung für Stadtentwicklung, Berlin (D), Takis Sgouros
142:	Cadimage Solutions Limited, Auckland (New Zealand), Campbell Yule
143:	digital electronic kühn GmbH, Dresden (D), Jens Kühn
144:	digital electronic kühn GmbH, Dresden (D), Jens Kühn
145:	Porr Immoprojekt GmbH, Wien (A), Claus Stadler
146:	Porr Immoprojekt GmbH, Wien (A), Claus Stadler
147:	Architekturbüro Werner Nußmüller, Graz (A)
150:	Architekturbüro Tadeusz Spychala, Wien (A)
151:	Architekturbüro Tadeusz Spychala, Wien (A)
152-153:	Fender Katsalidis Architects - FKAU, Sydney-Melbourne (AUS), David Sutherland
156:	Architektengemeinschaft Dürschinger & Biefang, Fürth (D)
158:	Architekturbüro Paul Katzberger und Michael Loudon, Wien (A)
159-160:	Drees & Sommer GmbH, Stuttgart (D), Hanspeter Sautter - Architekten: Freudenfeld+Krausen+Will, München (D)
161-162:	Architekturbüro Wiedermann, Innsbruck (A), Martin Lackner
164-165:	Architektengemeinschaft Triemli: Baumann & Frey Architekten, Zürich - Metron Architektur AG, Brugg / Bauherrschaft: Stadt Zürich; Amt für Hochbauten
166:	Hombo & Bañados Arquitectos, Santiago (CL), Pablo Bañados / Bauherr: Goverment of Chile
168-169:	Architekt Eduard Widmann, Salzburg (A) - InvestConsult Projektentwicklungs GmbH, Wien (A)
170:	Architekturbüro Gohm-Hiessberger, Hohenems (A), Otto Brugger
171:	Lund & Valentin Arkitekter, Stockholm (S), Lars Wahlström
172:	A-Konsultit, Helsinki (FIN), Eric Adlercreutz, Jyrki Iso-Aho, Päivi Vaheri, Heikki Prokkola
173:	Architekturbüro Walter Hoffelner, Wien (A), Jerzy Surwillo
174:	Architekturbüro Walter Hoffelner, Wien (A), Jerzy Surwillo
175:	Architekturbüro Walter Hoffelner, Wien (A), Jerzy Surwillo
176:	Architekturbüro Walter Hoffelner, Wien (A), Jerzy Surwillo
177:	Tadayyon Gilani mit AXIS Ingenieurleistungen, Wien (A), Christoph Friedreich
179:	Architekturbüro Werner Nußmüller, Graz (A)
180:	Architekturbüro Wimmer-Armellini, Bregenz (A) / Statik Ernst Mader Bregenz (A) / Bauherrschaft: Armellini Vermietungs und Verpachtungs GmbH
181:	Liljewall Arkitekter, Stockholm (S)
182:	Dietzel und Partner, München (D)
184-185:	maaars architecture, Innsbruck (A), Andreas Lettner, Stefan Knabel
186:	Arbeitsgemeinschaft Beneder-Fischer, Wien (A)
187:	Arbeitsgemeinschaft Beneder-Fischer, Wien (A)
189:	AXIS Ingenieurleistungen, Wien (A), Christoph Friedreich
190:	AXIS Ingenieurleistungen, Wien (A), Christoph Friedreich
190-191:	Architektur: Herbert Moser und Klaus Hagenauer, Linz (A) / Josef Pointner Architekturvisualisierungen, Linz (A) / Statik: Prof. Julius K. Natterer / Emanuel Panic Planungsbüro für Holzbau, Schleissheim (D)
192:	Architekturbüro Wimmer-Armellini, Bregenz (A) / Örtl. Bauaufsicht: Peter Speil, Göstling (A) / Statik: Friedrich Suppan, Strasshof (A) / Bauherrschaft: Hochkar Sport-Ges.m.b.H. & Co. KG, Göstling (A)
193:	Donald McDonald Architects, San Francisco (USA)
196:	Hans Hollein mit AXIS Ingenieurleistungen, Wien (A), Christoph Friedreich
197:	Architekturbüro Werner Nußmüller, Graz (A)
198:	Architekturbüro Werner Nußmüller, Graz (A)
198:	Richard+Wittschiebe Architects, Atlanta (USA)
199:	A-Konsultit, Helsinki (FIN), Eric Adlercreutz, Jyrki Iso-Aho,
200:	Päivi Vaheri
201:	Lund & Valentin Arkitekter, Göteborg (S), Bo Karlberg
202:	Thomas Forsthuber, Salzburg (A)
203:	Thomas Forsthuber, Salzburg (A)
204:	Atelier Katzberger, Wien (A)
206:	Ralph Baenzinger Architekten AG, RBAG (CH)
207:	Ralph Baenzinger Architekten AG, RBAG (CH)
208:	maaars architecture, Innsbruck (A), Andreas Lettner, Stefan Knabel
209:	Hombo & Bañados Arquitectos, Santiago (CL) / San Joaquín - Projektarchitekt: Pablo Bañados
210:	OrcuttWinslowPartnership, Phoenix, Arizona (USA)
212:	Baudenkstadt - Michael Alteneder, Wien (A)
213-214:	BEHF Architekten, Wien (A); Rigler Electric - Projektarchitekt: Armin Ebner / Messestand Shoe Fashion Group - Projektarchitekt: Erich Bernard / Restaurant Yume - Projektarchitekt: Stephan Ferenczy
215:	maaars architecture, Innsbruck (A), Andreas Lettner,

Stefan Knabel
216: Suben/Dougherty Partnership, New York (USA)

219- House+House Architects, San Francisco (USA),
220: Grand View Residence - Project Team: Steven House, Cathi House, David Thompson, Michael Tauber - Rendering: Shawn Brown / Roosevelt Way Residence - Design Team: Cathi House, Sonya Sotinsky - Rendering: Shawn Brown / Drucker Brownstein Residence - Project Team: Amena Hajjar, Steven House - Rendering: Kelly Condon

221: Rockefeller/Hricak Architects, Venice (USA)
222: Architekturbüro Gohm-Hiesberger, Hohenems (A), Otto Brugger
223: Architekturbüro Günther Domenig, Graz (A)
225: Architekturbüro Helmut Heistinger, Wien (A)
226: Mikula+Partner, Graz (A), Heri Pistotnig
227: Fa. Peter, Waidhofen/Th. (A)
231: STUDIOS Architecture, San Francisco (USA) / 450 Rhode Island - Design Architect: STUDIOS Architecture Madstone - Designer: STUDIOS architecture - Architect of Record: The Tricarico Group
231: Helin & Co Architects, Helsinki (FIN), Tom Cederqvist
232: Helin & Co Architects, Helsinki (FIN), Tom Cederqvist
233: Helin & Co Architects, Helsinki (FIN), Tom Cederqvist
234: BaulKultur, Linz (A), Michael Schamiyeh
234: Liljewall Arkitekter AB, Stockholm (S)
236: Architekturbüro Helmut Heistinger, Wien (A)
237: Rockefeller/Hricak Architects, Venice (USA)
237: Tillberg Design, Fort Lauderdale (USA)
239: LuminetIK, New York (USA), Kevin Cahill
240: LuminetIK, New York (USA), Kevin Cahill
241: LuminetIK, New York (USA), Kevin Cahill

242: LengyelToulouse, Köln (D); Korte Einrichtungen - Entwurf:
243: LengyelToulouse Architekten mit Agiplan - Visualisierung: LengyelToulouse Architekten / Bergwerks Götelborn: LengyelToulouse Architekten mit Agiplan / VDI-Geschäftsstelle - Entwurf: LengyelToulouse Architekten mit Agiplan - Visualisierung: LengyelToulouse Architekten
244: PAASTUDIO - Ivo Venkov, Santa Monica (USA)
245: PAASTUDIO - Ivo Venkov, Santa Monica (USA)
246: PAASTUDIO - Ivo Venkov, Santa Monica (USA)
248: Kimon Onuma, Tokio und Pasadena (JP/USA); Das Onuma Design-Team setzt sich aus einer Gruppe von Architekten wie auch EDV-Spezialisten zusammen.
249: Architekturbüro Gasparin & Meier, Villach (A)
250: STUDIOS Architecture, San Francisco (USA); Eigentümer/Entwickler: Wilson/Equity Office
254: M.A.D. oy, Helsinki (FIN); Samppa Hannikainen, Pasi Kiviniemi, Susanna Laasonen, Kalle Lievejärvi, Harri Mäkiaho, Raija Nevalainen, Jussi Niemi, V.-P. Ristimäki, Nina Västö
255: Ginder Akos Ignac / University of Belgrade (YUG)
255: Bogdan Ristivijevic - Zoran L. Pantelic / University of Belgrade (YUG)
256: Andrew Maynard, Stephen Mess u.a. / University of Tasmania (AUS)
256: Branislav Drgon, Trnava (SK)
257: Peter Bach und Peter Hadadi / Technical University of Budapest, Budapest (HUN)
257: Istvan Pölös und Marianna Illyes / NANA Architects, Budapest (HU)
258: Sam Rajamanickam, Design Collective Inc. (USA)
258: Hartmut Liebster und Bergit Hillner / HTWK Leipzig, Leipzig (D)
259: Andrei Radu / Technische Universität, Asachi (ROM)
259: Susanne Oeltjen, Wong Hong Chun und Lee Swee Wei / Universität Tasmanien (AUS)
261: Susan Pietsch, University of Adelaide (AUS)
261: Steve Johnson, Unitec Institute of Technology (NZ)
262: Steve Johnson, Unitec Institute of Technology (NZ)

262- Peter Bleier, Bob Martens und Jay Potts / Technische
263: Universität Wien (A) - Studierende: Sergei Bostandjan, Manuela Eitler, Klaus Lengauer, Jan Misek, Hannes Penn, Markus Piribauer, Martina Praznik, Daniela Wallmüller

264: Tom Cederqvist, Helsinki University of Technology (FIN)
265: Wolfgang Kurz, Technische Universität Wien (A)
268: Tina Mikrou, University of Edinburgh (UK)

269: Kloster Cluny I und II: ArgeProjekte SV, Wien (A),
270: Projektkoordination: Hans-Peter Walchhofer und Andreas Voigt - Modellierung und QTVR-Szenen: Helmut Hürner / Carnuntum: TU Wien, Institut für Örtliche Raumplanung und Multimediaplan.at, Wien (A), Projektkoordination: Manfred Schrenk und Andreas Voigt - Modellierung und QTVR-Szenen: Herbert Wittine

271- Bob Martens, Technische Universität Wien (A); Stu-
273: dierende: Daniela Wallmüller (Tempelgasse), Andreas Muttenthaler (Siebenbrunnengasse), Sabrina Frazetto, Willy Hochenbichler, Klaus Lengauer, Markus Piribauer, Florian Rode (Turnergasse)

277: Vito Bertin, Chinese University Hong Kong (HK)
278: Bruce Hill Ass., TurraMurra (AUS)

Index

Add-On, 67, 73, 138
AEC, 10

CAAD, 9-10, 16, 21-22, 37, 128, 183, 252, 260
Calculations, 21, 28, 36, 74, 89, 99, 107, 168, 210, 247, 281
Change of Scale, 81
Computer Driving License, 10, 21
Consultant, 120-121, 125, 155, 176-177, 196, 199, 216

Data exchange, 120-121, 145, 156, 252, 279
Database, 28, 30-31, 64, 86, 102, 105-107, 120, 126-127, 152, 182, 190, 209-210, 251, 280-282
Drivers, 115-116

Facility Management (FM), 31, 156, 182, 280-281
Favorites Palette, 85
Formats
    ARX Format, 44, 48
    DWG Format, 48, 121, 123, 129, 177, 196, 203, 207

DXF Format, 28-29, 48, 75, 79, 120-121, 123-124, 143, 177, 196, 203, 207, 252, 275
IFC Format, 48, 124-125, 199, 279-280
Multi-Platform, 26
O2C Format, 44
OFM Format, 44
Plot File, 117
Free Form Surface, 76

GDL Alliance, 61
GDL Object Technology, 43, 49, 66, 126, 167
GDL Product Catalog, 64
GDL Script, 44-45, 59, 66, 68, 262
Graphisoft Collection, 51

Interface, 120, 124-126, 245, 281
    API Interface, 70
    User Interface, 35, 49, 68, 252
Internet Browser, 47, 64, 109, 113, 182, 275

Modeling
    Three-Dimensional, 23, 25, 39, 42, 126, 192, 219, 223, 252
    Element-oriented, 30
Module, 60, 66-69, 124, 167, 209
    Hotlink Modules, 28, 66-69, 98, 124, 132, 147, 149, 155, 157, 174, 188, 194, 204

Nomenclature, 87

Object, 26, 28, 38, 43, 69, 126, 149-150, 160-162, 181-182, 188-189, 196-197, 202, 211, 215, 224-227, 247, 262, 265, 270, 276-278
    Library, 28, 38, 43, 51-57, 97, 105
    Library Element, 38, 43
    Object Portal, 64
    Real-life Object, 46, 60-62, 64-65, 182
Office Standard, 88, 120-121, 194, 214

Plan representation
    Layout, 118, 192
    Submission Plan, 99, 185
Planning Documents, 65, 79-80, 91, 100, 118, 123, 149, 161, 207, 272
Plug-in, 47, 70, 77, 114, 283
Product information, 62
ProjectXchange, 109
Point Clouds, 75
Publisher, 28, 47, 109

Room
    -reference book, 102-104, 155, 167, 174, 209
    -stamp, 102, 117, 162
    -XYZ Space, 38
    -zone, 102, 104, 154, 209

Simulation, 148, 159, 267, 274
Standard Tools, 38-39, 44, 66, 130, 157, 188, 224-225, 275

TeamWork, 24, 28, 83, 93-94, 97-98, 129, 145
Tool Palette, 71, 73, 76

Updating, 30, 37, 62, 69, 100, 105, 190, 220
    Automatic Updating, 37, 101, 152
    Dynamic Updating, 66, 118
User Friendliness, 20, 190

Virtual Construction Site, 35, 40
Virtual Building Concept, 28-30, 70, 80, 86, 91, 93, 100, 102
Visualization, 28, 34, 108-113, 126, 129, 136, 139, 147-148, 177-178, 189, 193, 211-212, 225, 228-230, 235-236, 238-239, 247, 259-260, 265-267
    Degree of Abstraction, 140
    Photo-realism, 35, 211
    QTVR, 28, 113-114

XREF, 28, 124, 132, 145, 157, 194, 204, 276

SpringerArchitecture

Andrew Watts

Modern Construction Handbook

2001. 312 pages. Numerous figures, partly in colour and numerous drawings.
Format: 21 x 29,7 cm
Hardcover **EUR 115,90**
Recommended retail price. Net-price subject to local VAT.
ISBN 3-211-83491-5
Modern Construction Series

The modern Construction Handbook examines a very wide range of construction options available to the contemporary designer in a concise, digestible format. It illustrates the wide spectrum of construction techniques in use, explaining how materials are chosen and the performance criteria that determine the way they are assembled. Throughout the book, built examples by high profile designers are used to illustrate generally accepted principles. The construction techniques described are applicable internationally. Each of the book's six chapters examines a particular aspect of construction from materials to structure, walls, roofs, environmental design and internal fittings. Specific elements are clearly explained, using a spread-by-spread approach, accompanied by fully annotated drawn details. The Modern Construction Handbook will provide a unique resource for the practising architect and student, as well as other members of the design team.

SpringerWienNewYork

P.O. Box 89, Sachsenplatz 4–6, 1201 Vienna, Austria, Fax +43.1.330 24 26, books@springer.at, **springer.at**
Birkhäuser c/o SAG, Haberstraße 7, 69126 Heidelberg, Germany, Fax: +49.6221.345-4229, orders@springer.de
Chronicle Books, 85 Second Street, San Francisco, CA 94105, USA, Fax +1.800.858-7787, sales@papress.com
Prices are subject to change without notice. All errors and omissions excepted.

Springer and the Environment

WE AT SPRINGER FIRMLY BELIEVE THAT AN INTERnational science publisher has a special obligation to the environment, and our corporate policies consistently reflect this conviction.

WE ALSO EXPECT OUR BUSINESS PARTNERS – PRINTERS, paper mills, packaging manufacturers, etc. – to commit themselves to using environmentally friendly materials and production processes.

THE PAPER IN THIS BOOK IS MADE FROM NO-CHLORINE pulp and is acid free, in conformance with international standards for paper permanency.